FAR FROM THE CALIPH'S GAZE

FAR FROM THE CALIPH'S GAZE

Being Ahmadi Muslim
in the Holy City of Qadian

Nicholas H. A. Evans

CORNELL UNIVERSITY PRESS **ITHACA AND LONDON**

First published 2020 by Cornell University Press

Library of Congress Cataloging-in-Publication Data

Names: Evans, Nicholas H. A., author.
Title: Far from the caliph's gaze : being Ahmadi Muslim in the holy city of Qadian / Nicholas H. A. Evans.
Description: Ithaca : Cornell University Press, 2020. | Includes bibliographical references and index.
Identifiers: LCCN 2019026545 (print) | LCCN 2019026546 (ebook) | ISBN 9781501715686 (hardback) | ISBN 9781501715693 (paper) | ISBN 9781501715709 (epub) | ISBN 9781501715716 (pdf)
Subjects: LCSH: Ahmadiyya members—India—Qādiān. | Ahmadiyya—India—Qādiān. | Faith (Islam) | Ethnology—India—Qādiān.
Classification: LCC BP195.A5 E93 2020 (print) | LCC BP195.A5 (ebook) | DDC 297.8/60954552—dc23
LC record available at https://lccn.loc.gov/2019026545
LC ebook record available at https://lccn.loc.gov/2019026546

Contents

Preface

In the Indian town of Qadian live a group of just over three thousand people who are absolutely certain that they are Muslims. They know that they are truthful followers of the Prophet Muhammad, and they are sure that their interpretations of the Qur'an are indisputable. They form a local branch of a global religious hierarchy in which disputes are routinely settled by appeal to higher authority. Moreover, they consider themselves blessed to know exactly where that authority lies, for they see the system within which they live as divinely ordained and their leader as God's lieutenant on earth. For these people, knowing how to practice their faith is straightforward, and truth is joyously self-evident. Moreover, the modern world does not present them with a challenge, for they see all of modernity's organizational, technological, and scientific accomplishments as a mere foretaste of what will come to pass with the global ascendency of the true Islam that they practice. Despite their confidence in being Muslim, however, these people face a very pressing difficulty, for in countries across the world, their Muslimness is contested and even denied. They call themselves Ahmadi Muslims; others describe them as heretics.

This book is about the challenges that Ahmadi Muslims face in proving their Muslimness. It is about their struggle to convince others of a truth about which they are absolutely certain; it is about the limits and possibilities of demonstrating what is known. My impetus for writing a book about the struggles that Ahmadis face in manifesting their Muslimness arose from the fact that I, like them, have often struggled with the challenge of convincing others. Specifically, I have often striven in vain to persuade my fellow anthropologists about the religious conviction that was displayed in my field site. Anthropologists, it seems, love to doubt certainty. Particularly within the anthropology of Islam, a keen attentiveness to the ambivalences of religious belief has become a hallmark of good ethnographic practice in the last few years, and any claim that people might relate to truth in a linear and straightforward fashion is met with skepticism. There is a good reason for this skepticism—after all, it is an attitude that cautions us to attend to the individuality of our interlocutors and thus prevents us from engaging in Orientalizing stereotypes. But this skepticism doesn't really help us to understand people like those I studied: members of a new religious movement who enthusiastically embrace self-essentialization and for whom certain aspects of their relationship to truth are stable and predictable.

A fundamental goal of this book is to show that if we want a better understanding of the lived religious experience of people like the Ahmadis, we have to broaden our definitions of religious doubt. I will argue that much anthropological thought, following a long Western tradition, tends to see doubt only in terms of one very particular relationship to truth: belief. Thus, we have tended to see doubt as the inverse of belief, a product of belief, a hindrance to belief, and, in some cases, a path to belief. But belief captures only one possible way of relating to truth. What if belief is not the aspect of people's relationship to truth that they problematize and worry over? What of situations in which people know how to believe in truth but are unsure of how to prove it, display it, demonstrate it, witness it, or even touch and experience it? In Qadian, truth is related to through an idiom of responsibility rather than belief, and this fact has a profound effect upon the doubts that people feel. Qadian appears to be a place of complete certainty only because of our poverty of imagination regarding doubt: it is in fact a place in which people constantly wrestle with their relationship to truth. This book is, therefore, about the possibilities of doubt beyond belief.

This book was made possible only by the hospitality and kindness of Qadian's residents. While many people in Qadian helped me with my research, all mistakes, misunderstandings, and inaccuracies are mine alone. To Arif, Athar, Basharat, Husam, Habib, Inam, Mahmood, Niaz, Dr. Majeed, Malik, Naeem, Osman, Shariq, Sohail, Shoaib, Rashid, Tahir, Yasir, Wahiduddin, and others, I owe a debt that cannot be repaid in words. Bilal deserves special mention for the many hours he spent teaching me the fundamentals of Urdu. Without the generosity of Qadian's senior officials, chiefly Nazr Talim Sb. and Nazr A'ala Sb., I could not have conducted this fieldwork. Mehfuz Sb. and his team at the Langar Khana, in particular Shivji, were a constant support. In the United Kingdom, Asim was a great help, especially in enabling me to arrange a meeting with the caliph. My research in India was also made possible only by the generous help of members of the Department of Sociology at Delhi University—in particular Rita Brara— where I was an affiliated researcher.

Adeel Hussain read an early version of the whole manuscript and was a consistently inspiring discussant. He helped me to see what I had overlooked— including the importance of sacrifice and the esoteric elements of Mirza Ghulam Ahmad's writings—and he motivated me to think on a bigger scale. Joel Robbins and Matthew Engelke both read sections of the manuscript and provided generous comments. Patrick McKearney read and commented on a number of parts of the book and also gave me support in the form of friendship. For three years at the Centre for Research in the Arts, Social Sciences and Humanities, Christos

Lynteris, Branwyn Poleykett, and Lukas Engelmann were wonderful companions, colleagues, and friends; I thank them for the many stimulating ideas that have directly ended up in this book, as well as for helping me to broaden my intellectual horizons and think beyond my specialism. In London, Nick Long has been a great support as I have attempted to balance the challenges of teaching and writing simultaneously.

Matt Candea, Jo Cook, and Paolo Heywood have all been inspiring discussants and friends, and our many conversations have helped to shape the ideas within this book. Jon Mair has been a wonderful interlocutor over the last few years, and conversations that we had together about what it means to speak ethically across borders have helped me to understand the challenges my Ahmadi interlocutors face as they attempt to speak across traditions to an often hostile world. Both Carrie Humphrey and Soumhya Venkatesan read the entirety of the manuscript in an earlier version, and their comments were probing, rigorous, and enlightening.

There are two people without whom this book would not exist. Susan Bayly has been a wonderful support and a brilliant teacher. James Laidlaw has nurtured this project since its inception, and with endless patience he has helped me to clarify my ideas over many years. His guidance has been invaluable, and the creativity of his thought has been inspiring.

An earlier version of chapter 5 appeared as "Beyond Cultural Intimacy: The Tensions That Make Truth for India's Ahmadi Muslims" in *American Ethnologist* 44, no. 3 (2017): 409–502. The fieldwork for this project was supported by the Economic and Social Research Council, grant number ES/I901957/1. At Cornell University Press, Jim Lance has been a wonderful editor, without whom this book would not have reached its full potential. I thank him and the production team for all their hard work. The three anonymous readers were sources of great inspiration and insight, and I thank them for their detailed engagement with my text.

My work has been nourished by the support of my parents and my stepfather, Ilaina, Charles, and Richard. Finally, it is to Claudia, with much love and admiration, that I dedicate this work.

Note on Names and Transliteration

Qadian is a well-known place with a relatively small Muslim population. I have therefore taken every precaution to preserve the anonymity of my informants, except for cases where I quote high-ranking individuals who act as spokesmen for the Jama'at in an official capacity. Consequently, this book contains relatively few distinct characters, and when I have introduced individuals into my narrative, I have kept details about their biographies as vague as possible.

Urdu and Arabic proper nouns with common English spellings are written following convention (e.g., Ahmad, Rabwah). Similarly, Arabic words that have entered the English lexicon are written as in the *Oxford English Dictionary*, and without italics (e.g., jihad, ulema). Elsewhere, I have followed an extremely simplified version of the *International Journal of Middle Eastern Studies* transliteration system. Diacritics have not been used with the exception of ' and ' to indicate respectively the 'ayn and hamza. For the sake of comprehension, I have in many cases used the English plural (-s) with Urdu and Arabic nouns (e.g., *mubahala* [singular], *mubahalas* [plural]). I have also capitalized proper nouns transliterated from Urdu and Arabic in line with English-language conventions.

FAR FROM THE
CALIPH'S GAZE

A TROUBLED RELATIONSHIP WITH TRUTH

There are few groups within contemporary Islam whose claim to belong to the faith is as endangered as that of the Ahmadiyya Muslim Community. This organization—which is spread across two hundred countries—claims to have "tens of millions" of followers and presents itself as a dynamic Islamic reform movement.[1] For many other Muslims around the world, however, Ahmadis (as members of the Ahmadiyya Muslim Community are known) are by definition non-Muslim. This is because Ahmadis follow the teachings of Mirza Ghulam Ahmad (c. 1835–1908), whom they revere as a messiah, a reformer, and, most crucially, a prophet after Muhammad. Within South Asia, where the Ahmadiyya community was founded, the Ahmadis' faith continues to be subject to verification in a public court of opinion, and in Pakistan the Ahmadis have suffered under state-led persecution for decades.[2] For a majority of South Asian Muslims, Mirza Ghulam Ahmad was an imposter; a false prophet who, they argue, was quite possibly working for the British rulers of India to bring discord to the Muslims of the subcontinent. For many of these Muslims, Mirza Ghulam Ahmad's self-declared prophethood is viewed as an insult to the finality of Muhammad's prophethood. Ahmadis, by contrast, reject all suggestions that their organization represents a new religion or a breakaway sect. Rather, they claim ownership over the center ground of Islamic orthodoxy and, through their publications, promote the idea that they are the continuation of the one true Islam as it was revealed to the prophet Muhammad in the Qur'an. This is a conflict over nothing less than who might claim the right to Islam.

In many non-Muslim majority countries, the Ahmadiyya Muslim Community (Jama'at-e-Ahmadiyya, hereafter Jama'at) is most commonly encountered through its attempts to promote Islam as a rational and universal religion that is compatible with modern democratic ideals. The Jamaʿat seeks to foster interfaith dialogue as a matter of theological necessity, and it employs mass media to communicate a message to all who will listen that Islam is a religion of peace. In a manner not unusual for a South Asian religious movement, it uses the branded slogan "Love for all, hatred for none," and it promotes what it sees as the true, beautiful teachings of Islam, be it through buying advertising space on the sides of London buses or hosting interfaith events in major cities around the world.[3] The Jamaʿat is thus engaged in both active proselytization and in what Matthew Engelke has described as public relations for God.[4] Many of the Ahmadis' efforts focus on staging events in the parliaments and assemblies of major democratic powers to present Islam as a revitalized, open, and outward-facing religion.[5] As a result of this promotional work, non-Muslim observers frequently speak of the Ahmadiyya Jamaʿat as the modern face of Islam, even though (and perhaps because of) the fact that the Ahmadis are treated as the paradigmatic outcasts of Islam in much of the Muslim world.[6] Liberal observers also often see in the Ahmadiyya community a reflection of their own values. For example, shortly before his election as the prime minister of Canada in 2015, Justin Trudeau attended a convention of the Ahmadiyya Jamaʿat in Ontario, where he praised the affinities between the values of liberal democracy and those of the Jamaʿat:

> Canada is a proud liberal democracy: a welcoming and peaceful nation. Canada is a country of open hearts and open minds: of fairness, justice and the rule of law. I speak to you today because I know the Ahmadiyya Community believes in those same values: diversity and inclusion, or as you put it so well, "Love for all, hatred for none."[7]

Unsurprisingly, this declaration was met by enthusiastic applause.

There are nonetheless certain key ways in which liberal suitors often seem to misunderstand how the values that they share with the Jamaʿat—of tolerance, openness, and cosmopolitan hospitality—arise from very different sources. I use *liberal* here only in its loosest sense to refer to a set of values structured around a belief in the autonomy and equality of citizens. In fact, members of the Ahmadiyya Jamaʿat are very open about the fact that their rhetorical insistence on such values as tolerance and integration does not arise from an egalitarian understanding of political subjectivity but is instead an act of submission to divine authority as embodied in the figure of their leader, the caliph (*khalifa*). The same process that enables affinities to emerge between Ahmadis and their liberal admirers thus also requires what I, together with Jonathan Mair, have previously described as a kind of "incommensuration": an arranging of things "vis-à-vis one another in such a way as to not admit comparison."[8] What is incommensurated in this case is the fact that the Ahmadis actively embrace many of the key hallmarks of liberal democracy to cultivate an attitude of absolute obedience to their caliph. It is the caliph who commands Ahmadis to be good citizens, and it is the caliph who demands that they exercise loyalty to the countries in which they reside. When Ahmadis reflect the values of the liberal democracies in which so many of them now live, they do so in order to manifest and demonstrate their loving subordination to their caliph. It is nonetheless another "illiberal" feature of the Ahmadiyya Jama'at that might shock their political suitors the most: the fact that many Ahmadis—despite their enthusiastic participation in pluralistic societies—remain uncompromisingly convinced of the absolute primacy of their own religious truths, and the corresponding *wrongness* of everybody else's. In other words, while they value conversation with others for its own sake, they remain committed to the idea that their doctrine is uniquely and universally superior to all other systems of thought. Most importantly, the Ahmadis about whom I have written this book were ill disposed to think of doctrinal doubt and skepticism as virtues.

My Ahmadi interlocutors' unwavering conviction is also the aspect of their religious lives that is most likely to lead to incredulity among anthropologists. Indeed, for many practitioners of our discipline, the fact that people might choose to snub doubt remains a far more shocking notion than the idea that they might seek liberation through self-subordination. Many anthropologists simply refuse to accept that absolute conviction is a possibility open to humans. As Michael Lambek has written, "while some theories of ethics seek firm grounds—and that is, in effect, what the practices we call religion try to offer—other thinkers, including me, think that certainty and sure grounding are ultimately unavailable."[9] He goes on to argue that "in any society, skepticism periodically shows itself—certainty is disrupted, alternatives appear, ritual action is demystified, and the sense that there is no firm ground for knowledge or value, threatens to prevail."[10] Lambek is not alone in expressing this idea, and I will show at the end of this chapter that there is a long tradition of Western thought that both assumes doubt to be a basic feature of human life and ascribes a moral value to it.[11] The fact remains, however, that the Ahmadis about whom I have written this book did display doctrinal certainty, and they demonstrated little interest in problematizing that certainty. These were people who have often been trained since a young age to engage in competitive polemics with opponents, people who savor the chance to best a rival's doctrine in debate, people for whom being always right and always certain is an uncontested mark of spiritual supremacy. These were people who knew that they were true Muslims, and they understood that this involved following their caliph as he tirelessly repeated the message that global peace could be achieved only through subordination to his authority. These were, in other words, people for whom there was no "crisis of authority" in modern Islam.[12] They were certain about what they should believe and how they should act.

The theoretical question that animates this book is thus how we might talk about this certainty. As I will show, much contemporary ethnographic work—particularly within the anthropology of religion—is premised on an idea that long-term and immersive ethnographic fieldwork will inevitably bring to light the real doubts, failures, and ambiguities that undergird our interlocutors' outward presentations of excessive certainty.[13] Not only that, but in much anthropological work on religion, there is an unspoken moral drive behind the discovery of doubt, for it is in doubt's existence that the gap between the fundamentalist Other and us is closed.[14] But what if, for just a moment, we stopped trying to discover the hidden doubts that we assume must wrack people like the Ahmadis? What if we accepted the idea that they might really be just as convinced as they claim? What if we begin to think about the ways in which the conviction of my Ahmadi interlocutors might coexist with an unclear, fragile, and apprehensive relationship to truth? What if this comingling of certainty and uncertainty is not, in fact, as paradoxical as it might appear?

The argument of this book is that we will only be able to appreciate the uncertainty felt by people like the Ahmadis if we stop trying to find out whether or not they doubt their beliefs. Indeed, I will argue that our default assumption that people should be doubters is a primary cause of our failure to understand other ways of experiencing uncertainty. Thus, rather than asking whether my interlocutors doubt, I will be asking what kind of relationship they have with truth and in what ways might it be troubled. In the rest of this introduction, I lay out the basic form of my interlocutors' troubled relationship to truth, before finally returning to the question of why this troubled relationship to truth might in fact be obscured by our understanding of religious "doubt." Doing this, however, requires that for a moment we turn away from what we think of as doubt and instead consider the relationship through which my interlocutors approach the truth of their religion: their relationship with their caliph.

A Sudden Dismissal

"Go back to England straight away and only come back when you have permission."

With these words, the chief secretary of the Ahmadiyya Jama'at in India dismissed me from the Indian town of Qadian and let me know that to continue my research I would require permission from none other than the caliph. It was January 2011, and I had spent a little over six weeks of what was to become fifteen months conducting ethnographic fieldwork in Qadian, a town in Gurdaspur District in Punjab, close to the border with Pakistan. At the time of my fieldwork, Qadian had a population of slightly fewer than 24,000, of whom about 3,000 people were Ahmadi Muslim.[15] This small number nonetheless belied the symbolic importance of Qadian, for Qadian is the birthplace of the Ahmadiyya movement. Qadian is the town in which Mirza Ghulam Ahmad was born, in which the Ahmadiyya caliphate was founded, and from which the movement began its worldwide expansion in the early twentieth century. The name of Qadian is now synonymous with the Ahmadiyya movement, and across the Indian subcontinent, other Muslims who would never have any cause to visit Qadian routinely refer to Ahmadis as Qadianis, even though (and often because of the fact that) the latter consider this term derogatory. Nonetheless, Qadian is also a place somewhat apart from the global Ahmadiyya movement, for during the partition of India in 1947, it was forever abandoned by its caliph. Huge tracts of land belonging to the Jama'at were lost to Hindus and Sikhs, and the Muslim population of Qadian fell dramatically. Nowadays, the Ahmadiyya caliph rules supreme from a base in south London, and Qadian remains far from his vigilant gaze.

When I was commanded to return to England by the chief secretary, I was initially quite puzzled. The Ahmadiyya community—a group that delights in telling the world that it is committed to open dialogue—seemed determined to send me away. As is common in ethnographic fieldwork, it was nonetheless this moment of confusion that ultimately led to a far greater clarity in my understanding of life in Qadian. This was the moment in which I realized that I was not relating to the caliph in the right way and that demonstrating a relationship to the caliph is an issue of great moral anxiety in Qadian.

The events leading up to my being asked to return home began several weeks earlier, when I had attended Qadian's Jalsa Salana, or "Annual Gathering." During this much-anticipated event, close to 25,000 Ahmadis congregated in the town for three days of edifying religious speeches in an atmosphere of communal belonging.[16] Most of the attendees had come from other parts of India, occasionally traveling by train for up to three days to reach Qadian, but there was also a substantial contingent of foreign guests, including many Ahmadis from Pakistan.[17] The Qadian Jalsa Salana is an extremely important event for Ahmadis, and parts of it are normally broadcast on the Jama'at's satellite television network (Muslim Television Ahmadiyya, or MTA for short) so that Ahmadis around the world might witness the spectacle. At some point during this event, an Ahmadi camera crew had filmed an interview with me about my experience of Qadian, and I was consequently featured in an international broadcast, identified only as a foreign guest from the United Kingdom. Jama'at officials in London saw this interview and were confused by my presence, for they had not authorized me—a British person—to attend the gathering in Qadian. As a result, the caliph's office in London sent an inquiry to Qadian asking who, exactly, I was.

The end result of this inquiry was panic in Qadian. On the day that I was told to return to England, I had been woken up early in the morning by a phone call from a junior member of the Jama'at instructing me to speak at once to the official who had been given temporary charge of overseeing my research. I arrived at this official's office, and he abrasively began to challenge what I was doing in the town. Until this point, everybody had been extremely welcoming, so the sudden hostile approach of this administrator left me bewildered. I responded in as deferential a manner as possible, and his attitude changed. He assured me that he liked me but that he had no other choice than to follow the rules. My presence in the town, he explained, was not sanctioned, and the situation was urgent. He thus advised me to write a letter directly to the caliph, asking for permission to stay in Qadian. I did this and then returned to his office, assuming that I would be able to send the letter through an official channel. From his reaction, however, I was immediately able to tell that I had committed a fresh mistake. He took the letter, crossed out a sentence naming him as the person who had advised me to write it, and then informed me that I was to send the letter to the general-purpose inquiries number of the caliph's office in London via a fax machine from a shop in the local market.[18] I left in a state of even greater confusion.

Until this point, I had negotiated access to the Jama'at via local administrators in Qadian. Equipped with my research visa and an affiliation to an Indian university, I had assumed that I had the necessary permissions to conduct my research. What became clear that day was that there was no way for me to gain access through local bureaucratic channels. Nobody in Qadian could attest to who I was; nobody could clear my research. In fact, there was only one person with the authority to do so: the caliph. Despite the many layers of administration that separated me from the caliph, my ability to conduct research would ultimately rest on the direct relationship that I would have with him. Over the next few days, word spread around Qadian that I had not secured permission from the caliph prior to my arrival in India, and for the first time I felt a sense of disapproval—even sadness—in the voices of my interlocutors as they asked me why I had not done what was for them an obvious thing. Significantly, I began to notice my interlocutors talking about the caliph in a way that I had never quite appreciated before. He emerged as an omniscient figure, capable of making decisions in ways that nobody else could and thus being the only person who could really resolve my situation. One cleric explained, "Only Huzur [i.e., the caliph] can give this [permission] because he knows everything that is going on. He knows the situation of each country and its Jama'at so he is able to give permission for people to travel between them." At the time, I found this hard to understand, for it implied that the caliph, with no knowledge of me and little time to consider me, would be able to make a better judgment about my research than those who had watched me conduct it for a number of weeks in Qadian. Perhaps tellingly, when I did finally secure the direct permission of the caliph (which involved several months of waiting and then finally a meeting in the caliph's offices in London), people's attitudes toward me changed dramatically. Where before they were guarded, now they were open and helpful. The same official who had refused to have his name mentioned in my letter to the caliph embraced me and exclaimed, "Please tell us everything you need, and we will do it for you."

A number of things became apparent to me during this episode. For a start, it sparked my realization that a good relationship to the caliph is one that is, ideally, unmediated. This episode was also when I first began to understand the moral weight that my interlocutors placed on correct bureaucratic process. As the chief secretary was later to explain, the Jama'at system is "divinely instituted": to follow its processes and rules is, for my interlocutors, an aspect of being Muslim. Perhaps most importantly, however, I learned something from the sudden panic that the administrators displayed when they realized that my presence might not be sanctioned by London. At stake was not just my ability to prove a relationship to the caliph but also theirs. As I would slowly discover over the coming months, the anxieties that were manifested during this event were about what it meant to make a relationship tangible, knowable, verifiable, and, in some crucial way, provable. In fact, I want to argue that what occurred during this event was a very obvious display of a particular kind of anxiety about how to relate to truth in Qadian. To understand why this was so, however, we need to know a bit more about the history of the Ahmadiyya Jama'at in South Asia.

Contesting Islam

Across South Asia, the question of what it means to be Muslim has never been more fraught. Reformisms, tied to global movements for the purification of Islam, have sought to purge the religion of Hindu or syncretic elements.[19] Amid this drive for purity, the Ahmadis are subject to hostility, false allegations, and occasionally violence. Among the Ahmadis' most hardened antagonists, the very mention of their name can arouse feelings of hatred. The reasons why a profoundly pacifist group can provoke such abhorrence is a continuing source of debate, but one thing that is clear is that the Ahmadis' supposed violation of Islamic norms is crucial to contemporary definitions of orthodoxy in South Asia. Indeed, the existence of the Ahmadis has provided many in South Asia—including those in alignment with the Pakistani state—with a way of defining a boundary that demarcates the Islamic from the heretical.[20]

The founder of the Ahmadiyya movement, Mirza Ghulam Ahmad, made bold claims to be the Promised Messiah of Islam and the *mahdi* (an eschatological figure popularly expected to come at the end of times). His most infamous declaration, however, was his claim to be a prophet after Muhammad, which most non-Ahmadi Muslims understand to contravene the finality of prophethood, or *khatam-e-nabuwwat*.[21] In other words, the Ahmadis are understood by their opponents to have stepped beyond the fold of Islam by denying the fact that Muhammad was the final prophet sent by God to earth. This is, however, a disagreement that goes beyond theology. Mirza Ghulam Ahmad is spoken of in a language of scatological repugnance throughout South Asia, and for many opponents, the Ahmadis' acceptance of a prophet after Muhammad is not just an abstract discrepancy but a matter of disgust that in a very visceral way appears to contravene the sanctity of the religion.

While passionate theological criticism has been leveled at the Ahmadis since the late nineteenth century when Ahmad first began declaring himself a prophet, it was only with the creation of Pakistan that the finality of prophethood became a political issue that could lead to the exclusion of Ahmadis from the mainstream of Islam.[22] Since then, the Ahmadiyya community has become the fulcrum on which attempts to define Muslimness in South Asia have rested. Charting the history of legal and governmental persecution of the community in Pakistan can help us to understand why this is so.

Low-level violence and discrimination are part of everyday life for Ahmadis in Pakistan, but since independence in 1947 there have been three important junctures to this persecution. The first episode occurred in the early years of Pakistan, when the Majlis-e-Ahrar, a group with pre-independence roots who had increasingly become preoccupied by the defense of the finality of prophethood, precipitated an agitation against the Ahmadis. In the early 1950s, this group formed the Majlis-e-Amal (or Action Committee) to agitate against the Ahmadis and, in January 1953, commissioned a deputation of ulema (Islamic scholars) to deliver an ultimatum to the prime minister of Pakistan demanding that Ahmadis be declared non-Muslim within the month and that prominent Ahmadis in public positions—in particular the foreign minister Chaudhri Zafrullah Khan—be removed from office. They threatened direct action if their demands were not met. The government rejected this proposal and on February 27, 1953, arrested a number of prominent leaders of the Majlis-e-Amal. As a result of this, disturbances broke out across the Punjab, which led to the imposition of martial law.[23] Government buildings were burned, and Ahmadis were lynched in the streets. The fallout from these riots established an important theme in Pakistan's modern history—namely, the linking of the question of Muslim identity to the Ahmadi "problem." The violence of 1953 led to the now-famous report of a court of inquiry, the Munir Report of 1954, which argued that it was impossible to define a Muslim in a way that could be agreed upon by all the ulema.[24]

The issue of the finality of prophethood continued to be a rallying point in Pakistani politics, although military dictatorship in the 1960s prevented excessive violence. In 1974, however, an altercation between Ahmadi and non-Ahmadi students led to a nationwide resurgence in popular support for the anti-Ahmadi movement and the second major upwelling of anti-Ahmadi sentiment.[25] In an attempt to settle the Ahmadi question, the Pakistani Parliament (with Zulfikar Ali Bhutto as prime minister) appointed a special committee to hold hearings. The question at this juncture was no longer how to define a Muslim but how to define a Muslim's antithesis: a nonbeliever.[26] The events of 1974 culminated in an amendment to the Pakistani Constitution, which made it punishable for any Muslim to deny the finality of prophethood but accorded Ahmadis minority status as non-Muslims. The constitution thus gave a definition of a non-Muslim without defining a Muslim.[27]

The third major shift in the history of Ahmadi exclusion in Pakistan occurred ten years later in 1984, when under the government of Zia ul-Haq a new ordinance was passed that made it punishable by imprisonment for Ahmadis to *pose* as Muslims by calling themselves Muslims or otherwise acting in a Muslim fashion, for example by calling their mosques "mosques" or by sounding the *azan* (the call to prayer). From a legal point of view, the most unusual and far-reaching feature of this legislation was that in the court cases that followed it, a notion of intellectual property was invoked to justify exclusive Muslim ownership over aspects of external behavior. The Ahmadis' "imitation" of Muslim ritual practice became a copyright issue. Thus when Ahmadis acted as Muslims, they could be compared to dishonest traders who were trying to pass off inferior goods as reputable brands.[28] As Andi Muhammad Irawan has shown, this idea has now become a part of the global discourse of anti-Ahmadiyya groups and associations. Analyzing the propaganda of a major opposition group to the Ahmadis in Indonesia, Irawan shows how they too accuse the Ahmadis of using tactics of "copyright infringement" and dissimulation to "hijack" the "brand" of Islam so as to lead others astray. For these opponents, the Ahmadis' claim to be Muslims is, Irawan argues, "a kind of falsification."[29] In 1984, the Pakistani government of Zia ul-Haq also introduced an amendment to another article (260) of the constitution, which resulted in a long-anticipated constitutional definition of a Muslim, as a person who believes in the unqualified finality of Muhammad and does not recognize any reformer or prophet after him.[30] This created a situation in which a new definition of religious identity gained state sanction in Pakistan: an

Ahmadi was one who imitated a Muslim, and a Muslim was a person who was not an Ahmadi.[31]

The actions of Zia ul-Haq's government in 1984 placed the fourth caliph in grave danger, and he was thus forced to flee Pakistan and seek exile in London, where he and now his successor have been based ever since. In the last few decades, large numbers of Ahmadis have spent periods in jail, including the current caliph, Mirza Masroor Ahmad, who at the time of his incarceration was working as an official for the Jama'at in Pakistan. The specific anti-Ahmadiyya provisions within the Pakistani Constitution are part of a broader set of blasphemy laws, which have been much lamented by both international observers and liberal Pakistanis and which carry a maximum sentence of death. Interestingly, during the period in which legal persecution of the Ahmadis was on the increase in Pakistan, a new set of discourses emerged which identified the Ahmadis as responsible for their own persecution. In particular, anti-Ahmadi activists argued (often with significant success) that they were the victims of Ahmadi claims to be Muslim, and that the Ahmadis themselves were responsible for provoking violence from an otherwise peaceful majority through the simple act of self-identifying with Islam.[32] In this way, the quotidian existence of the Ahmadis was transformed in the popular imagination into an incitement to public disorder that justified state intervention.[33]

Alongside government persecution in Pakistan, the Ahmadis suffer a daily rhetoric of hate speech from organized opposition groups, and at the time of my writing this, the new prime minister of Pakistan, Imran Khan, has given no indication that he will do anything other than allow this situation to continue.[34] Ahmadis are also frequent targets of vigilante violence and terrorism within Pakistan. A gruesome example occurred in 2010, when Taliban-linked gunmen killed eighty-six members of the Jama'at in coordinated attacks during Friday prayers in two Ahmadi mosques in Lahore.[35]

Qadian's Ahmadis, being situated just across the border in India, suffer from neither constitutional persecution nor daily acts of violence. During my fieldwork, Ahmadis in Qadian had little interaction with other Muslims and on the whole worked hard to maintain cordial if distant relations with the Hindus and Sikhs around them. Many people nonetheless had relatives in places where Ahmadis were actively persecuted; they feared abuse from other Muslims when they traveled around the subcontinent, and occasionally, there would be violence, riots, or kidnappings of Ahmadis in India.[36] A dramatic example of this was a communal riot in the town of Saharanpur in 2008 that led to most of that city's small Ahmadi population seeking refuge in Qadian.[37] At a quotidian level, other Muslims in India would constantly question the right of Ahmadis to speak as Muslims on behalf of Islam. As is the case in Pakistan, it is the Indian Ahmadis' supposed *dissimulation*—their imitation of Muslims—that comes under attack. Even if they do not experience ever-present danger, they live in the knowledge of being a persecuted minority, sharing the pain of those who lack freedom of expression. They are forever acutely aware of the insecurity of being a minority's minority in India.

As terrible as this persecution is, my Ahmadi interlocutors nonetheless understood it to confirm the truth of Ghulam Ahmad's message. They viewed oppression as something necessarily inflicted on the followers of true prophets, and they looked back at the history of Abrahamic prophets and argued that Moses, Jesus, Muhammad, and their followers all suffered from violent opposition. Persecution was seen to empirically prove the superiority of the Jama'at; it was a way of knowing the truth of Ahmadiyyat.[38] Describing the situation in Europe, where Ahmadis typically have peaceful relations with neighboring communities, an interlocutor in Qadian once told me, "Inshallah, there will be opposition." It was as if he desired the persecution of Ahmadis in Europe, because that would be a sure sign that the Jama'at was in the ascendency there. Among my interlocutors in Qadian, the knowledge of persecution only served to make their conviction stronger.

For all their conviction, however, Ahmadis do face a problem: how to prove to the world that which they know. In Pakistan, the law is such that what is judged is never what is seen. The same outward act of Muslim worship that proves the devotion of a Sunni will be understood to demonstrate the deception of an Ahmadi.[39] In India, even if the Ahmadis are legally free to call themselves Muslim, their being so is always contested. Across South Asia, Ahmadis are thus caught in a difficult situation, for the more they try to prove their Muslim identity through strict and observable public behavior, the more they end up confirming the beliefs of their opponents that they are imitations of Muslims. It is here that we can locate the core dilemma that the Ahmadis face, which separates them from other groups who are on the fringes of Islamic orthodoxy. The Ahmadis vociferously claim the center ground of Islamic orthodoxy, and in doing so, they deny any difference between themselves and Islam. They refuse to be labeled as a version of Islam, instead insisting that their religion is the one true Islam. The result is that what discredits them in the eyes of their opponents is not just the things they do differently from the Muslim mainstream but also the things that they do the same. It is from this dilemma that the idea of the Ahmadi as the counterfeit Muslim emerges: having a modern prophet may make the Ahmadis false, but praying in the same way as a Sunni is what makes them inauthentic.

The Ahmadis, in other words, face an uncertainty of surfaces: even if they feel no doubt about their own inner Muslimness, they are faced by a difficulty of demonstrating and showing this in public.[40] They must, on a daily basis, confront the question of how to translate inner life into something that can be evidenced in the surfaces of existence.

Being Ahmadi Muslim

So how do you prove you are Muslim? What kind of evidence could ever be sufficient of such a claim? How do you demonstrate what you already know to be true? A major argument of this book is that my Ahmadi interlocutors attempt to substantiate their Muslimness by making visible their devotion to their caliph. It is the caliph who gives certainty to the Ahmadi interpretation of Islam, who safeguards the accuracy of their doctrine, and who ensures that their Islam is the correct one. For my interlocutors in Qadian, to have a faithful, sincere, and disciplined relationship to him is thus to begin to approach something akin to tangible evidence for the indisputability of their Muslimness. As such, every aspect of communal life in Qadian has become a stage through which this relationship might be tested, verified, and known. More than anything else, the continued growth of the Ahmadiyya Jama'at as a unified global system (*nizam*) is taken as a profound and powerful proof of the devotion of Ahmadis around the world. The more the system grows, economically and materially, the more it is seen to demonstrate the bond that it is hoped exists between all Ahmadis and their leader. Members of the Jama'at have in effect turned a rationalized bureaucratic apparatus into an argument for their Muslim subjecthood. In the chapters that follow this introduction, I will further show how diverse activities such as polemical disputations with opponents are structured around a desire to cultivate a bond of love to the caliph and how members of the Jama'at utilize their satellite television network to broadcast images of this relationship to the world. In all these activities, Ahmadis seek to give Muslim subjecthood concrete form in the shape of a verifiable relationship.

The emphasis that modern-day Ahmadis place on the caliphate as a marker of Muslimness developed only after the death of their Promised Messiah, Mirza Ghulam Ahmad. Indeed, although modern-day members of the Jama'at describe the caliphate as the obvious continuation of Mirza Ghulam Ahmad's prophetic mission, the supremacy of the caliphate was a deeply contested issue for early adherents. When Ghulam Ahmad died in 1908, a close companion was elected as caliph (the literal meaning of which is "successor"). The first caliph's reign was, however, short-lived, and in 1914 he died. At this point, there was a huge disagreement over whether the community should continue to be led by a caliph, and when Mirza Ghulam Ahmad's inexperienced son was elected as the second caliph, a splinter group known as the Lahori Ahmadis broke off from the main faction in

Qadian, primarily because they felt that the caliph should not be the ultimate authority within the Jama'at.[41] It was only after this dissenting group left the community in 1914 that the second caliph was able to vastly expand the Jama'at's bureaucracy, its financial system, and the theological justification—largely absent from Mirza Ghulam Ahmad's own writings—as to why the caliphate was so vital.[42] The movement is now led by its fifth caliph, who exhorts his followers to be disciplined in heeding his message, and who is seen by them as a universal leader.

Unsurprisingly, my Ahmadi interlocutors constantly compare their own unity to what they see as the discord afflicting other Muslims around the world. For Ahmadis, mainstream Islam is a broken faith, which is riven by divisions and irredeemable violence. As they see it, Islam is sick, and their caliph offers the cure, for he promotes tolerance, an exclusively nonviolent interpretation of jihad, a commitment to open dialogue, and an insistence on loyalty as a defining virtue. In promoting these values as exceptional, however, Ahmadis frequently end up endorsing the idea that the Islam practiced by other Muslims must necessarily be the opposite of all these things.[43] Indeed, many Ahmadis in Qadian were deeply sympathetic to the idea that mainstream Islam should be seen as an enemy of democracy: one of my interlocutors justified the hostility that some Europeans express toward Muslim women wearing the burqa in public as a warranted form of suspicion toward a closed and violent religion. This was despite the fact that his own wife and daughters, along with every other Muslim woman in Qadian, wore the burqa in public. The Ahmadis' desire to present themselves as exceptional while casting mainstream Islam as defective has thus unsurprisingly led to them being celebrated by groups and individuals who are often accused of hostility to Islam. In India, they have been praised for their "tolerance and brotherhood" by Prime Minister Narendra Modi.[44] I also saw members of the Hindu nationalist organization the RSS (Rashtriya Swayamsevak Sangh) attend Ahmadi events: one interlocutor explained to me, "We are the enemies of their enemies [i.e., other Muslims]." For the Ahmadis of Qadian, such associations are deeply troubling—they know that the vision of Hindu society promoted by the RSS has no place for Islam. Yet they see such alliances of convenience as an often necessary part of their goal of demonstrating to the world that Islam can be redeemed, that it is a religion of peace, and that it contains the key to a truly peaceful society. The Ahmadis' exceptionalism thus has extremely interesting effects, in that it frequently ends up endearing them to politicians and public groups at opposite ends of the political spectrum. On the one hand are liberals, who celebrate the Jama'at for its tolerance and willingness to engage others in dialogue. On the other hand are those who are more likely to agree with my Ahmadi interlocutors in seeing the Muslim mainstream as problematic, backward, and violent. What is perhaps most interesting about the Ahmadis' exceptionalism, however, is that it results in the harmonization of a contrarian style of thought with an attitude of absolute subservience to authority. This exceptionalism thus provided my interlocutors with ways of displaying individual brilliance while also demonstrating total subordination to their divine leader. It became, in other words, another means through which they could call on their relationship with the caliph to carry an epistemic burden of proof.

The unique and exceptional relationship that Ahmadis cultivate with their caliph thus seems to offer them a way of evidencing Muslimness, especially when it can be compared to what Ahmadis see as the absence of unitary leadership among the mass of other Muslims in the world. As a form of proof, however, this relationship is not without challenge. After all, can one really take a relationship, which is by nature unknowable from the outside, and use it to inscribe a public and indisputable truth on the world? In fact, this is perhaps a more difficult task than my interlocutors were always willing to let on.

Being Muslim in Qadian

When the Jama'at was founded, Qadian lay within British India, where it remained for nearly forty years after Mirza Ghulam Ahmad's death. Throughout this time, Qadian was the center of the global Ahmadi system: it was from Qadian that the first missionaries were dispatched to the West, and it was in Qadian that the second caliph laid the financial and organizational foundations for the Jama'at as it exists today. This all changed in 1947 with the partition of India. When partition first began to seem inevitable, the caliph lobbied for Qadian to become an independent princely state, but this soon became obviously impractical.[45] Qadian's eventual location in independent India nonetheless presented the Jama'at with a problem, for it threatened to place the Ahmadis outside of the new center of Islam in the subcontinent. The caliph thus decided to abandon the town in order to stake a claim to membership of the Muslim state of Pakistan and thus affirm Ahmadi belonging within Islam.

The large and relatively wealthy Ahmadiyya community of Qadian thus followed the second caliph to Pakistan, together with the majority of Ahmadis from throughout Punjab. As a result, Pakistan is now home to what is almost certainly the largest number of Ahmadis in the world. While it is impossible to get exact figures, Pakistani Ahmadis today probably number in the millions.[46] By contrast, estimates for India given to me during my fieldwork were between eighty and two hundred thousand.[47] In Pakistan, the Ahmadis created a new city, Rabwah, upon supposedly barren ground.[48] The entirety of the Jama'at system, its international operations, its publishing and teaching operations, and its financial offices were moved to Rabwah, where they mostly remain to this day. The major exception to this is the caliphate, for as I have noted, in 1984 the fourth caliph was forced to seek exile in London due to increased persecution in Pakistan.

Qadian, by contrast, lost its burnish. During partition, exactly 313 men are said to have remained in the town to protect its monuments, its mosques, and the graves of the Promised Messiah and his companions.[49] The caliph of the time gave these men the honorific title of *derwesh* (ascetic or mendicant) in recognition of the years of extreme austerity that they endured following partition. The derwesh are heroic figures within the Jama'at, for their sacrifice and their forbearance. While they managed to keep much of the old town of Qadian in Ahmadi hands, they were impoverished and isolated in the years and decades that followed. In interviews I conducted with the remaining derwesh, I was told of the dangers, difficulties, and even periods of starvation that these men faced. When it came time to rebuild the community, they struggled to find wives, for no Ahmadi from elsewhere in India dared send their daughter to Qadian in those first few years. In the common historical imagination of the town, these were years of hardship and forbearance, when Qadian lacked any sense of integration into the broader global Jama'at. Isolated not just from the rest of the Jama'at but also a broader Muslim public, Qadian was understood by its residents as a last bastion of Islam within Indian Punjab.

Qadian, although still being considered the permanent home of the Ahmadiyya Jama'at, was thus physically separated from the global system. Despite the short geographical distance to Rabwah, for many years after partition Qadian struggled to maintain direct contact with the new Ahmadi center in Pakistan. Visa restrictions made it virtually impossible for people to travel frequently between India and Pakistan. Communications were limited, and at times, the Pakistani Jama'at had to communicate with India via third countries. Qadian went from being synonymous with the Ahmadi system to being a local outpost whose bureaucrats administered only the isolated Ahmadiyya population of India. This is a situation reflected in the academic literature on Ahmadiyyat in South Asia, which, despite Qadian's historical importance, has tended to focus on Pakistan, where the Ahmadis are most numerous and where they are most severely persecuted for their faith.[50]

For Qadian's Ahmadis, the most significant consequence of partition was their separation from the caliph. For over four decades after partition, the caliph did not visit India, and since then, caliphs have only visited Qadian twice.[51] The first of these visits, in 1991, was significant in that it was intended to inaugurate a new age of spiritual and material development, two forms of progress that are ideally seen as the same thing—worldly advancement should signal divine favor, and it is through the worldly progress of the Jama'at that Ahmadis point toward the truth of their doctrine.[52] This material progress did not, however, occur in the way that people in Qadian had hoped. During my fieldwork, people described how the caliph's visit led to only a marginal influx of capital, which nonetheless had the unfortunate effect of turning people's minds away from the simple and austere existence of the derwesh and thus corrupted the spiritual condition of Qadian. The result was a pervasive discourse of decline and degradation, caused not by the caliph's visit but by the fact that Ahmadis in Qadian felt that they had failed to cultivate the correct attitude toward him in the years that followed.

Since a second tour in 2005, the caliph has not set foot in the town. A proposed visit in 2008 was canceled because of the terror threat after the Mumbai terror attacks, even though the caliph had already arrived in India and carried out a tour of the southern Indian states. To this day, Qadian is thus marginalized from its caliph, a fact demonstrated by the intensity and longing with which people remember the fleeting visits that have been made. Indeed, the 1991 and 2005 visits continued to inform the lived geography of the town during my fieldwork. People would describe how the caliph had visited their houses and exactly where he had stood in their rooms. They would recall when they had met him and precisely what he had said to them. Qadian existed in a continual state of waiting for the caliph. Every year there is a hope that his participation in Qadian's Annual Gathering will be announced. In the last few years a private walled garden has even been constructed in the very center of the town for use only by the caliph and his family, should one of these long-awaited, yearned-for visits occur.

Ahmadis from elsewhere readily acknowledged the problems that had developed in Qadian due to its separation from the caliphate and the global bureaucracy. I met and spoke with a number of Ahmadis from Pakistan, who would laud the purity and systematicity of the Jama'at in the Pakistani headquarters of Rabwah—"we built it ourselves"—while lamenting the slow decay of Qadian. Even though Qadian would always be the spiritual home of the Ahmadis and the destination of their future global expansion, the system there, they said, lacked the purity of the system in Pakistan. Within Qadian itself, this decline was an intimate source of shame. It underlay the panicked reactions of the officials I described at the beginning of this chapter, and it underwrote everyday bureaucratic processes in profound ways. The question faced by my interlocutors on a daily basis was how, without a strong system, they could manifest their relationship to the caliph and how, without being able to demonstrate their devotion to him, they might make their Muslim identity visible and verifiable in the world.

Qadian's problem, in other words, was about more than just isolation from the caliph. In Qadian, the real question was whether my interlocutors ever felt that they could fully demonstrate that they were Muslim. As the spiritual and symbolic home of Ahmadiyyat, Qadian is a place where it matters more than most that Ahmadis are able to demonstrate their absolute Muslimness. Qadian is colloquially referred to as the *dar ul-aman*, a home of peace and sanctuary, and visiting Ahmadis praise it for a simplicity that enables them to feel closer to God. Qadian's mosques are the mosques in which the Promised Messiah prayed and in which he received revelations. Its major landmark, the White Minaret, is the most visible and widely recognized symbol of the global community, and Qadian is the prophesied center of a reinvigorated future Islam. Qadian is also, however, unique in its structural position, for due to its history it has been forcibly separated from its leader and the global system over which he presides. If evidencing Muslimness means demonstrating a relationship to the caliph, how can Ahmadis do this when their place within the global system is precarious? How can they demonstrate discipline to the caliph when their lives are structured around an anxiety of being forever too distant from him? Is it enough to just love from afar? What happens when Ahmadis in Qadian can never quite be sure of the relationship through which they are able to witness their own Muslimness? In short, Qadian is caught within a double insecurity of being Muslim: it is a place in which Muslimness is denied from without and yet also difficult to prove from within. Or to put this another way, it is a place in which it is easy to know the truth, but very hard to respond to it.

A Global Initiation

The complexities of relating to truth in Qadian were vividly demonstrated during my fieldwork by an event that has come, aesthetically, to represent the relationship between believer and caliph. This event was a global ritual that Ahmadis call the International Bai'at. The International Bai'at usually occurs during the Jalsa Salana (Annual Gathering) of the Ahmadiyya Jama'at in the United Kingdom, and it is broadcast live on the community's global television network, MTA.

The tradition of the Jalsa Salana was instituted by Mirza Ghulam Ahmad in 1891 in Qadian, and these gatherings are now organized around the world wherever there is a significant Ahmadi population. They have been held in at least thirty countries, although not in Pakistan since the intensification of legal persecution in 1984.[53] The Jalsa Salana is one of many community activities for which Ahmadis are expected to sacrifice financially, with all members donating 1/120 of their annual income toward its support. Ahmadi sources speak of Jalsa Salanas in ecstatic terms, and the religious significance of these gatherings goes far beyond their extensive programs of edifying speeches by celebrated clerics from the Jama'at. For my interlocutors in Qadian, the *jalsa* (gathering) mattered because it was the time of the year when the expansive and disciplined Jama'at system became most visible.

The UK Jalsa is nowadays by far the most important of these annual conventions. It is the "International Jalsa," which the caliph is guaranteed to attend and to which people from all over the world thus flock. Its importance also has subtle effects on the yearly calendar in Qadian. For example, it marks the beginning of the conversion year during which officers in charge of *tabligh* (communicating the message) count the annual numbers of Indian converts so that this figure can be announced by the caliph at the UK Jalsa.[54] For many in Qadian, the UK International Jalsa is looked forward to as a once-in-a-lifetime voyage: every year, some members of the Jama'at in Qadian, both male and female, are rewarded for their service with a sponsored trip to the UK to witness the Jalsa. Often, these are people who could never afford to pay for the trip themselves, let alone manage to get a UK visa without the sponsorship of the community. For the most part, however, Ahmadis far from London watch the International Jalsa via the continuous live footage played on MTA, and in Qadian, the rhythm of daily life changes to accommodate this broadcast.

In July 2011, I was in Qadian at the time of the UK Jalsa, and office hours in the Jama'at were curtailed slightly so that, allowing for the time difference between India and the United Kingdom, officials could leave work in time to see the live broadcast of the morning sessions. Televisions were placed in mosques to enable communal viewing, although most people watched from home. Walking through the Ahmadiyya neighborhood in the sweltering heat of the Punjabi summer, I did not miss a word of the Jalsa, for in every house, a television was tuned to MTA, and the sound carried through open windows so that it filled the streets and seemed to follow me as I walked. Moreover, there was a sense of local participation in this distant event, not unusual for MTA broadcasts but heightened during this period. When the caliph called for people to join him in prayer (*du'a*), those watching in Qadian would follow suit.[55] In the Ahmadi-owned teashops, which were the centers of male social life outside of the home and places where much of my research was conducted, televisions were switched from Bollywood music channels to MTA, and the caliph's appearance on screen would lead to older Ahmadis cautioning youngsters to be quiet.

Qadian's enthrallment in this televised event culminated on the final day of the UK Jalsa, when much of the town's Ahmadi population gathered in the two big mosques in the historic center of town, to partake in the global ritual of the International Bai'at. This ritual is a modern reformulation of a much older practice. *Bai'at* is the name given to an oath of allegiance and is most commonly encountered as an initiation into many Sufi sects. Mirza Ghulam Ahmad first took bai'at from his followers in 1889, during an event that is seen to mark the formal beginning of the Ahmadiyya community. Nowadays, new converts to Ahmadi-yyat continue to take bai'at as their entry into the community, but it is a bureau-cratic and formal process, and obviously not one carried out in the presence of the caliph. Once a year, however, the caliph appears on TV at the UK Jalsa to take the bai'at of Ahmadis around the world, both new converts and people born into the religion. This is the single annual moment of combined ritual in which all Ahmadis around the world are expected to synchronously participate. Unlike its formal counterpart, it retains elements of the original Sufi ritual of initiation, which was performed to create a link between devotee and master.[56] The International Bai'at was first staged in 1993, and it has since developed a very particular aesthetic form that is repeated, year after year, during its MTA broadcast.[57] In what follows, I describe it as a global ritual because it cannot be understood if viewed as simply a broadcast to which Ahmadis in Qadian responded. Rather, technical aspects of the live television broadcast needed to be performed correctly, and their improper implementation could lead to ritual failure. Camera angles, video editing, and even the placement of microphones and the sound mixing are parts of the ritual performance of this International Bai'at, as much as the responses of people sitting in the mosque in Qadian.

Each year, the International Bai'at is filmed using the same particular camera angles. The caliph enters the arena flanked by his retinue, wearing the original green coat that belonged to Mirza Ghulam Ahmad, which is preserved and used only for this occasion. Here, as elsewhere, the caliph is always shown walking toward the camera, until he arrives at the very front of the *jalsa gah* (literally meaning "gathering place," this is an enormous temporary structure erected to provide cover from the temperamental British weather), where he then sits on the floor before a low green table. Stretching out in front of him are single-file lines of men seated cross-legged on the floor, joining up with the larger crowd some way back, who fill the rest of the jalsa gah.

The caliph then places his hand on the table so that the devotees gathered around the table might join hands with him. The men in the lines then place their hands upon each other's backs such that they form an unbroken human chain going back to the main congregation, who likewise place their hands upon each other's backs. In this way, everybody in the arena is connected physically to the caliph. In the 2011 bai'at that I watched from Qadian, overhead cameras outside of the jalsa gah showed lines spreading out from the arena like the branches of a tree, composed of those on duty outside who had joined in this laying of hands.[58]

Once everybody is connected in this way, the caliph begins to read out the total number of converts to Ahmadiyyat over the previous year. The bai'at itself may then begin. The caliph recites the declaration of initiation, a phrase at a time, and this is repeated by all those present and ideally by all those watching on

TV.[59] He usually reads in English, although sometimes the Urdu text is also recited. At the end of each complete sentence, a discordant chorus sounds as translators in many languages proclaim the words simultaneously and at speed, as if trying to outdo each other in their passionate evocation of the caliph's words. This is a carefully produced part of the global ritual, during which the broadcast captures this exuberant eruption of sound in such a way that individual voices intertwine before occasionally separating into distinctive strands. The aesthetic goal is the creation of the global synchronicity of the ritual.

Each year, this moment in the ritual provides the opportunity for the creation of the most iconic image of Ahmadi devotion and subordination. Cameras on cranes slowly move across the mass of connected devotees, scanning the human lines emanating from the caliph, until finally the frame comes to rest directly above him. This bird's-eye image, with the caliph at the center and humanity radiating out from him, has become the defining aesthetic of the Ahmadiyya caliphate. Those close by and touching the caliph are seemingly chosen for their cosmopolitan appearance. As the camera focuses from above on the joining of hands, a multitude of headgear is shown. Some devotees will be wearing the typical Jinnah cap favored by Pakistani Ahmadis, while others may be wearing Saudi-style *kaffiyehs* or Indonesian *songkoks*. Likewise, European or African converts often feature prominently in these carefully composed scenes, their features being used to mark the universal success of the community. The picture shown by the camera thus mimics the broader ritual as it is intended to be: a moment when people from across the world simultaneously reaffirm their vows of obedience to their global leader.

At the end of this ritual, the caliph calls on his followers to prostrate themselves in thankfulness. As the congregation in the United Kingdom sink to their knees in *sajdah* (prostration), the camera usually rises up to pan across the arena. At this point, the microphones recording the event pick up something very specific: a quiet sobbing. Across the congregation, people weep as they reaffirm their connection to the caliph and, by extension, their relationship to God. This emotional outpouring is central to the aesthetics of the broadcast. It is also important that this is not a unidirectional emotional attachment, and the camera therefore often captures the moment when the caliph, rising out of his prostration, wipes tears from his own eyes with a handkerchief.[60]

In the mosque in Qadian where I watched the 2011 broadcast, a television placed in the south side of the building was watched by a packed congregation. Because of the television's placement, the congregation faced the side of the mosque, in other words, at forty-five degrees to the direction of the *qibla* in which Muslims normally pray. While watching the ritual on television, they did not join hands, and I was later told that the caliph, no doubt wary of accusations of idolatry, had explicitly forbade Ahmadis watching at home from touching the television screen. Instead, those present in the mosque refreshed their allegiance to the caliph by quietly repeating the words to the International Bai'at. As they recited this formula, they knew that across the world, Ahmadis in hundreds of countries were doing the same thing. Unlike Friday prayers, which must be performed at specific local times dependent on the position of the sun and thus can never be a universal phenomenon, this was a ritual in which the entire global Jama'at could simultaneously participate.

I was seated in the middle of the congregation, and when the caliph called for the sajdah at the end of the International Bai'at, the Ahmadis around me sank down to the floor of the mosque. I suddenly found myself looking out across prostrated bodies, the ceiling fans noisily turning above my head as occasional sobs rose from across in the mosque. Yet in that moment, something very interesting had happened. As this was a sajdah of thankfulness, there was no specified direction believers had to face. Those nearest the TV immediately prostrated in its direction, therefore facing south. Many of the men at the back of the mosque, however, seemed to pause for a moment, before a number of them turned forty-five degrees, and then only once facing Mecca did they kneel down in sajdah.

For my Ahmadi interlocutors, of course, one need not choose between the caliph and Mecca, for the caliph *is* the embodiment of true Islamic teaching. Yet the momentary hesitation of those at the back and the different positions that they chose to take point toward more fundamental questions about what it means to be Muslim in Qadian. How were Qadian's Ahmadis to evidence a truth of which they were convinced? How, in other words, were they to demonstrate their own Muslimness? As part of a global *ummah* of believers, signified by a universal orientation in prayer toward Mecca? As a group constituted through a shared ritual of allegiance on a television? Perhaps most importantly, however, this ethnographic vignette demonstrates that even when Qadian's Ahmadis should feel most unambiguously Muslim, they are confronted by a danger that in demonstrating that Muslimness, they might also undermine it. The International Bai'at is the yearly event through which the relationship between believers and the caliph should be most clearly demonstrable in all its aesthetic glory. It is when the global community marshals all its technological and economic capital to make this relationship visible in such a way that it produces a moment of unambiguous Muslimness. Yet in Qadian, it was accompanied by tension: a fleeting moment of uncertainty about how believers should position themselves toward their caliph and whether they could do so properly. The problem they faced was how to demonstrate their Muslimness in an unambiguous way such that the act of demonstration did not undermine a truth of which they were privately certain.

Doubt, Belief, and Anthropology

What I have so far described in this introduction is a troubled relationship to truth, which I think is characteristic of religious life in Qadian. We do, of course, have an English word for the troubled relationships that people have to truth: *doubt*. I have nonetheless chosen not to use this word. Understanding why I have chosen to do this, however, requires that we think a little more about what we mean when we use the word *doubt*.

Western thought does not lack engagements with doubt. Since its birth in ancient Greece, philosophy has sought to overcome doubt to arrive at knowledge. Philosophers have also frequently embraced doubt as a means through which to reach certain knowledge. René Descartes is the philosopher best known for using doubt as the method by which to arrive at certainty, but he was by no means the first to do so. Plato, Aristotle, and Aquinas all shared a similar methodological process of starting with propositions that might be doubted to then subsequently arrive at indubitable conclusions.[61] Within Western philosophy, doubt has thus been both a state from which philosophers have sought to emerge and also the means for its own transcendence. Knowing has always been dependent on doubt: certainty has been achievable only through doubt. For philosophers, doubt is a method through which a certainty stronger than that of faith might be achieved.[62]

A similar dynamic tension has structured much Western religious thought about the relationship between doubt and belief. A number of commentators have noted that believing necessarily implies the possibility of doubting.[63] The French ethnologist Jean Pouillon puts this succinctly: "to believe [*croire*] is to state a conviction; it is also to add a nuance to that conviction."[64] To say that you believe is, in other words, to signify that you are unsure. Indeed, within the long history of Christian thought, from St. Augustine to Kierkegaard, great emphasis has been given to the inescapable interdependence of doubt and belief, such that, for many Western thinkers, it can be hard to think about religion without doubt. The interconnectedness of doubt and belief in the Christian theological tradition can be illustrated through the much-interpreted story of the disciple Thomas. The inclusion of Thomas's doubts within the Gospel of John is representative of the way in which questions about the relationship between seeing, knowing, and believing lie at the heart of Christian scripture.[65] Throughout history, Thomas's story has also served as an endless source of inspiration for theologians and artists who wish to return to discourses on this subject. As one academic commentator has argued, Thomas can be seen as an "emblematic figure" for believers and nonbelievers alike: "his doubts are our doubts and his inconsistencies are our inconsistencies."[66] What the legacy of Doubting Thomas points toward is the fact that acts of recognizing and engaging with doubt have been integral to much

Christian theology. Indeed, doubt is often seen as the condition through which valued forms of religious practice are made possible. This is a position adopted, for example, by the popular historian Jennifer Hecht in a grand and wide-ranging narrative of the history of doubt.[67] Hecht argues that while belief existed prior to doubt, it was only the Greek's public culture of skepticism that made possible the idea of a religion structured around the active gesture of believing.[68] Standing back from this, we might say that while *doubting* has rarely been an aspired-to state for Christian theologians, a robust engagement with doubt, a willingness to entertain it, and a methodological embrace of doubt as a tool toward better faith have all been celebrated throughout the history of Christianity.

The various approaches to doubt from Western philosophy and theology that I have just referred to are diverse and in some cases irreconcilable with one another. They all, however, share one central feature: all these forms of doubt concern instabilities in a subject's capacity to either know or believe in a truth. There are ways of expressing this instability in more formal philosophical language. Epistemologists tend to divide doubt into two constituent parts: first-order doubts about one's beliefs and second-order doubts in which one questions the process by which one came to have those beliefs. This second type of doubt has been described as "epistemic self-doubt," and it refers to a state in which we doubt our ability to achieve true beliefs, a good example being Descartes's decision to doubt his own faculties of sense perception.[69] This division between first- and second-order doubt has led philosophers down interesting lines of investigation, for example, the question of epistemic akrasia. In brief, this is the question of whether a person can hold a belief in P even if they doubt their higher-order evidence about P, or to put it in even simpler terms: Can I believe something that I think I ought not to believe?[70] Likewise, philosophers have asked what we are to do when we discover "that our mechanisms for forming beliefs (and for revising them in the light of new evidence) are defective."[71] For many philosophers, an investigation into doubt is thus simultaneously an investigation into belief: each seems to require the other.[72] In other words, when philosophers talk about doubt, the default assumption is that it refers to the trouble people have with believing. People who doubt, it is assumed, are people who question their beliefs or people who question their reasons for having those beliefs.

Regarding religion, this assumption makes perfect sense in theological traditions in which the act of believing is a primary mark of faith and in which the challenges of belief are elaborated on and discussed at length. The situation does, however, become slightly more complicated in contexts where belief is not an object of intense concern and in which being religious is not just a matter of assenting to propositional statements. Indeed, in the past few decades, the work of anthropologists has been instrumental in challenging the idea that we might understand a religion simply by asking what beliefs it demands of its followers.[73] One prominent champion of this idea—the anthropologist Malcolm Ruel— quotes Wilfred Cantwell Smith to make this point: "The peculiarity of the place given to belief in Christian history is a monumental matter, whose importance and relative uniqueness must be appreciated. So characteristic has it been that un- suspecting Westerners have . . . been liable to ask about a religious group other than their own as well, 'What do they believe?' as though this were the primary question, and certainly were a legitimate one."[74] For Ruel, there is no single sta- ble Christian definition of belief across history, and transposing the notion of be- lief onto other religions is liable to make us misread the way in which people actually interact with the concepts and categories within religions. As Ruel notes (in a way that is prescient for the argument of this book), Islam is perhaps the religion that has the closest comparable concept to belief in the term *iman* (faith). And yet, the crucial act of Islam is to witness God rather than believe in him, and as such, "it is less the content of belief that has become elaborated in Islam than the duties of relationship."[75] It is possible to point out problems with Ruel's sweep- ing statement—after all, it seems to hark back to an Orientalist idea of Islam as rule bound and superficial—but it nonetheless signals an important point: if a religious tradition's key modality of relating to truth is testifying or witnessing rather than believing, its attendant forms of doubt are unlikely to be an elabora- tion on the struggles of belief.[76]

Since Ruel's path-breaking essay, a number of anthropologists have furthered his critique about the paucity of belief as a comparative term, and in doing so, they have shown that the drive to subsume religion into the category of belief has often assisted the interests of the powerful. Talal Asad famously argued that the idea of religion as private belief is ultimately a product of post-Enlightenment Christianity, which, while seemingly innocent enough, aided European domina- tion in many colonial settings.[77] The anthropologist Webb Keane has taken this argument even further, claiming that a Protestant notion of religion as private belief lies behind a globalized moral narrative of modernity that assigns value to a particular notion of individual agency.[78] In these accounts, the idea that reli- gion is solely a matter of private belief is historicized, contextualized, and shown to be a moral claim that originates in particular forms of (usually Protestant) Christian faith.

This body of literature has, in other words, historicized and contextualized be- lief. Furthermore, it has helped us to appreciate the fact that when belief is used as a comparative tool, it often ends up distorting the actual relationship that people have to concepts, ideas, and truths within their religions. But what has this got to teach us about doubt? Well, my point is very simple: Should we not also be ques- tioning our implicit linking of doubt to belief, that is, our assumption that doubt is a problem that people have in believing or knowing propositions? Should we not, in other words, be thinking about the ways in which our use of doubt as an analytical tool of cross-cultural comparison risks distorting the actual relationships that people cultivate to the concepts, ideas, and truths of their religion?

This argument certainly holds for Qadian. What I have described in this introduction is a troubled relationship to truth that does not involve anxieties over either belief or knowledge. These are people whose religious uncertainties seem to escape our definitions of doubt in a way that is deeply troubling for traditional social scientific analysis, for the fact remains that in many parts of the academy, extraordinary value is placed on the capacity that people have to doubt. In particular—within anthropology but also much more broadly within the academy—the possession of doubt is seen as a crucial marker of shared humanistic subjectivity.[79] In broader social discourses, doubt is often seen as that which separates the (neo-)medieval from the modern.[80] Its absence brands the fundamentalist "repugnant," while its presence renders the Other human.[81] There is, in other words, a tendency in much modern thought to tie the common humanity of the Other to their possession of a recognizable form of doubt. Indeed, contemporary thinkers are wont to agonize about whether we doubt too much, too little, or in the right ways and to condemn those who fail to do so. For example, the sociologists Peter Berger and Anton Zijderveld have made a plea for the necessity of doubt as a way of avoiding the excesses of both relativism (which produces dangerous forms of uncertainty, i.e., excessive doubt) and fundamentalism (which is altogether too certain, i.e., it lacks doubt). In making this argument, and in seeing doubt as a genuine source of tolerance, these authors place themselves within a much longer genealogy of thought that includes, for example, the ideas of Sebastian Castellio (d. 1563), a theologian who publicly quarreled with Calvin over religious freedom and who refused to see doubt as opposed to knowledge and faith, instead understanding it as a necessary step on the path toward truth.[82] Recognizable doubt is thus celebrated as an essential part of the human condition, and it is frequently seen as something that we must embrace if we are to grow politically and intellectually.

Indeed, within sociological and anthropological thinking, a lack of doubt has almost always been treated as something worrying and unnatural: as something that requires real explanation because it implies the presence of cultural factors that prevent people from indulging in their natural skepticism. By contrast, the presence of doubt has often been seen as a default mode of being human, which requires no explanation on the part of the social scientist. This has been particularly obvious in situations where social scientists have set out to study such groups as the Ahmadiyya community: new religious movements with strong hierarchical organizations and cosmologies that tend to differ substantially from their broader cultural context.[83] When examining these minority religious movements—or sects, as they are often known—sociologists have thus tended to ask how it is possible for sect members to lack doubts in spite of the fact that their beliefs deviate so broadly from accepted norms and in spite of the fact that these sect members must necessarily confront the incomprehension of outsiders on a regular basis.[84] The incredulity of the social scientist is often heightened in such situations by the fact that they find the beliefs of the people they are studying dubious. A standard approach to studying insular religious sects has thus been to investigate the mechanisms through which these sects manage to erase doubts in the minds of their followers.[85] Scholars of religion have consequently asked how certainty gets produced and what bearing it has on the relative flourishing or failure of new religious movements.[86] Fundamentally, the question becomes: What kinds of coercion and control are necessary for people to act in this way? Therefore, where doubt is not present, its absence is assumed to require explanation and quite possibly condemnation. We assume that doubt must be a central problem for the religious, and when the religious do not appear to be afflicted by it, its absence becomes a major problem for our analysis. The Ahmadiyya Jama'at is one example of a religious organization that would, in standard sociological theory, be seen to contain numerous "plausibility structures" to maintain certainty and ward off doubt.[87] Their conviction would be seen as 'unreal' unless enforced through social mechanisms that effectively curtail people's natural inclinations toward skepticism.

My goal in this book is to ask whether we might approach the Ahmadis' lack of obvious doubt in a different fashion. My argument is that our concern with doubt has narrowed our social scientific gaze and caused us to focus on only a particular and very specific way in which people problematize their relationship to truth. In other words, our analytical assumption that we need to explain a lack of doubt may in fact be built on a false premise, for we have been trying to explain why people do not doubt while all the while forgetting that "belief" might be a poor depiction of their relationship to truth. In this introduction, I have sought to show that, even though my interlocutors do not problematize their ability to either know or believe in truth (i.e., they entertained neither first- nor second-order doubts), their relationship to truth is far from untroubled. This is because they find themselves in the position of asking what they might owe to truth and whether they can fulfill their obligations to that truth. It is worth noting that despite what other Muslims might say of the Ahmadis, this is a very Islamic way of approaching the divine, for it is about being a witness to truth. As Emilio Spadola has observed, throughout history, "sources of Islamic discursive tradition repeatedly invoke the Divine call and define piety as responsibility to it."[88] The question is not whether you can believe in truth but whether you can respond to it. In Qadian, people wonder whether they can fulfill this responsibility by adequately demonstrating and proving truth. Their concerns and anxieties thus revolve not around belief, but around the nature of evidence, the viability of proof, and their own capacities to materialize truth within the world.

It is thus only when we start thinking about doubt beyond belief that we might begin to understand a place like Qadian as a location of all-to-human uncertainty. If we continue to see doubt only as the inverse of belief, the anxieties that are felt within groups like the Ahmadiyya Jama'at—hierarchically organized, insular, and with clear forms of religious authority—will remain inaccessible and veiled. They will appear to us as narrow-minded or fundamentalist, for there is simply nothing in the daily life of Qadian's Ahmadis that approximates what we expect doctrinal doubt to look like. Moreover, and more problematically, a narrow focus on doubt (as the opposite of belief) makes the curious mix of absolute conviction and troubled uncertainty that is so characteristic of life in Qadian appear unreal and paradoxical. I want to argue instead that in Qadian, a radical certainty about one's ability to know universal truth can and does coexist with a reflexive consideration of one's relationship to that truth. Fundamentally, the two are not incompatible, but if we want to understand how this is so, we need to cast aside our search for doubt, rethink the vocabulary we use to describe how people approach the truths of their religions, and begin to think about what uncertainty might look like if it is not simply a matter of belief.

Practice, Belief, and Religious Exclusion

My ambition to think about my interlocutors' doubts beyond belief also has a broader political goal of rejecting the obsession that opponents show in Ahmadi belief. Non-Ahmadi denials of the Ahmadis' Muslimness have, since the inception of the Ahmadiyya community, rested on assumptions of an inner truth that is masked by an outer deception. For example, Mirza Ghulam Ahmad's defense of colonial rule, his praise of the British system of governance, and his claim that jihad against the British was illegitimate have all been seized on by opponents as evidence that he was a British agent charged with neutering and dividing the Muslims of the subcontinent. This view, which continues to be widely held by South Asian Muslims today, rests on a notion of deception and dissimulation—that Ahmad hid his true purpose behind claims to prophethood. In anti-Ahmadi propaganda, it is common to hear accusations of deceit leveled against Ahmadis, who are said to deny their true goal of bringing down Pakistan.[89] Behind the appearance of being normal Muslims, the Ahmadis are thus accused of being agents of Israel, the United States, or Britain, intent on destroying Islam like a cancer from within. There is much productive work still to be done on the intertwining of anti-Ahmadi prejudice in Pakistan and discourses of anti-Semitism, and the ways in which each draws on notions of concealment and duplicity to present the other as an enemy within. This logic emerges, for example, in the Pakistani Constitution, which describes Ahmadis as "posing" as real Muslims. In all cases, Ahmadis are seen as fake Muslims, as dishonest imitations of authentic Muslims. The problem with Ahmadis, in other words, is felt to rest on a distinction between an (heretical) inner belief and a deceptive outer facade. Opponents claim to be able to see beneath the surface: to know what Ahmadis really believe.

This situation demonstrates the peculiarly modern nature of the conflict between the Ahmadis and their opponents, for this conflict relies on an anxiety about the sincerity of belief, a concern that has not always existed within Islamic traditions.[90] As Talal Asad (among others) has shown, a Muslim subject's social behavior and practice has historically been seen to matter more than their inner thoughts, and unlike in certain Christian traditions in which thoughts might commit blasphemy, in many Muslim societies, thoughts have been treated as inviolable so long as practice conformed to expectations.[91] Historically, orthopraxy rather than orthodoxy has thus been key to membership within the community of Islam. In light of this, the Ahmadi predicament is unique, for their orthopraxy is nowadays taken as evidence for their heterodoxy. What seems to matter to opponents of the Jama'at is the supposed insincerity of Ahmadis: the fact that their beliefs are not those of Muslims but that their actions are.

As the following chapters will show, my Ahmadi interlocutors feel only disdain for the obsession that others have with knowing their minds. To all those who declare them non-Muslim, they offer up their lives, their system, and their infallible devotion to the caliph as a challenge. *Come*, they say, *look at our system, and then tell us without hypocrisy that it is us and not you who are the unbelievers.* This is a challenge that they are certain none can answer.

Doing Ethnography in Qadian

This book draws on fifteen months of fieldwork in Qadian between November 2010 and April 2012. In addition, it makes use of insights gained during a number of years' acquaintance with Ahmadis living in the United Kingdom. Qadian has never been the subject of a full-length study before, and while it has been discussed in historical accounts of the Jama'at, its post-1947 condition has attracted little attention.[92] When mentioned, Qadian has been described as having stagnated due to isolation, with the attitudes of its residents unchanged since partition.[93] In this book, I show that Ahmadis in Qadian are equally concerned by the possibility of stagnation. A result of this is that Qadian's Ahmadis rethink and rework "traditional" forms of life as ways of staking a claim to the global modernity of the Jama'at and, ultimately, to being Muslim. This is most apparent in the strict observance of purdah (the separation of men and women) within the Ahmadiyya neighborhood of Qadian, the rigidity of which exceeded that of all other Ahmadi communities that I came in contact with. Anthropologists have shown that in much of the Muslim world, reformist movements have reframed veiling as an act that signals a consciously modern Muslim identity.[94] Qadian must be thought of in similar terms. Purdah is here not simply a hangover from an ancient past but a conscious attempt to demonstrate the *tarbiyyat* (education or cultivation) of the caliphate and thus make Muslimness demonstrable. This created limitations to my research, and consequently, this book is almost entirely about Qadian's male population. My interactions with women were limited to extremely brief exchanges of pleasantries with relatives of close friends. It was often inappropriate for me to even speak with the grandmothers of my friends. The small and cramped houses of the Ahmadiyya neighborhood made it exceptionally difficult for unrelated men to socialize in each others' houses while keeping purdah. This meant that Qadian's large and unattached population of young male students and missionaries would rarely socialize in domestic spaces. To my surprise, I once discovered that a bachelor friend, who was otherwise a popular and sociable young man, had spent most of the festival of 'Eid asleep. When I asked him why, he explained that it was a tedious occasion for a single man, because in Qadian, "we do not go to our friends' houses," and he therefore had nowhere to celebrate. One result of these restrictions is that Qadian has a vibrant culture of public male sociality that is informed by a reflexive concern about the kind of Islam that such sociality can demonstrate.[95] Much of this book is concerned with this public domain as an arena through which Ahmadis engaged the question of being Muslim.

Outline of the Book

Chapter 1 introduces the distinctive theology of Mirza Ghulam Ahmad, before exploring the historical processes through which the Ahmadi-caliph relationship became the dominant mode by which members of today's Jama'at attempt to evidence their Muslimness. In the early twentieth century, the second caliph directed a series of massive expansions to the Jama'at system and institutionalized key relationships of devotion, including a new scheme in which Ahmadis were encouraged to give their lives in service as *waqf*, an Islamic term normally reserved for endowments of property. Chapter 1 also explores the ambivalent political aspirations of the Ahmadiyya caliphate. Described by his followers as nonpolitical, the caliph nevertheless follows a Sufi tradition of exercising a spiritual sovereignty that overlaps with and potentially encompasses worldly power. Furthermore, I show that the Ahmadi-caliph relationship is understood to have its own political trajectory leading to the establishment of a new world system in which conventional secular politics are rendered defunct. For my interlocutors, this relationship is the Jama'at's revolutionary gift to the world.

As a result of the historical processes described in Chapter 1, life in Qadian is now dominated by the administrative system of the Ahmadiyya Jama'at. Chapter 2 examines how this system performs a crucial role in the Ahmadis' struggle to demonstrate their Muslimness: through the rational ordering of life, the system creates the intimate and direct relationship with the caliph that Qadian's Ahmadis so fervently desire. As such, this is an "enchanting bureaucracy," for it sacralizes life in the town. In explicit contrast with the Indian state, Ahmadis in Qadian argue that their Jama'at bureaucracy provides them with direct access to justice. This utopian vision is nonetheless impossible to sustain, and when it collapses beneath the weight of disagreements and resentments, the Ahmadi-caliph relationship that the system produced appears to be an imitation. In the context of my interlocutors' struggles to prove their Muslimness, the enchanting bureaucracy simultaneously produces both certainty and its antithesis. It might thus be considered to produce a *counterfeit proof* of Muslimness.

Popular criticism about the intellectual practices of South Asian Muslims often focuses on the fact that they do not appear to know how to doubt "properly." This is partly because much sectarian disputation between Muslim sects in South Asia has as its stated goal the shoring up of intellectual boundaries and the silencing of opponents. Chapter 3 examines the unexpected ways in which Ahmadis partake in this culture of sectarian disputation, and it explores how they cultivate an argumentative subjectivity that I refer to as "heroic polemicism." The argument of this chapter is that if we continue to approach this heroic polemicism through narrow categories of epistemic doubt and belief, we will miss the actual relationship to truth that Ahmadis in Qadian attempt to cultivate, alongside the uncertainties that they feel in discharging their obligations to truth. Furthermore, this chapter explores how Ahmadis embrace the modern world as a landscape of opportunity that offers almost unlimited resources through which they might expand the all-conquering truths of their Promised Messiah.

What happens when arguments fail and when polemics are insufficient to make a Muslim apparent? Chapter 4 looks at what appears to be a drastic last-resort attempt to prove Muslim identity in the form of an open challenge to all opponents issued by the fourth caliph in 1988. This was the *mubahala*, an ordeal that takes the form of a prayer duel to the death in which God is expected to smite the false party and thus make truth visible. Many Ahmadis believe that the (still unexplained) 1988 death of the president of Pakistan, General Zia ul-Haq, was a direct result of this mubahala challenge. In spite of this seeming victory, however, it would appear that the fourth caliph actually challenged his opponents to this ordeal *in order to let the ritual fail.* Chapter 4 examines how an ordeal designed to produce testable and empirical proof of Muslimness ended up functioning through its failures rather than its successes. In issuing this challenge, the fourth caliph was ridiculing his opponents and mocking their claims to know the minds of the Ahmadis. In fact, I show that the call to mubahala was an argument for the demonstrability of Muslimness through the quality and nature of a person's social relations.

Chapter 5 explores how Qadian's Ahmadis attempt to inscribe their Muslimness in the world through the cultivation of an exemplary aesthetic of universal devotion to the caliph. Since the creation of the community satellite television network MTA in 1994, Ahmadis have increasingly been placed in situations in which they are called on to witness the truth of Ahmadiyyat by watching images of themselves performing this exemplary aesthetic. Chapter 5 asks what happens when Qadian's Ahmadis are presented to the world as "proof" even though they feel their actions to be imitative of genuine exemplarity. What happens, in other words, when they are called on to witness truth in their own "counterfeit proof"? I show that in such moments, they are in fact able to achieve a certainty that otherwise eludes them, for in these broadcasts they are comforted by belonging to the only system capable of enforcing truth upon them. Being a witness to truth means opening up the self to this authority.

The conclusion to this book develops the idea that my interlocutors' worries over manifesting and demonstrating truth often give rise to what I describe as counterfeit proofs, which simultaneously prove and undermine Ahmadiyya Muslimness. I explore how such counterfeit proofs might help us to rethink the place of doubt in anthropological theory, and I argue that anthropology's poverty of imagination regarding doubt has had two consequences. First, it has resulted in a situation in which much anthropological work is driven forward by a desire to discover doubting subjects that resemble us. Second, it has meant that when we encounter people (such as the Ahmadis) whose relationship to truth is foreign to us, we have often been unable to recognize them as holding very human forms of uncertainty. Moving forward, I argue, requires that we provincialize our own celebration of an interior-orientated doubting subject to recognize the presence of other archetypal doubting subjects, such as the Ahmadis' heroic polemicist. Doing so will broaden our appreciation of the various kinds of trouble that people might have with truth.

THE HISTORY OF THE AHMADI-CALIPH RELATIONSHIP

In the monumental opus *What Is Islam?*, Shahab Ahmed attempts to capture a way of being Muslim that flourished from the end of Islam's classical period until about 1850. It was, Ahmed argues, a form of being Muslim that was creative and explorative, that could openly embrace contradiction, that did not need to legitimate itself through a mimesis of pristine authenticity.[1] In short, it was a way of inhabiting a religious identity that has never been available to Qadian's Ahmadis. Indeed, it was only after the collapse of this self-confident and taken-for-granted understanding of what it meant to be Muslim that the conditions emerged in which the creation of the Ahmadiyya Jama'at could be dreamt of. Mirza Ghulam Ahmad belonged to a generation of Indian reformers and religious thinkers who began their careers in the period after the rebellion of 1857, when the last remnants of the Mughal Empire were finally destroyed, and Islam's fall from primacy in the subcontinent was laid bare. After these calamitous events, a number of self-conscious attempts were undertaken to reform Islam and to recapture a sense of surety in being Muslim. Two of these reform movements in particular are often cited as representing contrasting responses to the need to reform Islam. These were a modernist embrace of the west, as typified by the establishment of Aligarh Muslim University, and a reactionary retreat into tradition, often associated with the establishment of the Islamic seminary at Deoband.[2] In this broader context, Mirza Ghulam Ahmad's lifework must be seen as an attempt to recuperate Muslim confidence, in particular through a muscular and argumentative engagement with Hinduism and Christianity. The community he founded was part of a larger set of cultural movements that sought to recapture a surety about what it meant to be Muslim when faced with a situation in which such identity could no longer be assumed in an unproblematic fashion. For his modern-day followers, Mirza Ghulam Ahmad is understood to have achieved this goal with astonishing success, for he removed the inconsistencies that had crept into Islamic theology over the preceding centuries and delivered to his followers a body of religious truth that could be known and understood in a clear, rational, and uncomplicated fashion. As we saw in the last chapter, this does not, however, mean that my interlocutors in Qadian enjoy a straightforward relationship to truth. While the truths of Ghulam Ahmad may be eminently knowable, they are not always provable, and consequently, contemporary Ahmadis in Qadian attempt to evidence truth by cultivating the demonstrability of their relationship with the caliph. The importance of the Ahmadi-caliph relationship nonetheless developed only slowly in the decades following Ghulam Ahmad's death: quite how this relationship came to be such a foundational aspect of what it means to prove truth in Qadian is the subject of this chapter.

The Promised Messiah

We can say with certainty that Mirza Ghulam Ahmad was born in Qadian, but other details about his entry into this world are a matter of modern-day dispute. Ahmadi sources as late as 1914 place his birth date in 1838 to 1839,[3] and yet nowadays, the Jama'at argues that his date of birth was February 13, 1835, claiming earlier estimates had been wrong due to a lack of records from the period.[4] This issue is contentious because Mirza Ghulam Ahmad prophesied that he would live to be more or less eighty years of age.[5] Non-Ahmadis continue to argue that he was born in the late 1830s and that his prophecy was therefore fraudulent. For Ahmadis who insist on the earlier birth date of 1835, however, this is an example of a glorious fulfilled prophecy.

According to his own writings, Ahmad's family had been the major landholders in the area of Qadian during the Mughal period but lost their holdings in 1802 due to Sikh political ascendency in Punjab.[6] The family was forced from Qadian and lived in impoverished exile until 1818, when they were allowed to return in exchange for military service. After the family sided with the British in the rebellion of 1857, their fortunes were somewhat reversed, and seemingly because of this, Ghulam Ahmad remained loyal to the British throughout his life.[7] Indeed, Ghulam Ahmad repeatedly celebrated the British in his writings and insisted on the justness of colonial rule in India.[8] This family history continues to inform present-day understandings of colonial history in Qadian, with many Ahmadis seeing the British as the saviors of Muslims from Hindu and Sikh oppression.

Moreover, Ghulam Ahmad's defense of the colonial state forms the basis of the Ahmadis' firmly held doctrine that Muslims should pledge allegiance to a ruling government so long as it guarantees religious freedom (a doctrine that, from the outside, looks very much like secularism). Among opponents in present-day South Asia, however, these are some of the most vilified aspects of Ghulam Ahmad's writings. For these critics of the Ahmadiyya Jama'at, this doctrine is evidence that Ahmad was an agent of colonial powers, tasked with dividing the Muslims of India.

Ghulam Ahmad lived the first few decades of his life in relative obscurity but rose rapidly to prominence in 1880 with the publication of the first volume of what Ahmadis regard as his magnum opus, the *Barahin-e-Ahmadiyya*, or Proofs of Ahmadiyya.[9] It was at this time that he began to make his first and most modest claims to a special spiritual standing, by implying that he was the *mujaddid* of the era.[10] A mujaddid, often assumed in Islamic tradition to be a scholar, is thought to live at the turn of every century in the Islamic calendar and to act as a reformer.

In the decades after the publication of *Barahin-e-Ahmadiyya*, Ghulam Ahmad embarked on a career of religious debate, argument, and disputation that was, even for this time, "remarkable."[11] He published an extensive catalog of books, pamphlets, and tracts; he issued challenges to his enemies, and he engaged in public debates. At first, Ahmad positioned himself as a defender of Islam, but he also began to increasingly debate and argue with other Muslim reformers. A number of these debates were high profile and controversial, and they were also frequently inconclusive.[12] In 1896, Ahmad predicted the death of a Hindu polemicist of the reform group the Arya Samaj, with whom he had clashed in the past. This Hindu reformer was assassinated within six months of the prediction by people unconnected with Ghulam Ahmad, but the coincidence of the prediction with the assassination was enough to attract the notice of the police.[13] If Ahmad's goal had been to bring attention to his spiritual claims, then through his long career of disputation and prophecy, he had succeeded. In engaging in arguments with Muslim, Christian, and Hindu opponents, in issuing challenges, and by virtue of his unique theology, Ahmad had by the beginning of the twentieth century aroused the hostility of every other reform group in Punjab.[14] Throughout this period of remarkable public activity, Ahmad refined and gradually enlarged his own claims to special spiritual standing. Had he claimed only to be a reformer, he could have remained simply an unconventional defender of the faith, but it was his eventual insistence on his own prophethood that signaled what many Muslims continue to interpret as an irreparable break from Islamic tradition.

Ghulam Ahmad's claims to special spiritual standing were complex and multilayered. Most importantly, he argued that he was the embodiment of two eschatological figures, the Promised Messiah and the mahdi, and he claimed that in being so, he was a prophet. Ghulam Ahmad's claim to prophethood has aroused enormous ire within the Muslim world because it is seen to contradict the notion that Muhammad is the seal of the prophets. This phrase is taken from the Qur'an (33:40) and is generally understood to imply that Muhammad was the final prophet of all time. Consequently, any claimant to prophethood after Muhammad must necessarily be a false pretender, delusional, or both. Ghulam Ahmad, however, argued that his prophethood was completely consistent with Muhammad being the seal of the prophets.[15] Ghulam Ahmad applied the words *nabi* (prophet) and *rasul* (messenger) to himself and even wrote a pamphlet to clear up misconceptions among his followers that he might not be claiming to do so.[16] For Ghulam Ahmad, there was no great theological distinction between nabi and rasul. He argued that the important difference instead lay between law-bearing prophets and non-law-bearing prophets. By this, he meant those prophets who bring a sharia and those who do not. This is where his interpretation of "seal" differs from Sunni Muslims. Ghulam Ahmad understood seal to mean that Muhammad was the most perfect of prophets, that it was only by following Muhammad that anybody else could achieve subsequent prophethood, and that Muhammad was the final prophet to bring a sharia, or divine law, to the world. In other words, Muhammad was the last law-bearing prophet, whereas he, Mirza Ghulam Ahmad, brought no new law. Ghulam Ahmad thus claimed to be a prophet, but a very specific kind of prophet. He was a prophet without his own sharia, for he attained his own prophethood only by his absolute faithfulness to the sharia of Muhammad. His prophethood was thus a "shadow" (*zill*) of Muhammad's. In making this claim, he was arguing that Muhammad's status as the seal of the prophets meant that all doors to prophethood have been closed bar one: the annihilation (*fana'*) of the self in the Prophet Muhammad.[17] Only in absolutely loosing himself in his devotion to the Prophet could Ghulam Ahmad thus attain prophethood, and not, he was careful to maintain, by way of any personal attribute. Ghulam Ahmad's identification with the Prophet Muhammad was thus a result of his becoming a *buruz*, or manifestation of the latter.[18] For many opponents, this was not just an act of self-aggrandizement but also a dangerous theological move, for they argue that Ghulam Ahmad's position ultimately implies that the perfection of Muhammad's prophethood was dependent on Ghulam Ahmad achieving this status.[19]

Ghulam Ahmad's claim to prophethood has dominated academic discussion of the Ahmadiyya Jama'at, and the protection (or defense) of the finality of prophethood continues to be the major focus of anti-Ahmadiyya activity in Pakistan. Ghulam Ahmad's claim to prophethood was nonetheless a secondary result of his claim to be the Promised Messiah, which to this day remains far more important for his modern followers in Qadian. There, he is almost always referred to as simply the Promised Messiah (Masih Mau'od). Ahmad's other major claim was to have been the mahdi. There have been, and still are, many claimants to this title; at one point, Iran reportedly had three thousand mahdis in jail.[20] Literally meaning "the guided one," the mahdi is expected to come at the end of days and fight the Antichrist, or *dajjal*. A commonly cited hadith reports that the mahdi "will break the cross, kill the swine, and abolish war."[21] Ghulam Ahmad stripped this hadith of its apocalyptic and violent dimensions and instead interpreted it to mean that as mahdi, he would be victorious over the Christian belief in the crucifixion and resurrection of Jesus. Thus, Ghulam Ahmad wrote, "the creed of the cross would come to an end and complete its life span, not through war or violence, but exclusively through heavenly causes, *in the form of scientific reason and argument*."[22]

My goal is not to probe the claims of Ghulam Ahmad in greater depth. Other scholars, particularly Yohanan Friedmann and Adil Hussain Khan, have done so in remarkably comprehensive detail.[23] Rather, in the remainder of this section, I highlight aspects of Ghulam Ahmad's argumentative style that remain important to the possibilities and aspirations of ethical life in contemporary Qadian. A number of historians have shown how interreligious debates between reform groups in colonial Punjab led to new forms of communal identity and new kinds of public.[24] In studies of the Jama'at, what has been less remarked on is the fact that to this day, Ahmadis continue to draw on an almost mythological reading of nineteenth-century Punjab as a place of disputation in which Ghulam Ahmad stood alone as an all-conquering polemicist. As a result, for Qadian's contemporary population, Ghulam Ahmad's celebrated status as a polemicist continues to create specific possibilities for being Muslim. Most importantly, Ghulam Ahmad's claims and his style of argument paved the way for a particular understanding of exemplary action in the modern Jama'at.

In order to justify his prophethood in a combative culture of disputation, Ahmad developed an extraordinarily rich theology of proofs. To this day, these proofs constitute the arsenal of arguments deployed by Ahmadi missionaries in their disputes with opponents, and the glorious efficiency of these arguments in silencing hostile challenges is much lauded among Qadian's Ahmadis. One of the most remarkable features of these proofs is the centrality of the figure of Jesus (Isa) to Ghulam Ahmad's attempts to conclusively disprove both Christianity and other forms of Islam. Indeed, Ahmad's own claim to be the Promised Messiah is dependent on his historical thesis that Jesus died not on the cross but of a natural death in Kashmir. This thesis is most clearly laid out in Ahmad's treatise of 1899, *Masih Hindustan Main*, or *Jesus in India*.[25] The book describes in detail how Jesus could not have died on the cross, for to do so would be an accursed death. Instead, Ghulam Ahmad argues that Jesus was crucified for only two hours, before being taken down and healed, so that he could subsequently travel east to continue his work of ministering to the lost tribes of Israel. In the course of Jesus's search for these scattered tribes, he traveled through present-day Afghanistan and Punjab and arrived in Kashmir, where he died at the age of 120. Ghulam Ahmad further speculated that Jesus may have traveled as far as Tibet, Nepal, and even Varanasi. Ghulam Ahmad was not the first to suggest that Jesus traveled to Asia: he based his work on preexisting ideas about Jesus's lost years in India. He was, however, the first to propose that Jesus traveled to India after the crucifixion.

To understand why Ahmadis see this argument as obliterating any opposition to Ghulam Ahmad's prophethood, we need to first understand mainstream Muslim ideas about Jesus. Jesus is mentioned in multiple places in the Qur'an and is understood by all Muslims to be a prophet. There is a tradition, accepted by most Muslims, that Jesus did not die on the cross but was instead taken up to heaven by God, where he awaits the end of days.[26] When Ahmad was engaging in his polemical defense of Islam in colonial Punjab, these widespread ideas about Jesus made it extremely hard for Muslims to defend themselves against Christian missionaries' arguments that a living Jesus, as compared to a dead Muhammad, proved the superiority of Christianity over Islam.[27] In the single act of proving that Jesus died a natural death, Ahmad saw himself as achieving multiple victories over his opponents. First, he disproved the Christian notion of the resurrection and thus the divinity of Christ. In doing so, he provided evidence for the Muslim notion that Jesus was merely a prophet of God, not God's son. Second, he disproved the disquieting notion that Jesus, a prophet of lower rank than Muhammad, should be alive while the latter was dead. Third, he opened the way for Jesus's return in a metaphorical rather than literal sense. This third point was crucial to the development of Ghulam Ahmad's full claim to prophetic rank. Most Muslims believe that the awaited messiah of Islam will be Jesus himself, who will descend from the heavens, where he currently resides.[28] Ghulam Ahmad's claim that Jesus in fact died on earth means that the second coming of Jesus must be metaphorical. Ghulam Ahmad thus declared that he was this metaphorical second coming of Jesus: he claimed to both resemble the earlier messiah and to have received revelation that he had been transformed into Jesus.[29]

What is most interesting about Ghulam Ahmad's thesis regarding Jesus, however, is that it was only partly founded on revelation. In order to justify his claims, Ghulam Ahmad had turned historical investigator and in the 1890s made a series of empirical "discoveries" that would eventually culminate in the publication of *Jesus in India*. In the introduction to the book, he thus argues that the thesis deals in "established facts, conclusive historical evidence of proven value, and ancient documents of other nations."[30] Indeed, to structure this argument about Jesus, Ghulam Ahmad drew on a wide variety of evidence from Christian and Muslim scripture, medieval medical texts, and historical accounts. From scripture,

Ghulam Ahmad made the claim that Jesus had to be taken down from the cross before he had died because of the coming of the Sabbath. Blood spurting from the spear wound in Jesus's side was used as medical evidence that Jesus still lived. Ghulam Ahmad then argued that once taken down from the cross, Jesus was treated with an ointment mentioned in medieval texts, the *marham-e-Isa*, which was of such potency that within three days Jesus was able to walk again, hence the Christian confusion over the resurrection. Ghulam Ahmad additionally provided numerous historical, anecdotal, and speculative etymological arguments to show that the people of Kashmir and Afghanistan were indeed the lost tribes of Israel. Furthermore, Ghulam Ahmad attempted to prove definitively that Jesus was not, as some had argued, influenced by Buddhism; rather, his preaching was incorporated into Buddhism, and Jesus later came to be conflated with the person of the Buddha.

There is a good deal of conjecture in this text, and many observers have not taken it seriously.[31] Yet to dismiss it is to overlook its real importance; we have here a claim to prophethood made not just as revelatory statement but as a sustained thesis drawing on multiple different forms of source material. It is presented as a clearly structured empirical case that makes appeals to logic and reason. It is a single-minded defense of an idea; an exposition or treatise that is designed to present the reader with an argument that is above all else robust. It is an argument for an enchanted rationality in which prophethood is equated with analysis and evaluation.[32]

Another strand of Ghulam Ahmad's thought that is much promoted by the contemporary Jama'at is his rejection of violent jihad. This doctrine was linked to his theological argument that the mahdi is a nonviolent figure. It was also related to another of Ghulam Ahmad's major theological claims: the idea that verses of the Qur'an do not abrogate (*naskh*) one another. The Qur'an contains multiple verses on violent jihad, some of which seem to imply that it is always necessary, others that it is to be avoided apart from in defense. The traditional scholarly interpretation of this discrepancy rests on the idea that the Qur'an was revealed over a long period: later verses therefore render earlier (and conflicting) verses null. Ghulam Ahmad rejected this theology of abrogation and argued that the Qur'an is perfect and consistent. To preserve this unity, he reasoned that Qur'anic verses apply to the circumstances in which they were revealed. Thus, violent jihad would only ever be valid in a situation of grave danger akin to that which the early Muslims faced.[33]

Ghulam Ahmad's efforts to claim that Islam is a religion of peace were undoubtedly linked to attacks from both Christian missionaries and Hindu reformers, who in the nineteenth century claimed that Islam was an inherently violent religion.[34] Such assertions about Islam have obviously not gone away, and subsequent Ahmadi caliphs have elaborated extensively on the idea of nonviolent jihad.[35] Nowadays, an insistence that Islam is a religion of peace structures the community's continuous efforts to engage the non-Muslim world in ethical conversation.[36] This doctrine is condensed to its most basic form as a slogan—"love for all, hatred for none"—and used by the Ahmadis to court power in countries where Islamic extremism is seen as the dangerous other. This reduction of Ghulam Ahmad's theology to a slogan nonetheless contains an elision. For Ghulam Ahmad, jihad may no longer have been violent, but that did not mean it was nonconfrontational. Ghulam Ahmad's polemics against his opponents were his jihad, and they were at times full of fierce imagery and descriptive terminology. For Ahmadis living in Qadian and speaking Urdu, Ghulam Ahmad's ferocious polemics are celebrated and emulated (see chapter 3). It is only as discourse is shifted to English—when the Jama'at hopes to speak to India's cosmopolitan urban centers or foreign audiences—that polemics cease to be celebrated and Ahmadis focus solely on the simple message that Islam is a religion of peace. I am not the first to note this discrepancy. The theologian Yohanan Friedmann, writes, "In its relationship with the non-Muslim world, however, the Aḥmadiyya is primarily engaged in defending Islam and depicting it as a liberal, humane, and progressive religion, wrongfully calumnied by non-Muslims. Understandably, these elements figure much more prominently in the publications of the movement in English than in those in Urdu or Arabic."[37]

The Establishment of the Caliphate

The theological claims outlined above continue to be important points of contention between the Ahmadis and their opponents, but being Ahmadi Muslim in contemporary Qadian is about more than theology. Being Muslim in Qadian is fundamentally a matter of belonging to an organization, being disciplined within that organization, and bearing witness to the organization's unity and strength under a single global leader. This particular vision of what it means to be Muslim developed after Ghulam Ahmad's death, particularly during the reign of the second caliph, Mirza Basheer ud-Din Mahmood Ahmad, and it continues to be advanced through the present caliph's weekly sermons, which emphasize discipline and obedience to the system within which Ahmadis live. The rest of this chapter charts the development of the vast global apparatus of the Jama'at system, to ask how it created the very specific relationship that today defines Ahmadi claims to Muslimness.

The foundations of the present organization were laid in March 1889, when Ghulam Ahmad held a ceremony during which a small number of his followers pledged their allegiance to him. Apart from this formalized process of initiation (bai'at), Ghulam Ahmad left few clear instructions as to how he envisioned the community functioning after his death. As a result, much has been made of a single and rather ambiguous text published in 1905, *al-Wasiyyat*, or *The Will*.[38] In the barest of terms, this pamphlet stipulated a system of inheritance that Ghulam Ahmad hoped would provide financial stability for the nascent community. Believers were encouraged to bequeath between one-tenth and one-third of their assets to the Jama'at, and for doing so they would be buried in a special plot of land in Qadian, the heavenly graveyard (*bahishti maqbara*). This scheme still exists today, and in accordance with Ghulam Ahmad's instructions in *The Will*, only those of piety may partake, with Jama'at officials insisting that rigorous character checks take place before any money may be donated. This new scheme of financial contributions demanded some kind of management, and thus in order to administer this new source of community wealth, Ghulam Ahmad published an appendix to *The Will* in which he created a new formal body, the Sadr Anjuman Ahmadiyya, or Executive Ahmadiyya Committee.[39]

Ahmad wrote *The Will* in anticipation of his passing, and yet its ambiguous nature meant that the exact form of the community's future organization was very much up for debate. In *The Will*, Ghulam Ahmad explained that his immanent death had been revealed to him but asked his followers not to grieve, for it was only through his passing that a second *qudrat* (translated by the Jama'at as "manifestation") of God would occur.[40] It was the job of all those who remained faithful to witness this manifestation. Ghulam Ahmad did indeed die soon after, in Lahore, in 1908.[41] The nascent community took qudrat to imply a form of succession, and thus Ahmad's closest companion and devotee, Hakim Noor ud-Din, was elected as his first caliph. Noor ud-Din was known for his pious and devoted character, and his succession as caliph thus appears to have been uncontroversial among members of the Jama'at.[42]

Noor ud-Din died in 1914, at which point it became clear that the widespread acceptance of the caliphate had been only a temporary suspension of the question of the Jama'at's future, made possible by the first caliph's unobjectionable character. The subsequent election of Ghulam Ahmad's twenty-five-year-old son, Mirza Basheer ud-Din Mahmood Ahmad, as the second caliph led to a public airing of different interpretations of the movement's future and eventually a schism. For those who remained loyal to Mahmood Ahmad as the second caliph, the second manifestation (qudrat) was held to necessarily stand in the same relation to the executive committee (the Sadr Anjuman Ahmadiyya) as had Mirza Ghulam Ahmad himself.[43] This group maintained control of the Jama'at in Qadian—hence, they are often described as the Qadian faction—and they formed the basis of the Jama'at-e-Ahmadiyya, the subject of this book. The dissenting party, by contrast, argued that this executive committee alone should guide the movement. Led by the editors of the movement's English-language journal, they broke off and formed what is now known as the Lahore Ahmadiyya Movement, which I briefly mentioned in the introduction. This breakaway sect continues to exist as a separate faction today, although its numbers are far, far smaller than those of the Jama'at-e-Ahmadiyya, and its global reach is negligible. For its part, the Ahmadiyya Jama'at continues to see the Lahori secession as a cynical political move motivated by personal rejection of the second caliph.[44] The Lahori faction has been described elsewhere, and I will not discuss it at any further length in the present study.[45]

Three major points of difference appear to have underwritten the schism: first, the Lahoris rejected the idea that Ghulam Ahmad had claimed to be a prophet; second, they disagreed with the extent of the caliph's authority; and third, they took exception to Mahmood Ahmad's (the second caliph's) seeming description of all non-Ahmadi Muslims as unbelievers.[46] This debate effectively reopened existing tensions in the Jama'at regarding Ghulam Ahmad's prophethood—that is, as to whether it should be accepted as prophethood, per se, or whether it should be qualified in some fashion.[47] In response to their rivals' demands to qualify Ghulam Ahmad's spiritual station, the Qadian Jama'at maintained that the Lahoris' rejection of Ghulam Ahmad's prophethood was merely a politically motivated act that occurred after they decided to reject the caliphate of Mahmood Ahmad.[48]

The Expansion of the System under the Caliphate

In a 2015 book on the Jama'at, Adil Hussain Khan has suggested that an anti-intellectualist attitude may have informed many of those who sided with the young caliph. As recent converts to the movement, they were not particularly interested in the finer points of a debate over prophetology but rather "wanted to share in a familiar type of spiritual satisfaction that corresponded with their folk Sufi, Sunni, Punjabi backgrounds."[49] In light of this, it is perhaps unsurprising that the schism became the springboard from which Mahmood Ahmad transformed Ahmadiyyat such that the role of the caliph became paramount. In the following years, he instituted a series of reforms that led to the Qadian Jama'at becoming far more centralized under his control. Starting in April 1914, Mahmood Ahmad solidified his control over the Ahmadis loyal to him by holding a meeting in which all executive power in the organization was transferred to him.[50] In the following decades, he gradually instituted the extensive bureaucracy that today characterizes the system of the Jama'at, which is understood by my interlocutors to be divinely inspired and which is now absolutely central to their ethical lives. All this while, he was engaged in a steadfast defense of the ideological centrality and necessity of the caliphate.[51]

It was in these decades prior to partition that most of the administrative units of the modern-day Jama'at were first established. In 1919, various departments were created within the executive committee, which laid the basic foundation of the organizational structure that persists to this day.[52] In 1934, Mahmood Ahmad established the Tehrik-e-Jadid (the New Movement) to oversee missionary activities oversees.[53] This is itself divided into a number of subsections, which manage the revenue, properties, and activities of Ahmadi communities outside of the Indian subcontinent. Mahmood Ahmad created a further organizational apparatus, the Waqf-e-Jadid, or New Dedication, after partition in 1957, with the intention of bringing Ahmadiyyat to the rural and Hindu populations of Pakistan, although this too is now a global administrative structure. Nowadays, the missionary works undertaken by these two organizations are extensive. In India, the Jama'at focuses its missionizing on poorer, rural populations. Globally, Ahmadis usually understand West Africa to be the place most receptive to their message, and they claim to have large numbers of converts there.[54] European converts exist in smaller numbers but are often prominently featured in MTA programming.

Mahmood Ahmad's efforts to centralize and regulate the lives of his followers through the creation of an ever more complex administrative system led to the Jama'at becoming increasingly self-reliant and disassociated from a wider Muslim public. The historian Ayesha Jalal has described how Mahmood Ahmad's efforts to unify "temporal and spiritual authority" overstepped what was acceptable to many other Muslims, for Mahmood Ahmad was increasingly "running the local administration on the lines of an Ahmadi mafia."[55] The organizational changes described above give some indication as to how the Jama'at gradually developed into a transnational bureaucracy during Mahmood Ahmad's reign, but the specific character of the community that developed under him becomes clear only when we consider the kinds of religious subjectivity that were fostered within these new administrative systems.

These new religious subjectivities can be most clearly discerned in Mahmood Ahmad's institutionalization of a relationship of devotion to the Jama'at system through his introduction of a scheme known as Waqf-e-Zindagi. *Waqf* means "dedication," but it traditionally refers to an inalienable endowment, usually in the form of land or property that has been dedicated to a religious cause, such as a madrasa or mosque. *Zindagi* means "life," so the whole phrase translates loosely as "life devotion." To apply the concept of waqf to persons rather than just property was one of Mahmood Ahmad's most original organizational modernizations.

It has resulted in a situation in which individual Ahmadis give their labor, time, and attention as an inalienable gift to the Jama'at. Lives given as waqf are given in perpetuity, and for a life devotee to break their bond to the system is a hugely shameful act. Individuals wanting to become Waqf-e-Zindagi must apply directly to the caliph, who frequently, and to the great disappointment of many whom I met in Qadian, will turn such applications down if there is no available work. Those who are successful are sworn to serve the Jama'at for the rest of their lives. Most importantly, those who become Waqf-e-Zindagi must live where their caliph commands and accept without complaint any and all work he assigns them. They cannot express personal desire, and they must show no sign of trying to control their future. Their pay is minimal, for it is heavenly rewards that they seek. Being a Waqf-e-Zindagi means living as a functionary within the gradated and hierarchical system of the Jama'at, but it also means seeing oneself as a personal devotee to and servant of the caliph. The tensions that this creates are explored in the next chapter.

Most, although not all, of the Ahmadis employed in the Jama'at system in Qadian had given themselves to the movement as waqf. Two broad categories of Waqf-e-Zindagi predominated in Qadian during my fieldwork. The first and numerically smaller group was comprised of professionals, trained in secular institutions and in possession of skills that were seen as beneficial to the community's continual global expansion, for example, doctors, engineers, or administrators. The second and much larger group was composed of members of the Jama'at's clergy, known as *mubalighs* in Urdu, or "missionaries" in English.[56] These men, all of whom were Waqf-e-Zindagi, had been trained in Qadian's theological college (the Jamia Ahmadiyya), which was established by Mahmood Ahmad in the 1920s. The institution of Waqf-e-Zindagi has, in other words, resulted in the formation of a fixed and regulated clergy. The duties of these missionaries go far beyond proselytization or acting as imams within Ahmadi mosques. Indeed, in Qadian, the vast majority of these missionaries held desk jobs in the Jama'at bureaucracy, where they were responsible for administrative and accounting work.

The present system of Waqf-e-Zindagi, in which adults dedicate their lives to the service of the Jama'at, dates back to the time of Mahmood Ahmad. In 1987, however, the fourth caliph instituted a new form of waqf, shortly after he had fled Pakistan and established a new home in London. This new scheme was called the Waqf-e-Nau (the New Dedication), and it aimed to create a new cadre of life devotees who would help to bring about a new and explosive growth in the global Jama'at. Under this scheme, parents dedicate their as yet unborn children (boys and girls) as waqf to the movement. At the time of my fieldwork, I was told that there were about two thousand to twenty-five hundred children enrolled in this scheme in India alone. As part of their upbringing the children must learn a

FIGURE 1. Students from the theological college in Qadian, who have dedicated their lives as waqf to the Jama'at, restore their energy with a cup of tea between lessons.

particular syllabus, which includes points of basic Islamic doctrine, ritual practice, and etiquette. Language learning is stressed heavily, as it is seen as key to the community's expansion. After the age of fifteen, the children must retake their pledge to serve the Jama'at. Workers in the administrative office of the Waqf-e-Nau scheme told me that in the history of the scheme in India, only about four to six children had ever refused to continue their service. Most strikingly, because they are expected to spend their lives in service of the Jama'at, these children may only pursue career paths seen as beneficial to the Jama'at. A list produced for the Waqf-e-Nau of India details thirty acceptable careers. Becoming a missionary is highly encouraged, as is training in one of the professions, but there are also some more surprising options available to the devotees, for example, the study of archaeology and Egyptology. These subjects may seem like unusual choices, but are in fact crucial to the production of a new generation of Ahmadi scholars who are capable of producing the historical and archaeological proofs of religion that were pioneered by Ghulam Ahmad in his treatise *Jesus in India*. Whatever career the child devotee chooses, they must first consult the Waqf-e-Nau office in Qadian before embarking on study or work so that they might receive the permission of the caliph. From the moment they are born, these children are reminded that they must obey their caliph and sacrifice everything for him.

The waqf schemes have obviously been hugely important in binding specific individuals to the caliphate and the Jama'at system. The second caliph nonetheless also created another series of institutions, which have arguably had an even greater impact on the religious subjectivities of the majority of Ahmadis around the world. These were the so-called auxiliary organizations of the Jama'at. Mahmood Ahmad established the first of these, the Lajna, in 1922. This is an organization to which every Ahmadi woman over the age of fifteen belongs. Ahmadis often describe the Lajna as giving women independence and autonomy within the Jama'at, and its offices and hierarchy to some extent mirror those of the wider system, which is run entirely by men.[57] Due to the absolute nature of purdah in Qadian, this was a separate social world to which I (as a male researcher) had no access. Mahmood Ahmad subsequently established similar organizations for men—the Khuddam for those aged fifteen to forty and the Ansarullah for those above the age of forty, in 1938 and 1940 respectively. With a stated aim of promoting moral and spiritual training, these auxiliary organizations have the effect of institutionalizing the social life of Ahmadis and promoting a sense of a life lived wholly within the boundaries of the global system (the Nizam-e-Jama'at). They are also an essential means through which the Jama'at surveils and disciplines its members. The local leaders of these organizations keep track of people's engagement with the Jama'at, their attendance at mosque, and their devotion to the caliph. When individuals are seen to slip in their devotion, these officials may intervene.

The Boundaries of the Jama'at System

The various organizational units just described are supported by the financial contributions (*chanda*) of all Ahmadis. These donations are given in addition to and not instead of zakat, the standard form of almsgiving in Islam. The basic donation (*chanda am*) is paid by all members of the Jama'at with independent means and amounts to one-sixteenth of monthly income. This is not optional. For example, if a woman does not work (as is usually the case in Qadian), she must still pay chanda out of whatever allowance her husband chooses to give her.[58] To be exempt from paying chanda, an Ahmadi must get permission directly from the caliph. Any Ahmadi who fails to pay will be disciplined by the Jama'at and prevented from holding office within the Jama'at system. If they continue in their refusal to pay, then the caliph can expel them from the Jama'at.[59] All Ahmadis must also pay an obligatory chanda to support the Annual Gathering (Jalsa Salana) in their country, at the rate of 1/120th of their annual income. Ahmadis who have willed money to the Jama'at under the aforementioned *al-Wasiyyat* scheme are required to pay between one-tenth and one-third of their monthly income as chanda. A consequence of these obligatory contributions—levied on Jama'at members in a manner akin to income tax—is that individual members of the Jama'at have little financial privacy from the organization to which they belong. In addition to the obligatory chandas, there are many other voluntary schemes, to which all Ahmadis are heavily encouraged to donate. These include donations to support the various different Jama'at organizations described above, donations to support the satellite TV network and the Jama'at's English-language journal, donations to help build new mosques and mission houses, donations to aid girls from poor families in marriage, and donations to help the poor at 'Eid. The Jama'at promotes donations through ceaseless reminders of the importance of financial sacrifice (*mali qurbani*), and my interlocutors in Qadian would quote the Qur'an, their Promised Messiah, and their caliphs to argue that monetary donations have both spiritual and worldly rewards. Financial sacrifice is seen to be of such benefit to the giver that it is the refusal of the Jama'at to accept donations from those who have been disgraced and excommunicated that is said to be the most painful aspect of their punishment, more so even than the inevitable social ostracism that follows their dismissal from the Jama'at.

The compulsory nature of financial sacrifice means that there is no intermediate position for a person to occupy if they are neither in nor out of the Jama'at. Individuals may not agree with the hierarchy or the doctrine, but if they do not pay their chanda, there is no place for them in the Jama'at. Indeed, it is through this demand for financial sacrifice that the boundaries of the present community are most clearly policed. The Ahmadiyya Jama'at first began to be sequestered from the wider Muslim community during the lifetime of Ghulam Ahmad, who initiated his followers and asked them to declare themselves separately in the Indian census, which they did for the first time in 1901.[60] It was during the caliphate of Mahmood Ahmad, however, that ever more rigorous boundaries were drawn around the Jama'at. Most importantly, Mahmood Ahmad forbade Ahmadis from praying behind a non-Ahmadi imam, which effectively turned their theological difference from the mainstream into a ritual difference.[61] To this day, this prohibition is rigorously upheld by my interlocutors in Qadian, who argued that its continued observance is due to the fact that a non-Ahmadi imam might direct his prayers against the Promised Messiah and that any congregants (Ahmadi or not) would be implicated in this act of rejection. Another act of boundary creation instituted in the early years of Mahmood Ahmad's caliphate was the prohibition against Jama'at members marrying non-Ahmadis.[62] This rule also continues to be followed, although it is nowadays mainly applied to Ahmadi women wishing to marry outside of the sect. In cases that occur throughout the global diaspora, when Ahmadis try to marry a member of another community, a conversion to Ahmadiyyat by the spouse is normally enough to legitimize the marriage. It is not, however, always possible for other Muslims to undertake such a conversion, due to family pressure and the intense distrust with which Ahmadis are viewed from outside. In cases where no conversion takes place, the caliph has the power to excommunicate. Sometimes, expulsion is extended to those who are seen as accessories to the offending marriage, as for example in the case of an Ahmadi boy attempting to marry a Hindu girl in Kerala in 2012, when anybody attending the ceremony was threatened with expulsion.[63]

The Jama'at's rigid policing of its external boundaries explains its silence regarding some of its most famous Western converts. Ahmadis lionize and celebrate some of their most accomplished members—in particular the Nobel Prize–winning physicist Abdus Salam—and yet other names that might be familiar outside of the Jama'at are rarely spoken of within it. This is particularly the case for U.S. Ahmadis involved in the arts. The Jama'at sent its first missionary to the United States in 1920, who was treated with suspicion and initially imprisoned by the authorities but who found a willing audience among African Americans, for whom Ahmadiyyat represented "an *alternative* universal history to which to pledge allegiance."[64] As Ahmadiyyat expanded among African American communities, it came to be an early influence on Malcom X and also became a part of life for many famous Jazz musicians, among them Yusef Lateef, Ahmad Jamal, and Art Blakey. Indeed, it is probable that the philosophical potentialities opened up by Ahmadiyyat were influential in the composition of John Coltrane's *A Love Supreme*.[65] These figures represent some of the Jama'at's major historical influences, and yet they remain unspoken of by many Ahmadis of South Asian descent. Rarely were they fully committed lifelong members, and moreover, many of them practiced an art form that, while neither forbidden nor encouraged, is seen as a gray area of potential moral danger.[66] As figures who represent the potential for porosity in the community's boundaries, these famous African Americans thus remain largely overlooked or ignored in many of the Jama'at's own official narratives of itself.[67]

In sum, the massive organizational changes that occurred during the premiership of Mahmood Ahmad had two major consequences. First, Ahmadi articulations of Muslim identity were increasingly phrased as declarations of devotion to the caliphate. Secondly, human flourishing was now understood to occur through the institutionalized relationships of an all-encompassing administrative organization, which had clear and enforceable boundaries.

The Caliphate, Political Islam, and Sufism

Throughout Islamic history, caliphates have been politico-religious institutions, with caliphs claiming leadership (in theory if not practice) over the entire Muslim community. The last widely acknowledged claimant to the title was the Ottoman sultan, leader of a worldly empire. Since the collapse of the Ottoman sultanate in 1924, there has been no single accepted source of worldly authority for Sunni Muslims, a situation that has led many contemporary Islamist thinkers to call for the creation of a new caliphate. This has become a major goal for many of those who espouse what is often described in English as "political Islam." Common to many of these calls is the idea that this new caliphate will be a replacement for the existing international order of nation-states. A good example is the transnational movement Hizb ut-Tahrir, which was founded in East Jerusalem in 1952 and which aims for the immediate creation of a universal caliphate, albeit through peaceful means.[68] Hizb-ut-Tahir is a global movement, which has historically had much appeal for educated first- and second-generation Muslims in such countries as the United Kingdom. In many Muslim-majority countries, however, it is suppressed for its challenge to state power.[69] Other proponents of the reestablishment of a caliphate have been more inclined to violent means. In 2014 the short-lived Islamic State (Daesh) declared itself to be the seat of a worldwide caliphate. For members of the Islamic State, the establishment of a caliphate was seen as a pressing political necessity, to be achieved at all costs through violence. Other jihadist groups, however, were more cautious. Even Al-Qaeda expressed reservations, arguing that a long period of proselytization was necessary before the formation of the caliphate.[70] There are nonetheless shared assumptions behind many Islamist calls for the reestablishment of a caliphate, chief among them being the sweeping away of an existing political order, the harking back to a golden age of Islam, and the creation of a polity in which religion and statehood are indissoluble.

The Ahmadiyya caliphate shares some theological inspiration with its Islamist competitors. Like many Islamist Sunni Muslims, Ahmadis understand the caliphate to be the successor institution to the Prophet Muhammad, as well as an inheritor to the traditions of the first four "Rightly Guided Caliphs" after Muhammad (the Rashidun caliphs). In other aspects, however, Ahmadi and Islamist interpretations begin to diverge dramatically. Unlike some but not all Islamists, for example, Ahmadis reject all historical claimants to the title of caliph between the Rashidun caliphs and their own. At the time of the collapse of the Ottoman empire, the Ahmadis thus never recognized the claim of the Ottoman sultan to be the caliph, which in the context of South Asian politics was a source of great tension between them and other Muslims who, through the Khilafat movement, had sought to pressure the British into enabling the survival of the Ottoman caliphate.[71] The most important difference between Islamist and Ahmadiyya versions of the caliphate, however, is the latter's outward insistence that the caliphate does not seek to supplant an existing world order. In many ways, this is an example of the Ahmadis' exceptionalism: the official organs of the Jama'at compare the nonviolent and nonthreatening Ahmadiyya caliphate to that of other Muslims in an effort to placate the fears of non-Muslims (including, for example, the Hindu majority in India).[72]

In their official and outward-facing communications, the Ahmadis thus insist on the nonpolitical nature of their caliphate. This is almost certainly a result of the fact that opponents in Muslim countries have historically been quick to identify the Ahmadiyya caliphate as a direct political threat and use this as a justification for anti-Ahmadiyya measures. As Ali Usman Qasmi has argued, the danger posed by the Jama'at to the nation-state was invoked as one reason for the passing of anti-Ahmadiyya legislation in Pakistan in 1974, when such Jama'at titles as Secretary in Charge of Foreign Affairs were taken to imply the presence of a parallel government structure operating among the Ahmadis.[73] In private, however, things are slightly more ambiguous. Ghulam Ahmad did not directly address conflicts between his authority as a prophet and that of secular power, instead phrasing his relationship to the British colonial state as one of loyalty.[74] The caliphs have also traditionally been vague on the question of whether the caliphate will one day evolve into a political power. The fourth caliph went the furthest in arguing that the Qur'an endorses a separation of religion and state, although his concern was more about theological boundaries than questions of his own sovereignty.[75] During my fieldwork, Qadian's Ahmadis tended not to speculate on what the fate of nation-states will be once Ahmadiyyat achieves its inevitable dominance in the world, although they did draw on certain statements by caliphs to indicate that Qadian would be the center of a new global order. Often, speculations about the political future of the caliphate were couched in the vague language of dreams. One interlocutor, for example, told me of a dream that he once had about a coin stamped with Mirza Ghulam Ahmad's face and name, "just like a king's face." Whether this implied hope for a future Ahmadiyya polity he left open to interpretation, saying only, "It could happen, no?" The result of these ambiguities is that, in their efforts to appeal to democratic states and publics, the Ahmadis often present themselves—or at the very least allow themselves to be presented—as secular. At least among my Indian interlocutors, however, this declaration of secularism does not always directly equate with an understanding of the Jama'at as nonpolitical. As one Ahmadi man in Qadian explained to me, "other Muslims don't like us being *secular* [using the English word *secular* in an otherwise Urdu sentence]. They don't like us talking to all communities and people and showing everybody love and respect." Note that the definition of secular employed by this man drew on a very specific genealogy of Indian secularism "as a continuous search for a non-antagonistic ground between religious communities, for toleration and respectful coexistence."[76] This secularism was thus not based on a rejection of religion in politics but a recognition of the need for coexistence between groups.

The ambiguity of the Ahmadiyya caliphate's relation to politics is in fact best understood not through a comparison to contemporary theories of the caliphate but to the long history of Sufism in South Asia. As I have shown in this chapter, the caliphate that developed in the Jama'at after Ghulam Ahmad's death was not explicitly based on a Sufi model. Indeed, as the next section of this chapter will show, Mahmood Ahmad's intellectual inspirations were as much modern European political ideologies as they were Sufi theology. Ahmadis in Qadian today will explicitly state that their caliph is nothing like the Sufi *pirs* venerated across Punjab. They see their relationship to the caliph as an attempt to establish an indisputable Islamic orthodoxy: for them, the caliphate is an argument, rendered in a universal language of loyalty and discipline, for Ahmadiyyat being the only orthodox form of Islam. In this respect, they agree with their own Islamist critics: the religion found in Punjab's shrines has nothing, they argue, to do with Islam. Nonetheless, the influence of Sufi philosophy on Ghulam Ahmad is now well documented, and a number of previous commentators have noted how the Ahmadiyya caliphate appears to share crucial features with Sufi devotional practices that are widespread in South Asia.[77] Small details point toward this fact, for example, the Ahmadis' initiation ritual (bai'at) resembles Sufi initiation, and food that the caliph has touched is often treated as blessed (tabarruk).[78] It is, however, in the caliph's relationship to worldly power that we might discern a deeper inheritance from longstanding Sufi practices in South Asia.

The idea of a dynamic interplay between Sufi saints and political leaders has been a staple of anthropology for some time, particularly among scholars of North Africa. E. E. Evans-Pritchard and Ernest Gellner both saw it as a fundamental structuring principle of North African political systems, while Abdellah Hammoudi argued that Sufi practices were essential to what he described as the stability of authoritarian rule in the Arab world.[79] Interactions between Sufi sheikhs and political leaders have also been a subject of much interest for historians of medieval North India. Throughout the medieval period, Sufis were frequently called on to legitimize ruling sovereigns.[80] They also frequently exercised a form of spiritual rule (*wilayat*) that ran parallel to the sovereignty of kings, refusing to allow themselves to become beholden to a specific ruler. As one historian of the Delhi sultanate has argued, "it was below the shaykh's dignity to be seen as being under the king's patronage, indicated through such gestures as accepting royal grants or attending his court."[81] Neither could the Sufi sheikh be seen to attend on the king in court, for such a visit "would involve the observance of court etiquette designed to emphasize the supremacy of the sovereign over all who attended."[82] Indeed the Sufi desire to retain autonomous and parallel authority to the king can be discerned in a story about the famous sheikh Nizamuddin (d. 1325), who was reported to have refused to allow the sultan to visit him, stating, "The house of this weak one has two doors. If the Sultan enters by one door, I will go out by the other!"[83] In medieval India the relationship between kings and Sufis was one of ambivalence and sometimes unease, for their sovereignties overlapped in unclear ways. For all the sultan's actual superiority in wealth and arms, the sheikh could claim to be necessary to and outside of his power. The indifference a sheikh showed to his sultan could be a source of great humiliation for the latter, whereas through his blessings the Sufi could act as kingmaker.[84] The Sufi sheikh thus both encompassed and rejected worldly politics.

While the nature of political sovereignty in South Asia is much changed from these medieval accounts, a similar kind of relationship has nonetheless been observed in ethnographic accounts of the engagements between Sufi sheikhs and politicians in Pakistan. Writing of a modern transnational Sufi cult with origins in Pakistan, Pnina Werbner argues that Sufi attitudes to politics continue to be "highly ambivalent, a mixture of moral superiority and pragmatic accommodation."[85] Moreover, the Sufi saint of her ethnography continued to interact with politicians in a manner strikingly reminiscent of the aloofness of his medieval predecessors. First, he would refuse to ask the name of any visitor to his *darbar* (court), even if they were evidently important Pakistani politicians. Second, he would refuse to make himself a client of politicians, always rejecting gifts, no matter how extravagant. As Werbner observed, "he is a giver, never a taker," and this was calculated to emphasize his power over the temporal.[86] At the same time, however, he was willing to entertain these politicians, for their presence—their need to come to him—was what confirmed his power and station as a *wali*, or friend, of God.[87]

While most Ahmadis explicitly reject the idea that their caliphate is a reformulation of Sufism, it is worth noting that the relationship between Sufi saints and temporal politics I have just described better encapsulates Ahmadi aspirations for their own caliph than does the rather bland notion of the "nonpolitical" found in their own English-language promotional material. In many ways, the above descriptions of medieval Sufi sovereignty echo the kind of power that is aspired to by the present-day Ahmadiyya caliphate. The caliph is simultaneously aloof from and yet deeply involved in worldly politics. In Britain, where the caliph resides, but also during his tours of other countries, the Jama'at work hard to arrange meetings and audiences between the caliph and secular authorities. These meetings are nonetheless never constructed as two-way exchanges. Rather, as in the case of the saint described by Werbner, the caliph alone is seen to give. He addresses politicians, and in doing so he gifts them his message of justice and peace. As I will show in chapter 5, Jama'at reportage of these events—both in print and on their satellite television channel—is above all concerned to present these politicians as witnesses, not interlocutors. The emphasis is always on their reactions to the caliph's message and his personage. Yet despite this, the caliph, like the medieval Sufis before him, does not seek to replace these temporal witnesses to his power. Moreover, as for his Sufi predecessors, his is a spiritual power that admits and allows the existence of a pluralism within society that other, more political theories of the caliphate do not.[88] Also, like medieval Sufis, the caliph's sovereignty is not tied to a territory, and in situations of conflict with worldly sovereigns, he may simply move elsewhere, as the fourth caliph famously did in 1984.[89]

A New World Order

In Qadian, the caliphate is thus seen as simultaneously separate from *and* encompassing of temporal politics. Ahmadis saw their nonpolitical caliphate as having the potential to transform the global political system. Whenever I spoke to Ahmadis in Qadian about the relationship between their religious system and politics, one text remained a stable reference point and inspiration: a transcription of a lecture delivered by the second caliph, Mahmood Ahmad, in Qadian in 1942, titled *Nizam-e-Nau* (*The New System*).[90] Set against the backdrop of the Second World War, the lecture was an argument for how the administrative system of the Ahmadiyya Jama'at could replace the dominant political ideologies of the twentieth century. It thus provided a theoretical framework for a new Islamic system, which my interlocutors in Qadian still understand themselves to be embodying in their daily practice. It is by far the most unambiguous statement of political intent found among the Jama'at's large corpus of texts, and its popularity—taken together with contemporary statements that the Jama'at is secular and nonpolitical— helps to explain the caliphate's ambiguous relationship to worldly power. As one man in Qadian exclaimed when he saw me reading a copy, "this is a very great book. After World War Three, this book will rise up and have its time."[91]

While my Ahmadi interlocutors in Qadian often presented their theological and political views as being the dehistoricized products of prophecy, *Nizam-e-Nau* was clearly part of a more general movement within late colonial South Asian Islam to engage with European ideologies of fascism and communism and to transform Islam into an equivalent and mutually exclusive ideological unit. Indeed, this lecture was delivered only a year after the foundation of another movement that was greatly influenced by the organizational models being promoted by fascists in Europe—Abul Ala Maududi's Jama'at-e-Islami.[92] Maududi was to become the leading proponent in the subcontinent of the idea that Islam could be understood as a complete system (or nizam) for the economic, social, and political regulation of a society.[93] The idea of Islam as an objectified system was likewise taken up by a range of thinkers across the Muslim world, most notably Sayyid Qutb in Egypt, whose works were foundational in the development of the modern-day Muslim Brotherhood. Like these Islamist thinkers, Mahmood Ahmad proposed a systematized version of Islam that was in dialogue with European political movements of the 1930s and 1940s.

Mahmood Ahmad's original 1942 lecture was broad and expansive. It began by establishing that modern industrialized society had resulted in a crisis of redistribution; inequality was rampant, and something needed to be done. The vast majority of Mahmood Ahmad's audience would have been drawn from rural Punjab, and thus he proceeded in simple language and with illustrations drawn from local agricultural life, to illustrate the various theoretical responses that had emerged in Europe to inequality. He began with a brief account of liberalism and socialism, before introducing the ideas of Karl Marx. A discussion of Marxism led to a brief description of the Russian Revolution, and the conflicting ideologies of Boleshevism and Menshevism. Having made his audience aware of some of the weaknesses of these ideologies, he then turned to the other political systems at that time in power in Europe: the fascisms of Hitler, Mussolini, and Franco. While he had been somewhat open toward the benefits of the various forms of socialism, he was far more critical of fascism, both for its narrow national and racial outlook and for its potential for a new form of extractive imperialism, particularly within South Asia. He then summarized what he saw as the proposals contained within other religions for solving the problem of inequality. Judaism, he argued, is too constrained by a racial logic, Hinduism hampered by the caste system, and Christianity simply impractical.

Mahmood Ahmad then introduced Islam, which he characterized as an economic system of redistribution, to compare it to the political ideologies at war in Europe. He praised zakat—the alms that every Muslim is obliged to pay—but then argued that this was not sufficient for ending present-day inequality, and he thus argued that within Islam there had always been the provision for the emergence of a more extensive kind of system. For Mahmood Ahmad, this Islamic system would be comparable in a strictly formal sense to European political ideologies, and yet at a deeper level it would be fundamentally incomparable in its completeness and internationality. At this level, Mahmood Ahmad's proposal was very similar to ideas that would be proposed by such Islamist thinkers as Sayyid Qutb, who also advocated for the idea of Islam as a political system.[94] Mahmood Ahmad's point of radical departure from his contemporaries, however, was in the relationship between the system he proposed and the sharia. The vast majority of arguments for treating Islam as a system are made in terms of sharia being rendered as a code that can then be applied to society as a whole.[95] In contrast, while Mahmood Ahmad's proposal may have been in accordance with Islamic law, it ultimately extended well beyond the sharia.

Mahmood Ahmad's basic argument was that a new world system already existed, and it was to be found in Ghulam Ahmad's *al-Wasiyyat* (*The Will*).[96] As explained earlier in this chapter, *al-Wasiyyat* was the short treatise written late in Ghulam Ahmad's life, which described a system of inheritance through which the future growth of the Jama'at could be funded. Mahmood Ahmad's original intellectual contribution in *Nizam-e-Nau* was to argue that this form of inheritance could constitute the basis for a new global system that would be comparable to yet wholly different from Marxism, Bolshevism, and fascism. He was not just positing the Jama'at system as a replacement for the global order of nation-states: he was arguing that the most basic relationship of devotion within the Jama'at would constitute the foundational building block of a new global order. The main argument of *Nizam-e-Nau* was that this system of inheritance would be capable of creating a fully redistributive economic system that did not suffer from the major problem that Ahmad saw when he looked to the Soviet Union— it would require no compulsion, for all property would be given to the system voluntarily and joyfully. Mahmood Ahmad envisioned that if everybody were to give one-third of their assets in this way, in a few generations, most property would have accumulated in the hands of the Jama'at for the benefit of all humanity. He was, in other words, arguing that this system of inheritance could form the basis of a wide-ranging and potentially global economic system. It would be specific to no country; it would, rather, encompass all humankind. Summarizing this argument in present-day Qadian, an Ahmadi official boldly declared to me, "Wasiyyat is going to replace capitalism."

The English translation of *Nizam-e-Nau* appeared in 1943—a mere year after the original Urdu lecture—and yet it contained substantial differences, the most obvious of which was its distinctive new subtitle, *New World Order of Islam*.[97] It was translated by Muhammad Zafrullah Khan, the highest-profile Ahmadi of his day, who after partition became the first foreign minister of Pakistan. In an introductory note to his text, Zafrullah Khan explained that he reduced repetition in the text to transform it from an oration to a written document. Yet the alterations in style that emerged through his translation hint at the significant developments within Jama'at thought that were crystalizing during this period. First, Zafrullah Khan's translation had the effect of delocalizing the text. Ahmad's original Urdu discussion of Marx, for example, had been emplaced by examples known and understood to his Punjabi audience.[98] Thus the violent appropriation of the means to production was illustrated in the original speech with an ex-ample of irrigation canals in an agricultural setting. In the English translation, however, Zafrullah Khan abstracted the text into the language of political theory. Likewise, in the original speech, when Ahmad related anecdotes and stories, he had slipped into the first-person perspective of his characters to demonstrate their emotional state.[99] This is an idiom that would work in English, but Zafrullah Khan instead chose to make the text far more theoretical. He kept speech quotations from the original but condensed anecdotes.[100] Examples were almost universally shortened and sometimes omitted entirely. The text became less vivid, and meta-phors were truncated. Moreover, Zafrullah Khan introduced into his translation technical terms, such as *secular*, which have no direct parallel in the original. In doing this, Zafrullah Khan was emplacing *Nizam-e-Nau* within and against a ge-nealogy of political writing in English. Where the original had explained social-ism and Marxism in the most basic of language, the English translation directly invoked a vocabulary of universal revolution, class, and struggle. Thus, *Nizam-e-Nau* was transformed from an expansive and conversational lecture into a terse political treatise. Zafrullah Khan's translation thus furthered the process by which a form of private inheritance was transformed into a totalizing political and eco-nomic system. Moreover, he applied an English-language vocabulary of political theory to the disciplinary relationships that had been developing in the Jama'at for the previous half century. Zafrullah Khan therefore enabled the political the-orization of a private relationship of devotion such that this relationship could form the basis of a new imagined global utopia.

Ultimately, the uniqueness of *Nizam-e-Nau* lay in its ability to envisage a world in which public structures of governance had been rendered void by the global-ization of a personal relationship of devotion. In this sense, it was both a prod-uct of the colonial setting in which Mahmood Ahmad and his father lived and a challenge to it. In the decades after 1857, the British colonial state had begun to restrict the operation of religious law to a carefully demarcated private sphere. Islamic criminal law effectively ceased in the subcontinent after the implementa-tion of the Penal Code of 1862, and sharia was restricted exclusively to what the colonial state defined as the personal realm.[101] This was most apparent in the es-tablishment of spheres of customary law that remain in existence in India today, for example, Muslim personal law. In other words, Muslims in North India went from having an emperor of their faith to being told that their religion could reg-ulate only that sphere of life that the British colonial state deemed personal. This personal space included marriage and also the regulation of inheritance. In *Nizam-e-Nau*, Mahmood Ahmad did not challenge Islamic law's relegation to a private sphere but instead proposed a transformation of the global economic system based precisely on religion's regulation of the personal. Out of this personal sphere emerged a system that, in its political ambition and coherence, was said to out-systematize European ideologies of fascism and communism. In other words, *Nizam-e-Nau* both emerged from and exceeded a colonial classification.

As explained above, the vast majority of Islamist thinkers who have proposed that their religion be treated as a system (nizam) have done so from the point of view that any separation of the political and the religious is fallacious. Likewise, contemporary Islamist arguments about the need for the caliphate are frequently based on an assumption that the religious and the political are indistinguishable. The Jama'at does something quite different. It makes claims to neither statehood nor politics, for it implicitly accepts an order of the world in which the caliph's sovereignty overlaps with that of worldly nations. And yet it simultaneously proposes a radical unsettling of politics, for it proposes a basic relationship of devotion that, expanded on a global scale, will render conventional politics defunct. Understanding Mahmood Ahmad's *Nizam-e-Nau* can thus help explain the complexities of the Ahmadiyya caliphate and the face-value contradictions that seem to structure the way in which it is talked about in Qadian. It can help explain why my interlocutors see the end of politics within a system they often explicitly describe as nonpolitical and why they argue that Qadian will one day be the center of a new global order while all the time insisting on their absolute loyalty to the nation-state of India. In *Nizam-e-Nau* the Ahmadiyya caliphate is not presented as a direct successor to worldly political systems: rather, the caliphate is seen to give rise to a private relationship of devotion that has the power to render secular politics defunct.

The Contemporary Caliphate

Given that global renewal rests on the relationship individuals can cultivate with their caliph, it is unsurprising that there is a tension between the individual caliph and the office he holds. Ahmadis in Qadian insisted that the caliph was an institution. The caliph should not be thought of as an individual person but as the Nizam-e-Khilafat, or as the embodiment of the Silsila-e-Ahmadiyya. This was also reflected in the ways that people would speak about the caliph. His followers always refer to him with the honorific *huzur*, and they frequently do so in a way that makes no distinction between individual caliphs. Older Ahmadis will tell stories of how their life has been interweaved with that of their huzur while making no distinction about the particular huzur they are referring to. Likewise, I heard stories in which people would describe dream visions of the caliph and make no linguistic distinction between the huzur of their dreams and the actual man. This avowed attachment to the institution nonetheless sits side by side with a veneration of the individual man. Each caliph is admired for his personal qualities, and people engage with him on an intensely aesthetic level. Pictures of all five caliphs hang in most homes and shops in Qadian. When people meet the present caliph, they often describe the light that radiates from his face. One interlocutor even told me how he had identified the specific perfume worn by the caliph, sought it out, and then bought it so that he could be more like his leader.

Somewhat mediating this tension is the extreme moral censure placed on anybody who is heard to compare the different individuals who have occupied the office of the caliphate. On assuming office, the present caliph gave a sermon in which he reminded his followers that it is forbidden to draw attention to the deficiencies and weaknesses of any one caliph.[102] Everybody I spoke to was extremely careful to avoid any form of comparison, although statements that could be read as comparisons inevitably slipped into conversations when Ahmadis praised a particular caliph. Once, an Ahmadi missionary spent some time describing the immense abilities of the previous incumbent, Mirza Tahir Ahmad. He explained that when Tahir Ahmad was asked to name an unborn child, he would, unlike the present caliph, reply with only a single name, for he was able to determine in advance the sex of the baby. My interlocutor suddenly grew flustered and fell silent. "I am not trying to make a comparison," he told me, obviously worried that what he had just said could be seen as a slight on the present caliph.

For most of my interlocutors in Qadian, to make a comparison between caliphs was to demonstrate that one had not understood the nature of the institution. Another young Ahmadi told me a story to demonstrate this. He had been a young child when the present caliph, Mirza Masroor Ahmad, assumed office, and the first thing he noticed about this new caliph was that upon election he did not have a beard. At this point, my interlocutor paused and then quietly reflected, "I probably shouldn't be saying this," before he carried on with the story. He told me how, in the months after the election, he slowly began to get used to the idea of Mirza Masroor Ahmad as the caliph, particularly given the fact that the new caliph began to grow a beard immediately upon being elected. And yet my interlocutor still felt that something was lacking, so he confided to an older relative that he found the new caliph to be less "handsome" (he used the English word) than the previous one. He was immediately admonished for this remark. Now, looking back, he told me that he felt great shame for having ever made such a comparison, for it sprang from a childish misunderstanding of the nature of the office. His hesitation in telling the story, he explained, was not because of an abstract rule against making comparisons: it was because he now understood the caliphate in a way that he had never done as a child, and this understanding carried with it an emotionally charged appreciation of the fundamental equality between caliphs.

A similar logic operates regarding speculation about who will be the next caliph. Several people with whom I spoke claimed to have had dreams in which they foresaw a future caliph, yet any discussion about these dreams prior to the investiture of a caliph is deeply taboo. On the death of a caliph, an electoral college comprised of senior officials meets to elect a successor. For Ahmadis, the very legitimacy of the institution rests on this electoral process. No prior canvassing is allowed, and nobody may express interest in becoming caliph. The ideal candidate should fear the responsibility of being caliph and should be compelled to assume the mantle. There is an obvious reason why people may not disclose dreams about who should be caliph; to do so could be conceived as a form of canvasing. It might even be seen as a distortion of the divine process of electing a caliph, for Ahmadis argue that while the physical election is carried out by the hands of men, it is God who steers the choice of the electors. Yet the prohibition against describing dreams about future caliphs extends far beyond the centers of power within the Jama'at, to people who could have no conceivable influence over the election process. Once again, this prohibition is only an explicit articulation of what a person who has understood the caliphate should have realized: obedience to the office is more important than one's personal preference as to who should be caliph. To understand the caliphate is to realize that it is a relationship that extends beyond personal likes or dislikes, opinions, or desires. Rather, it is a path to God and a precondition for living as a disciplined Muslim. Thus, even dreams that correctly predict the election of a caliph are not always shared after his election. I was told that in 2011, eight years after the election of Mirza Masroor Ahmad as the fifth caliph, there were still people who had not divulged true dreams foretelling his election. Such dream-visions (*ruya*) were ultimately a personal matter, kept quiet out of spiritual humility.[103] The election of a new caliph was not a chance to aggrandize the self by boasting of receiving a true vision from God; it was rather an opportunity to subordinate the self in discipline to a divine office.

Since the schism of 1914, every caliph of the Jama'at-e-Ahmadiyya has belonged to the lineage of Mirza Ghulam Ahmad. The second caliph was Ghulam Ahmad's son, and the third and fourth caliphs were both sons of the second. The current caliph is a great-grandson of Ghulam Ahmad. The Ahmadiyya caliphate has thus come to take on a loosely hereditary structure, although the Jama'at—perhaps wary of any comparison to Shia imams—strenuously denies this. For many Ahmadis, the fact that the role has remained within a single family is felt to be evidence of the efficacy and incorruptibility of their electoral process: it is evidence of the fact that God is indeed responsible for the election of the caliph. One Jama'at official in Qadian explained this to me as follows: after the election of every caliph, it is possible to look back with hindsight and say that the new caliph was the person who took the most benefit from a close, obedient, and loving relationship with the previous caliph. For my interlocutors, it was obvious that those who could cultivate the most perfect relationship of discipline to a caliph would be members of the same family (*khandan*). It is this family that carries the living memory of what it means to live in closeness and discipline to a prophet: it is this family that most truly displays the tarbiyyat, or cultivation, that emerges out of their closeness to a divine leader. It is thus only expected that caliphs should be drawn from the one single family that demonstrates the most exemplary relationship: a relationship that is seen to make a person Muslim.

The incumbent caliph, Mirza Masroor Ahmad (official title Khalifat ul-Masih al-Khamis, or the Fifth Successor to the Messiah), was born into the family of Ghulam Ahmad in 1950. He attended agricultural college in his native Pakistan before serving the Jama'at in Ghana. Ahmadi sources make much of the fact that he was involved in an experiment that successfully grew wheat in that country for the first time.[104] Prior to his succession, he was the chief secretary (*nazr a'ala*) of the Pakistani community. This is the second highest-ranking position in the Jama'at after the caliph, but as the next chapter will show, the difference between the caliph and other senior officials in the Jama'at is one of kind as well as degree. Like his predecessor, he resides in Southfields, London, and is unable to return to Pakistan for fear of government persecution. Far from being a hindrance, the caliph's exile in London is seen as a great blessing to the community. The caliph now lives in one of the most cosmopolitan cities in the world, whence he ceaselessly reiterates a universal message. From London he is said to speak to governments and advise the leaders of the free world. For my interlocutors in Qadian, the political problems of the world were overwhelmingly understood to have arisen due to governments and people ignoring the message of the caliphate. The caliph has spent much time appealing to world leaders, and the letters he has sent them—advising on how to achieve world peace—have been widely published by the Jama'at.[105] In Qadian, the future of the world and the dawning of a new global order are said to rest on the willingness of individuals and nations to embrace the caliph as their one true global leader.

The Caliphate and Qadian

This chapter has charted the historical development through which Ahmadis came to understand devotion to the caliph as the core means through which to articulate their Muslimness. In this context, the growth of the Jama'at system as an extensive transnational bureaucratic apparatus is not merely a side effect of the caliphate but a necessary aspect of what it means to live a godly life. This system creates a hierarchical framework through which people can live as servants of their caliph, particularly through the waqf schemes that provide the means for Ahmadis to make themselves into the property of the Jama'at. Yet the importance of this system extends much further than this simple fact. The existence of the Jama'at system is a physical proof through which Ahmadis can know the truth of their religion. For people whose primary ethical concern is with the evidencing of religious truth, this system functions as a global, material trace of divine favor that they can look at over and again so as to know that they are following the true Islam. When my interlocutors in Qadian wanted to convince me of the truth of Ahmadiyyat, it was to this global system that they pointed: to the fact that across the world, individuals within this system led absolutely disciplined lives beneath a single, universal leader. For my interlocutors, this system was a truth to which they could make themselves responsible. By extension, its existence placed an obligation on the world to respond to the truth of Ahmadiyyat. When natural calamities or war broke out across the world, they would locate the cause of these disasters in the failure of people to heed the caliph's message of universal leadership. The extensive and global system of the Jama'at provided the evidence through which Ahmadis attempted to make their own Muslimness irrefutable.

The global Jama'at system is the most perfect example of a more general desire to live within the confines of a system. In Qadian, people frequently judged various nations by the extent to which they enabled their citizens to live within an organized system. Such comparative discourse rarely favored India. I experienced a striking example of this when an Ahmadi visitor to Qadian, now a long-term resident of Germany but originally from Punjab, recounted with great pleasure how the German police had once arrived to question him about a business transaction following a tip-off that it might be illegal. I had expected him to show some annoyance that the police were intruding into his privacy. Rather than berate the German state for being intrusive, however, he spoke with absolute delight about how the police involved themselves in his business and questioned him. How good it was, he told me, to be regulated. Herein, he explained, lay Germany's evident superiority over both other European countries and India. This kind of speech is extremely prevalent in Qadian and can take on some unusual forms. For example, Ahmadis in Qadian often told me that due to the systematized nature of life in Europe, Europeans are actually far more Islamic than Muslims, for it is in Europe that they saw people demonstrating precisely those qualities that also make the Jama'at into a shining beacon of Islam.

As I argued in the introduction, however, a seemingly paradoxical mix of absolute conviction and deep uncertainty characterized the relationship that my interlocutors in Qadian had with truth. In this regard, it is perhaps unsurprising that the connection people had to the global system could be both a source of doctrinal certainty and a cause of ethical concern. This is particularly acute in

Qadian because of the liminal yet central position that the town occupies within the transnational Ahmadiyya system. In many respects, Qadian's Ahmadis live in what should be one of the most systematized places in the global Jama'at. The creation of the Jama'at administration under Mahmood Ahmad occurred in Qadian in the early decades of the twentieth century, and nowadays, an extensive bureaucracy structures life in the town. In Qadian, the Jama'at runs schools, the hospital, courts, and even a bank. It provides security for those who have fallen on hard times and scholarships for study. Furthermore, the Jama'at is the only major employer of Muslims in Qadian, and the donations that are taken from individuals amount to what is effectively an income tax. In sum, the Jama'at functions very much as a self-regulating local government in Qadian. In this way, my interlocutors sought to make Qadian into an exemplary demonstration of the Jama'at system: a model of what an Islamic society can be. That they lived under this parastate apparatus has to be seen not as a desire to liberate themselves from the Indian state but to liberate themselves through dependence on their caliph.[106] Yet in spite of the extensive nature of the Jama'at system in Qadian, the history of the town since 1947 has left it in a uniquely isolated position from the global caliphate. With the partition of India, the entire organizational structure of the Jama'at moved to Pakistan, and to this day it is from Pakistan that the vast majority of the movement's global missionary activities are coordinated. The rupture caused by partition—the complete division of Punjab by a border that to this day lacks real permeability—meant that Qadian could no longer be a part of the same organization as the rest of the global Jama'at. To maintain its property, the Jama'at in India necessarily had to form an independent legal entity. As a result of partition, the Indian Ahmadiyya community effectively functions as a parallel organization to the rest of the world. It is led by its own chief secretary, has its own board of directors, and nowadays reports directly to London.[107] Consequently, during the first four decades of independence, the Indian Jama'at was largely isolated from the globalizing movement spearheaded by missionary activities from Pakistan. The hard border running through Punjab and separating Qadian from the Pakistani headquarters of Rabwah meant that the Indian community was alone in the world in finding itself separated from a movement that was otherwise characterized by an abundance of transnational connections.

Indeed, such has been the fall in the town's fortunes that the fact that I was even doing fieldwork in Qadian was sometimes questioned by its inhabitants. Why, I was asked, had I chosen to come to Qadian when the Jama'at system was so much more exemplary in Pakistan? Or why did I choose to situate my research away from the caliph, when my university was so close to his residence in London? People seemed confused by the fact that I had left a place where the presence of the caliph made a prophetic society possible, to come to a place that was somewhat unmoored from his influence. For Ahmadis to have surety in a Muslim identity requires the organizational and economic resources to create a perfect system that exhibits discipline to the Caliph and enables truth to be manifested and witnessed. In spite of its historical and symbolic importance, Qadian was felt, due to its history of post-partition isolation, to lack such resources. If my job as a scholar was to witness truth and to make myself responsible to it, I had, I was frequently informed, come to the wrong place. In many instances, I felt that Ahmadis told me such things to warn me: they hoped that I would not confuse the arrogance (*takabbur*) of individuals in Qadian who had strayed from caliphate with the humility of the global Ahmadiyya Jama'at.

Compounding all these worries was a sense of being left behind by the global Jama'at. In Pakistan, Europe, and North America, Ahmadis are often educated, upwardly mobile professionals.[108] In Qadian, this is less commonly the case. At partition, the core of educated and wealthy Ahmadi families left Qadian in the care of just a few hundred young men who were chosen for their strength, not their education. In a worldly sense, Qadian thus clearly fell behind the global movement, and increasingly, its residents seem to fear that the same may be true in a spiritual sense. When, during my fieldwork, the official in charge of the "India desk" in London—that is, the man who mediates between the caliphate and Qadian and who just so happened to be the caliph's son-in-law—came to inspect the town, a sense of concern, anxiety, and inadequacy was palpable in the administration.[109]

Tiny, innocuous details of life in Qadian point to the central absence of the caliph in people's lives. When I first arrived in the town, I was surprised by the uniformity of the blue-tinged whitewash that had been used to paint all the Ahmadi houses in the central neighborhood, which stood in stark contrast to the multicolored paints used to decorate houses in the Hindu and Sikh parts of town. When I first asked somebody why this was so, he laughed and told me that I was being a typical social scientist and reading too much into things. Only later did I discover that the uniform color had been a conscious choice dictated by the Jama'at to beautify the town in anticipation of a 2008 visit by the caliph that never came to fruition. Qadian exists in a perpetual state of waiting for its caliph to return. People assured me that it will one day be the center of the new global order dreamed of by the second caliph in *Nizam-e-Nau*. For the time being, it is a place to which the elderly often migrate so as to spend their days in quiet prayer before being buried in the heavenly graveyard by the side of their Promised Messiah. Qadian continues to await its caliph.

AN ENCHANTING BUREAUCRACY

The Ahmadiyya caliphate stands at the heart of an extensive transnational system (Nizam-e-Jama'at) that encompasses peoples' lives from the moment they are born to that in which they die. In Qadian, children are dedicated to this system while still in their mothers' wombs, and most adults aspire to will property to the system at death so that they might be buried in its heavenly graveyard (bahishti maqbara). The Jama'at system surveils its members, effectively taxes them, structures their lives, employs a good deal of them, and monitors and controls the presence of outsiders within Qadian.[1] Far from being resented, the intrusion of this system into the everyday is celebrated in Qadian for bringing order to life, for redistributing material resources, and for creating obligation between Ahmadis.[2] Most importantly, the Jama'at system is said to fulfill obligations in a way that the Indian state never can. In Qadian—where, as in much of India, stories of government corruption serve as everyday currency for small talk—the state is noticeable for both failing to meet basic obligations to its citizens, and obstructing their daily lives.[3] In comparison to this, the Nizam-e-Jama'at is described as an ideal bureaucratic model: a redistributive system that provides employment and administers an India-wide class of religious clerics. This system functions as a parastate within Qadian, and it is celebrated for its efficiency, its justice, and its centralized order.

For many of my interlocutors in Qadian, the key to the wondrous nature of the Jama'at is that it functions as an administration without mediation. This is not an uncommon utopian ideal in India. William Mazzarella has described how early forays into e-governance in India seemed to promise a "politics of immediation" that could bypass a corrupt bureaucracy.[4] Other ethnographers have shown how some relations of clientelism, influence, or bribery might be understood as attempts to create direct ties of unmediated personal obligation in situations where the Indian state is otherwise indifferent or illegible.[5] In the Jama'at, utopian directness is a result of the intimate relationship that each and every follower is said to have with their caliph. He guides the administrative system down to the minutest detail; he makes the bureaucracy responsive to the needs and desires of Qadian's inhabitants; he fulfills the obligations of the system toward its members; he is the guarantor of justice (*insaf*). This is a direct relationship, shorn of any mediation: it is from the caliph that orders flow, and it is to the caliph that all appeals and petitions are made. The result of this situation is that every decision of importance within Qadian's administrative system is attributed to the caliph, and because of this, every decision taken may be said to lead the Jama'at further toward spiritual and material prosperity. To quote an officeholder, "Every Ahmadi is living proof that the khalifa [caliph] of the time is the most beneficial person alive." It is through this unmediated and direct relationship to the caliph that Qadian's Ahmadis hope to demonstrate their authentically Muslim identity.

My interlocutors thus desire to live under the benign authoritarianism of their leader, which they see as a benevolent and sacred form of sovereignty. From him, material and spiritual gifts flow (via the administrative system of the global Jama'at), and in return Ahmadis offer their obedience. This is a model of sovereignty that draws extensively on older South Asian models of kingship, premised on a personal relationship of unequal reciprocity in which the justice of the sovereign is made available to his people through the act of petitioning.[6] Such an image of life beneath the caliphate is, however, an idealized picture. My interlocutors want the caliph to direct what they do, to authorize their actions, and to control their lives, but he is far distant, and they must therefore always struggle to capture and expand the power he has over their lives. For them to subordinate themselves to the caliph thus requires effort and determination: it is not simply a case of passive submission.[7]

Understanding how Ahmadis make themselves ruled necessitates that we turn to the materialities of bureaucratic practice in the town, for it is through a "regime of paper documents" that the caliph is emplaced in everyday life in Qadian.[8] The rationalization of life through bureaucratic processes in Qadian has not led to disenchantment in the Weberian sense.[9] Qadian is instead the site of an enchanting bureaucracy, for the administrative system is the essential means through which the caliph is made present in the intimate spaces of everyday life in the town.[10] Indeed, the unmediated relationship between follower and caliph is made possible through the bureaucracy that separates them. Only by way of bureaucratic mediation can the caliph emerge as an idealized and archetypal patron: a font of "selfless munificence" whose direct relationship to each and every Ahmadi is the key to their spiritual and material prosperity.[11] This chapter thus builds on anthropological work on bureaucracy to see the Jama'at's administrative system as "a central site for the forging of the personhood, affective life and sometimes the radical potential of contemporary citizens."[12] It is, in short, an attempt to account for how a hierarchical and rationalized ordering of society might be a response to a longing for a life that is enchanted with a transparent, immediate, and sacred sovereignty.

Behind this enchantment of life there is nonetheless a contradiction, which has wide-ranging consequences for what it means to be Muslim in Qadian. To state this contradiction in the simplest terms: the caliph is present in the daily life of Qadian only because he is not. The reason for this is that just as the bureaucracy makes the caliph immanent, so too does it threaten to reveal his actual distance (both physical and spiritual) from the town. For Qadian's Ahmadis, who see in their relationship with the caliph an assurance of their contested Muslim status, this contradiction is particularly dangerous. In Qadian, bureaucratic practice simultaneously holds out the promise of a verifiable Muslim identity while also functioning as a form of evidence that might reveal, once and for all, the irreparable rift that opened up between the town and the caliph at partition. In my interlocutors' struggle to make themselves responsive to truth, bureaucratic processes are therefore productive of both certainty and its antithesis.

The Separation of Qadian

Within the global Ahmadiyya system, Qadian is home to an administrative apparatus that is second only to the community headquarters of Rabwah in Pakistan. The reasons for this, as discussed in the last chapter, are historical. When the caliph moved to Pakistan, Rabwah became the networked center of the entire global community, and the newly impermeable border running through the Punjab separated Qadian not just from the caliph but from the global system as a totality. As such, there could be no bureaucratic connections between Qadian and Rabwah, and the administrative structures of Rabwah therefore had to be emulated in Qadian. Alone in the world, Qadian is the center of an Indian bureaucracy that parallels that of the larger global Jama'at system.

Far from being a cause for celebration, this special status is deeply troubling for Ahmadis in Qadian, for it is a continuous reminder of their separation from the global Jamaʻat and hence the caliphate. The Ahmadi conception of the caliphate is premised on the idea that if human society is bereft of divine guidance, it will inevitably decline.[13] Left on their own, people will naturally move away from godly practices toward innovation and idolatry, while the caliphate is the institution that guards against such decline. It is thus through total obedience to the caliphate that a pristine Islamic society might be maintained. A number of times during my fieldwork, Ahmadis used the metaphor of a solar system to illustrate the social function of the caliphate. The caliph is said to be like the sun, the huge gravitational body around which his followers orbit like planets. The closer a person is to the center, the faster his or her orbit will be, or to put it in more human terms, the more exemplary his or her behavior will be. The result is that it is only among those closest to the caliph that we find the true society of God—that is, the society that bears the imprint of prophethood and revelation. This is an image of society in which all goodness is understood to spring from the caliph, while negative actions begin to emerge as a result of human action in the cold outer reaches of the "solar system" where his gravitational pull is weaker. For Ahmadis in Qadian, this is no abstract model but, rather, an explanatory device for world politics: war in the Middle East and insurgency in Pakistan are a result of Muslims in both places rejecting Ahmadiyyat and failing to heed the messages of obedience preached by the caliph. When a terrible earthquake and tsunami ravaged Japan in 2011, there was quiet agreement among Ahmadis in Qadian that its cause lay in the failure of the Japanese people to turn to Islam, Ahmadiyyat, and the leadership of the caliphate. On the other hand, there are said to be major benefits for those non-Muslims who heed the word of the caliph. In Qadian, this was understood to have happened close to home. Indian Punjab underwent a period of violent turmoil in the 1980s during the height of separatist calls for it to become the independent Sikh state of Khalistan. In Qadian, It was rumored that the dampening of this violence in the 1990s was a direct result of the 1991 visit to Qadian by the caliph—the first since the partition of India. He is said to have held talks with many leaders of the insurgency and advised them in such a way that they ceased their violent course. The caliph is thus thought to have a profound impact on world history, both when people choose to build a relationship with him and when they refuse the obligation placed on them to do so.

Time and again, I was confronted by narratives that seemed to imply that the wrenching of the caliphate from Qadian in 1947 had precipitated an inevitable collapse in the moral substance of the town. Pakistani Ahmadis seemed surprised on coming to Qadian both by how much standards had slipped in Qadian and by how concerned Qadian's Ahmadis were to make the caliph present in their lives. I was told that while Qadian was an acceptable place for me to carry out my study because of its history, if I really wanted to experience Ahmadiyyat, I would have to go to London, where the caliph presently resides. Central to these narratives was a fear over the declining *tarbiyyat* of the town. Referring in the simplest sense to training, the Urdu term *tarbiyyat* was at the center of Qadian's Ahmadis' fears about their own cultivability. As a form of upbringing, tarbiyyat exists and is preserved within families. Historical family linkages to the caliphate from before partition are thus seen as repositories through which new generations might be brought up with the right moral training. This tarbiyyat was nonetheless also seen as something that once lost could not easily be regained without direct physical proximity to the caliph. The gradual loss of tarbiyyat lies at the heart of narratives of decline in Qadian. I heard stories of how, in the 1970s, the final member of Mirza Ghulam Ahmad's family (khandan) to remain in Qadian ordered the children of the derwesh who had spread out across India to return to Qadian. The derwesh, being the men who had been personally ordered by the second caliph to defend Qadian at partition, were the last remaining links to a time when the caliphate existed in Qadian, and their families were therefore crucial repositories of a tarbiyyat appropriate to the caliphate. The fear was that as they spread out into India, their tarbiyyat would be lost or diluted, and so too would the tarbiyyat of the town.

In the latter decades of the twentieth century and since, as Qadian has begun to expand and grow economically, it has attracted increasing numbers of Ahmadis from across India. The Jama'at offers employment, and it provides a measure of social security deeply desired by those who can only make a precarious living in India, while for others Qadian is a refuge—a safe place to be Ahmadi Muslim. This migration of Ahmadis from across India means that the town is nowadays increasingly populated by those who do not trace their lineage back to the derwesh and who therefore lack a family link to a time when the caliphate was based in Qadian. Such families might have been Ahmadi for decades, and yet even so, I occasionally heard members of older families describing them as new converts. It did not matter how long they had been in the Jama'at—if their family had no direct link to the caliphate, they were also suspect of being new, of being outsiders. Consequently, their continued influx was seen by some to take the town ever further away from a state of pure communion with the caliph.

Confronted by this inexorable sense of decline, Ahmadis in Qadian fought for closeness and intimacy with their leader. Their efforts were always underwritten by a sense that they would forever fall short in their relationship to the caliph and that he would always be far more concerned about maintaining a relationship with them than they were with him. His was a love that his remote and isolated followers in Qadian could not match.[14]

Faxing the Caliph

Faced with a historical separation from their leader, Qadian's Ahmadis strove for a realization that only through their adherence to the caliphate might they succeed in spiritual and worldly spheres. The desired relationship that people sought to realize was said to be stronger than that between child and father. Ahmadis in Qadian spoke of crying at the death of a caliph in a way they had never done for relatives. They described how, were they to be found guilty of some bad deed, they would feel more shame before the caliph than in front of their own parents. At the heart of such emotions was the moral concern that each individual have a personal and intimate relationship to their caliph. Cultivating discipline to the caliph meant listening to his weekly sermons and acting on his moral message, but those in Qadian—more so than any other community of Ahmadis I met—also strove to allay the threat of distance by cultivating a relationship of intimacy with the caliph through the writing of letters. In one sense, the writing of personal letters was a deeply private exercise, but it was also subject to community regulation and surveillance by the Jama'at bureaucracy. In their monthly field reports, missionaries must specify whether they have written to the caliph, and if they say they have not, they will be asked why. Likewise, in each neighborhood of Qadian, the local leader of the men aged fifteen to forty will ask those men if they have written to the caliph for prayers, and then include in his monthly report the percentage who said yes.[15]

Overwhelmingly, letters to the caliph would be sent to London via fax, which throughout my fieldwork in 2010–12 was the major technological means for both personal and bureaucratic communication with the caliph. This anachronistic technology produced material traces of communication with the caliph, which were key to both the enchantment of everyday life in the town and to the dangerous possibility that this enchantment could be exposed as a fabrication.

The most I ever heard of anybody faxing the caliph was twice a week, while, at the other end of the spectrum, some people barely ever wrote. Many of my interlocutors endeavored to write at least once a month, although they tended to be more punctual in this during times of anxiety, for example, before a wedding or during school exams. The basic feature of any letter to the caliph is a request for prayers. The caliph is not seen as an intermediary between humans and God, but his prayers are accepted with greater regularity than those of normal humans. In difficult periods, people will ask the caliph to pray that their personal or family problems might be resolved. They might ask that he pray that they are able to be true servants to the Jama'at. Perhaps the most common thing that people ask for is that the caliph pray that they become better servants of him. While individuals will frequently write to request prayers before making a big decision, they also ask the caliph for advice. Should they marry a particular person? Should they accept a job? Should they study engineering or English at university? Sometimes, people will even write with very specific personal requests. One young boy, a final-year student at the theological college in Qadian, wrote to the caliph asking whether the latter could recommend any books for his thesis.

Structuring these requests for prayers or advice is a sense of unmediated correspondence with the caliph, who is said to read and take time over individual supplications. People worry that if they send too many faxes in a single week or month, they could cause the caliph trouble, or they might worry that excessive amounts of correspondence might not look good. While some people will share deeply personal worries with the caliph, others will not include such details in their letters because of the shame they feel before him. In each case, there is a sense of personal intimacy and accountability before the caliph that drives their decisions. For many in Qadian, there is a sense that just as the caliph cares for them through his attention to their supplications, so too must they care for him as an individual; letters often begin by offering prayers for the caliph's health, and when members of his family die, Ahmadis in Qadian send him condolence (*t'aziyat*) letters.

Sometimes the caliph replies; oftentimes he does not.[16] Occasionally, he will respond to requests for advice with a definitive answer. Other times he will simply advise his followers to pray such that they make the best decision. Certain requests are almost always answered; for example, most newborns in Qadian are given names directly recommended by the caliph in one of his replies. When individuals ask for prayers, he might reply to say that he prayed for them, and when they send him condolence letters, he may respond by asking them to pray for him, thus stressing that this is a relationship of mutual support, of intimacy, and of unequal reciprocity. Replies, when received, are treasured. One man in Qadian who had kept every reply he had ever received from the caliph described how the file holding these letters "contains my whole life." The fact that these replies are usually written by a private secretary and only signed by the caliph is not seen as important; these letters are seen as coming directly from the Jama'at's divine leader, and in this sense they prove his extraordinary ability to maintain a personal relationship with all his many followers, to know who they are, and to be able to speak directly to the conditions of their lives.[17]

Whether or not the caliph actually replies to people's faxes, the act of writing them is a crucial technique through which Ahmadis learn to live lives that are filtered through their relationship to the caliph. This is a point often explicitly made by parents, who tell their young children to write to the caliph to form a habit that will grow into a genuine connection when the child is older. The goal is to create an inner disposition in which every decision a person makes is colored by their connection to the caliphate.[18] It is about structuring life around this relationship with the caliph in such a way that a person realizes that he or she is, as one Jama'at employee put it, worthless (*bekar*) without the caliphate. This is what people refer to when they describe how they came to realize or understand the importance of the caliphate to their lives. A life devotee in Qadian explained to me that when he first began to study at university, he didn't truly understand the meaning of the caliphate. At this time, his grades were on the whole low. But then a change within him occurred, for he began to understand the caliphate; he began to write to the caliph on a regular basis, and suddenly his grades improved. His life was transformed in both spiritual and material terms once he began living it through the knowledge of the connection he could share with the caliph. I likewise came across elderly Ahmadis who would tell the entire story of their lives as that of a relationship with the caliph. Indeed, people in Qadian are frequently defined by this relationship such that it comes to encapsulate the essence of their being. On a nondescript Friday during my fieldwork, I sat in the main mosque in Qadian, waiting to hear the weekly local sermon, when a death announcement was made. An elderly woman had passed away; all that was mentioned of her was that she had been greatly attached to the caliph's sermons.

Effacing a System?

The idealized relationship between caliph and Ahmadi admits of no intermediary presence, and as such, practices of letter writing in Qadian frequently have the effect of effacing the bureaucracy that bridges the gap between individual believers and their leader. For example, after Ahmadis in Qadian watch the coverage of overseas events on the Jama'at's satellite television network—for example the annual gatherings (jalsa salanas) in Europe—they will often send a congratulatory fax to their caliph. In these moments, the complex hierarchies of individuals who actually make such events happen disappear. The caliph alone is held to have caused the event and to be responsible for its success. In instances like this, the entire bureaucracy of the global Ahmadiyya Jama'at disappears such that an idealized image of devotion and love between individual and caliph can emerge.

Furthermore, for an intimate and reciprocal relationship to exist between Ahmadi and caliph, the latter must necessarily be seen to have almost superhuman attributes. For starters, his memory is said to exceed that of an ordinary man. People tell narratives about the caliph instantly recalling details from individuals' letters when he meets them for the first time and asking them specific questions relating to those issues. He is also said to be able to advise individuals on any topic (not just spiritual matters), while his ability to run a global organization, counsel world leaders, give weekly sermons, hold daily meetings with his followers, and still attend to every individual letter he receives are all held up as signs of his immense physical and mental abilities. Indeed, so prevalent were ideas about the superhuman attributes of the caliph that a supposedly genuine copy of the caliph's daily routine—detailing how he manages to do all this while also keeping up to date on current events—was circulating around Qadian when I did my fieldwork. Unsurprisingly, the caliph is reputed to barely sleep at all. Common to all these narratives is the idea that the caliph, by being immensely powerful, is able to attend to his individual relationships with followers in a way that they, as flawed human beings, can never match. In all these stories, the caliph alone is held to be singularly responsible to and for his global community of millions. The system through which his actions are carried out is discursively erased, and he alone is recognized as a generative force within the world.

The system is not, however, always so easy to efface, and this fact could be troubling for my interlocutors. Take the example of a convert from Hinduism who belonged to one of the Ahmadi communities in South India. When I first met him, he had been an Ahmadi for only two years. His conversion had been dependent on the caliphate, for like many who choose to embrace Ahmadiyyat, his decision had been influenced by a dream in which he vividly saw the caliph. Despite having been an Ahmadi for two years, however, he had not yet written to his leader. He had in fact been planning to do so for a year, gathering his thoughts, and working out what to put in his first letter. He wanted to explain in this letter how he felt before taking bai'at (the act of joining the community) and how he felt after having done so.[19] And yet in spite of his careful planning of this first letter, he was hesitant to send it, for he was worried that the caliph might not read it. He planned to wait until he knew that the caliph was in London before faxing the letter, but even then, he had no guarantee that the letter would not simply be lost in the system. Such worries pointed toward the fact that between the individual and the caliph operated an entire system that just as easily produced distance between them as it could intimacy: despite the superhuman powers of the caliph, people still worried that he simply might not be able to read their letters.

It is hard to estimate the exact number of letters and faxes the caliph receives every day, but once when I was attempting to contact the caliph's office to gain permission for a spell of fieldwork, I was informed by his personal secretary that it was several thousand. As instructed, I had sent my request by fax, and I was told that the influx of communication was so great that if I did not immediately call the office to alert them to my fax, it would likely be buried in an ever-increasing pile and never be seen again.

A number of myths circulated in Qadian about how the caliph engages with letters and faxes. Often, my interlocutors would insist on the enormous capacity of the caliph to get things done; his ability to read each and every letter was a result of his superhuman work ethic and his keen memory. Many Ahmadis in Qadian seemed to assume that the caliph pays attention to each and every letter, but others doubted that this was possible. Some people argued that there are three secretaries in London sorting letters into piles; others, that the letters were summarized and then indexed by a single private secretary. These ideas were only ever speculations. Crucially, the exact mechanisms through which the caliph might attend to his followers on an individual basis remained purposely obscure: the mechanics of the intimate relationship between caliph and Ahmadi were a matter of studied ambiguity. Such was the case that some of my interlocutors even downplayed the communicative aspect of letter writing. The important thing, they argued, was not that a letter ever reached the desk of the caliph but that the individual follower sat down with an intention of writing that letter. I heard stories, for example, of how prayers were answered even before the letter could have arrived in London and thus before it was possible for the caliph to have read the supplication.

These fears over faxes and letters being lost in the system, the studied ignorance on the issue of exactly how the caliph managed to read thousands of pieces of correspondence a day, and the insistence on prayers being answered even if letters did not arrive all point toward a tension at the heart of my interlocutors' relationship to the caliph: that the immediate, personal, and intimate relationship between believer and caliph was possible only because of the vast bureaucratic apparatus that separated the two. Indeed, any relationship of intimacy to the caliph that is not mediated through the bureaucracy becomes deeply problematic. This means that relationships that existed with a caliph prior to his election must be effaced once he assumes office. An Ahmadi man in Qadian, for example, showed me a picture of his father that he had found after the latter's death. The picture quite clearly showed the father as a young man in Pakistan sitting outdoors with a friend. That friend was Mirza Tahir Ahmad, who would one day become the fourth caliph. "My father never mentioned this friendship when he was alive," he told me. "He kept completely quiet all his life. I only discovered it when he died." When I asked why, he replied, "Because it is not good to tell people this. Had he been a politician or another public figure it would have been fine. But he is the spiritual leader. It is not good to go around telling people that he was or is my friend." Personal attachment built on friendship, in other words, can be dangerous and disruptive once the caliph is elected and the individual is transformed into the office that he holds. Rather, the idealized intimacy that should exist between Ahmadi and caliph must be generated through, mediated by, and cultivated within the apparatus of the Jama'at system.

Enchanting the Bureaucracy

For all the importance of personal letters, the most significant way in which the caliph was made present in the quotidian life of Qadian was through the administrative workings of the Jama'at system. In every space in which the system operated, the caliph's decisions were said to affect people's lives, and his direct instructions were understood to guide Jama'at employees. I first began to notice the constant presence of the caliph in Qadian during conversations in which employees and life devotees of the Jama'at told me about their administrative postings throughout the Indian system. These devotees had given their lives to the Jama'at (or had been pledged to the Jama'at while in their mothers' wombs) as waqf, a term normally used within Islam to describe not a person but an inalienable endowment.[20] As a result, their own desires, hopes, aspirations, and sense of autonomy had to be effaced; they were servants of their caliph to do as he commanded. For many, this was a tough life characterized by hardship and sacrifice. Some of these devotees were trained in professions in demand by the Jama'at system: doctors, teachers, or engineers. The vast majority, however, were

FIGURE 2. One of Qadian's newer administrative offices. This picture was taken at the time of Qadian's Annual Gathering; hence, the figures sat talking on the grass.

missionaries trained by the Jama'at in the theological college in Qadian.[21] Their complete lack of autonomy over their lives was a celebrated characteristic of their disciplined responsibility to truth, but it also meant that they could never anticipate whether they would end up working a desk job in Qadian, being attached to a mosque in Mumbai, or attending to a newly converted flock in rural Bihar. All of these prospects could be terrifying for different reasons. A rural posting brought with it a threat of privation and alienation; I heard stories of missionaries going mad from the extreme conditions in India's hinterlands. A desk job, by contrast, could be a distraction from one's calling as a missionary, while a city job presented its own unique challenge: how to provide one's family with the semblance of a middle-class lifestyle in an expensive city on only the meagre wages given by the Jama'at. These men could not, however, complain, for as one young missionary told me, "it is not about where I want to go, for wherever I am sent, I will go. This is my duty."

This life of sacrifice is made bearable because life devotees understand themselves to be serving the caliph directly. The first few times I heard Ahmadi devotees describe new postings by saying that the caliph had ordered them somewhere directly, I did not think much of it. But the more I paid attention to the precise manner in which people described their duties, the more I noticed quite how much of life in Qadian seemed to be a result of direct orders from the caliph. There was an unmistakable concern to locate the source of orders with the caliph and thus to be carrying out his orders directly. People would not just say that they were being posted to a particular village or assigned a particular duty; they would say, "Huzur [the caliph] has sent me," or "Huzur has ordered me." These orders were described as coming personally from the caliph.

In fact, there were large areas of life in Qadian in which the presence of local intermediaries seemed to be completely forgotten, such that people talked only of directives as if they came straight from the caliph's office. For example, there was a period of a few weeks in my fieldwork when the students at the theological college were waiting nervously for their exam results. When I spoke to them, they unanimously described the process as one of waiting for their caliph to issue their results. None of them seemed quite sure of what his role had actually been: Was he the chief examiner? Was he checking the marks? Was he legitimizing the marks already awarded? Or was he setting the pass mark? That the marks had almost certainly been awarded locally was of little concern for these students; what mattered to them was the fact that their marks were coming directly from their leader. Should they pass or fail, this was a matter entirely between them and their compassionate leader.

Once again, these stories point to two very distinct facts about the caliph. First, his relationship to his individual workers is said to be immediate and intimate.

No matter what their position, high or low, they speak of their orders coming directly from the caliph; they serve only him, and his use of their labor is based on his familiar knowledge of them. Second, he emerges as all powerful within the realm of Qadian's system. His decisions are final and total; nothing happens without him, and everything happens because of him. He is the be all and end all of life in Qadian.

Only slowly as I conducted my fieldwork did it become obvious quite how much effort and labor was required to produce this image of the caliph's intimate power. As I encountered more and more instances in which people attributed extensive local occurrences and events to the caliph, it became clear that the caliph's will was being created in Qadian through a laborious form of bureaucratic practice. This bureaucratic labor sought to erase its own traces, but there were moments when its presence became brightly illuminated.

A particularly clear instance of this occurred during the elections for a leadership position in one of the auxiliary branches of the Jama'at. Every Ahmadi belongs to one such auxiliary organization, as determined by their age and gender. It is through these auxiliaries that many internal Jama'at activities are organized. The auxiliary organizations also concern themselves with the devoutness of their members: it is the auxiliaries in Qadian that record whether individuals have been writing to the caliph or praying regularly in the mosque. The election in question was for the position of vice president (*naib sadr*) of the local branch of the auxiliary organization for Ahmadi men in Qadian over the age of forty. As is the case for all elections in the Jama'at, including that of the caliph, strict rules were in place stating that nobody could promote himself for office; individuals could neither submit their own candidacy nor campaign for election or show a desire to be elected. Instead, other people had to nominate those who they expected would do a good job. In this case, these strict rules resulted in the election of a man who was extremely popular for his kindness and humility but who would almost certainly never have volunteered his own name. As in all Jama'at elections, however, the vote was seen as nothing more than an advisory mechanism, for it was only the caliph who ultimately had the power to create a new vice president, and in this case, the caliph declined to give the elected man the role.

When I first heard that the caliph had overridden the result, I was surprised, if only because it seemed odd that such a loyal and popular servant of the Jama'at had been refused such a prominent role. I asked why this had happened, but people seemed content with an explanation that privileged the caliph's intimate control and power over Qadian: "Huzur did not give him the role." It was only when I began pressing people and really asking them why this was the case that an interlocutor finally told me what would have been obvious to anybody from Qadian: "Actually, the chief secretary [*nazr a'ala sahib*] must have recommended against it because he [the elected man] is very busy. So the caliph [*huzur*] will have taken his decision based on this."

The man who had been elected was simply too busy to do the job due to his other Jama'at duties. He thus clearly did not have time for this new position, and although he could not express himself openly, he no doubt felt trepidation at the idea of another huge responsibility falling on his shoulders. The chief secretary would have known this and most likely sent a fax to the caliph advising him to reject the election results. This was, in other words, a local decision taken on the basis of local knowledge, rubber-stamped by the caliph's office in London.

It is quite clear from this example that the average Ahmadi is under no illusion about the complex network of actions that lies behind decisions.[22] The work of the bureaucracy in Qadian is not hidden; rather, its dependable labor of documentary work enables Ahmadis in the town to give what they see as an ethical explanation to events. Indeed, what occurs in Qadian can be compared to one of the most celebrated anthropological accounts of how people assign responsibility: Evans-Pritchard's *Witchcraft, Oracles and Magic among the Azande.*[23] Evans-Pritchard famously described how, even though his Zande informants were well aware of the fact that termites cause grain silos to collapse, they still saw such an interpretation as insufficient to explain the misfortune of why a grain silo should collapse on a particular person at a particular time. Hence, in order to give a moral explanation to the phenomenon of collapsing grain silos, they invoked witchcraft. Likewise, the Ahmadis in Qadian would be able to give a rational account of how their bureaucracy causes local events to happen in Qadian, but they would view such an account as insufficient for explaining how the Jama'at's global system continually functions so as to produce good, just, and effective—in short, perfect—decisions. In each case, people are asking moral questions about responsibility. For the Azande, an explanation is not an explanation until responsibility is assigned to a human: for the Ahmadis, their system is not sacred until it is seen to emanate from the caliph.[24] He must be made responsible for all the many successes of the Jama'at as they unfold on a daily basis in the local spaces of Qadian.

In this way, the bureaucracy of Qadian functions so as to enable the caliph to emerge as responsible for minute, everyday goings-on. When a decision taken in Qadian is considered to have potential effects or ramifications (and sometimes this is true for even the most mundane, bureaucratic tasks), a fax will be sent to the caliph with a recommendation. For example, in the selection of a candidate for an office in the Jama'at, the chosen candidate's name will be sent to the caliph with a recommendation from the chief secretary in India. One result of this top-heavy system is that the caliph's office receives a huge quantity of bureaucratic requests and reports daily. In London, faxes requiring the caliph's approval are organized and presented to him by his private secretary. To give his permission, the caliph often simply ticks the application or scrawls a quick OK (*thik hai*) at the bottom of the paper to signal approval, before the whole thing is once more faxed back to where it originated. This process effectively means that all decisions can ultimately be traced back to the caliph, no matter how small his input may have been. One senior administrator explained that even the smallest matters are put before the caliph for permission, the reason being that "he is the representative of God. If he gives the answer yes, things can't go wrong, but if we make decisions, things can go wrong." As a result of this centralized impulse, the many decisions actually being made in Qadian on a daily basis can be discursively erased. The offices of Qadian generate huge quantities of paper—reports, notes, and, above all, letters, which are circulated between departments until they may eventually be faxed to the caliph, at which point they can be transmuted into decisions. In this way, the endless paper labor of the bureaucracy enchants life and creates the sacred bond between the townsfolk and their leader. The caliph can be held accountable for an enchanted life, and the routinized labor of the bureaucracy can be forgotten.[25]

Many of the Jama'at employees in Qadian see this centralized system as a utopian safeguard against human error. The administrator just quoted above described how, if there was any problem in his department, he immediately asked the caliph for guidance via fax. As a result of this, he explained, "there is no gap between this department and the caliphate. We have never been stuck by any problem because of this." Later in the same conversation, he told me, "Our brain is the khalifa [caliph] of the time: we merely carry out his instructions." The beneficence of the caliphate is thus said to lie in the fact that the caliph can give advice on any topic, even secular ones. At times, this means that the caliph's advice might even override that of a specialist, as the following example will show. In India, homeopathic medicine is considered a professional occupation, and to become a homeopathic doctor requires many years of institutional training.[26] The Jama'at in Qadian employs homeopathic doctors in its hospital, and most Ahmadis have a high degree of confidence in this form of medicine, for it was championed by the fourth caliph. Indeed, homeopathic doctors are accorded a similar respect to their allopathic peers. One of these homeopathic doctors told me a story. He had been treating a cancer patient with a course of medicine that he thought correct based on his extensive training and experience. At the same time, however, the patient's family wrote to the caliph, explaining their situation and asking for advice. The caliph replied with a recommendation for a different homeopathic medicine. When the patient brought this letter to the doctor, he initially rejected its recommendation; after all, he was the trained doctor. That night, however, he suddenly realized the terrible thing he had done; he had sought to override advice by the caliph. He thus contacted the patient the next day and told her to take the medicine recommended by the caliph.

The processes described above can also help us to understand the continued use of fax in the administration of Qadian. This antiquated technology continued to be used, despite the fact that almost all the offices in Qadian had at least one computer at the time I was conducting my fieldwork. It is true that fax was a trusted and reliable technology that was in place across the global Jama'at and that was often used to communicate with places where—unlike Qadian—internet connections might not have existed. But its continued use also had another benefit due to its very material nature. Fax enabled the caliph's presence to be embedded in bureaucratic modes of writing through his ability to inscribe himself on paper.[27] Fax thus enabled a fundamentally impersonal mode of bureaucratic writing to be transformed into a vessel for the caliph's will that could enchant every aspect of daily life in Qadian. Physical inscriptions made by the caliph's hand could be literally dispersed through the offices of Qadian as copies of faxes passed between them. Modern utopian dreams of bureaucratic systems that function without mediation have often been associated with attempts to govern through the internet in such a way that citizens as consumers can be directly connected to their state.[28] The Ahmadis, by contrast, consciously reject new forms of networked connection and instead rely on a paper technology for the creation of immediacy, for their goal is not just to create lines of connection but to emplace the caliph within Qadian and to make him accountable for their lives.

When I spoke to a former private secretary of the fourth caliph, he explained more of the process that led to the caliph approving faxes. The crucial aspect of the private secretary's role had been the presentation of information to the caliph in such a way that the caliph was merely facilitated in making his decisions. Importantly, this meant that the secretary had to be extremely careful not to alter or change information in such a way that the caliph's sovereign ability to assess the facts for himself was interfered with. The private secretary argued that the caliph, in yet another example of superhuman ability, had been able tell when the system was working in such a way as to disrupt his unmediated link to his followers or to disrupt his sovereign ability to make each and every decision. The private secretary would often present a summary of a letter to the caliph, but the original letter would always be presented alongside it, as a security. And, the secretary told me, the caliph would on occasion spot mistakes in such summaries and correct them, despite being able to give each letter only a few seconds of attention. This is just one such instance in which a feature that seems to make the Jama'at grossly inefficient from an outside perspective—namely, its top-heavy reliance on a single overworked individual—is precisely what is celebrated in the Jamaʿat for making it the most efficient system in the world.

The prohibition against violating the sovereign decision-making ability of the caliph is not just confined to his close associates but percolates down throughout the system. The national committees of all the auxiliary organizations in India once a year hold a consultative council, or *majlis-e-shura*.[29] Such councils are important mechanisms for advising the caliph within the Jamaʿat system. They are avenues through which the opinions of the caliph's followers may be made known to him, important sites for the resolution of potential conflict, and occasions when elections can be held for national positions of authority. Fundamentally, however, these councils have no executive power, for that is the sovereign right of the caliph. After meetings, members of these councils will thus categorically refuse to talk about what the council has recommended or whom the council has elected until such a time as the caliph has given his approval. Votes cast in a council are treated as if they have no ability to precipitate events; final decisions must always rest with the caliph alone.

Antonio Gualtieri, an academic commentator who was evidently shocked by the caliph's "excessive" workload, describes with awe how the fourth caliph managed to achieve everything he did with only two or three hours' sleep a night, a fact that the Ahmadis attributed to God's favor.[30] While the caliph's duties are immense, this face-value interpretation somewhat misses a crucial point that the caliph's unmediated control over the global movement is not just a result of his work but of all those around him. The bureaucracy must continually work to discursively erase its own presence as it emplaces the caliph's will in the crevices of local bureaucratic practice. Individuals, meanwhile, must continue to attribute responsibility for the total actions of a sprawling global system to the split-second decisions being made as the caliph glances at faxes arriving from all over the world. What Gualtieri missed, in other words, was the ethical work demanded of the bureaucracy as it enchants the world with the caliph's presence. Qadian's Ahmadis' refusal to speculate on the role of the bureaucracy in mediating the caliph's agency can, moreover, be compared to another case in the anthropological literature— namely, the commonly encountered "opacity of minds" in Melanesia.[31] This refers to the frequently observed tendency of Melanesians to choose not to speculate on the thoughts of others, not because they are unable to but as a way of maintaining the autonomy of others. To refuse to speculate on others' minds is, in other words, to take an ethical stance on how relations between people ought to be structured. When Ahmadis refuse to speculate on the mechanisms behind the caliph's power, they are of course taking an ethical stance on what kind of relationship should exist between them and their leader.

In respect to this ethical stance, Qadian is perhaps unique in the global Jama'at. When I described my observations to an employee of the Pakistani Jama'at at Rabwah, he agreed that he had often noticed that people in Qadian refer extensively to the caliph as being responsible for local events, in a way that simply did not happen elsewhere. References to the caliph being responsible for local actions occurred only rarely in Rabwah, he observed, and then only "ceremoniously" so as to indicate the dignity of labor under the caliph. Distance from the caliph, it would appear, is felt more keenly in India than Pakistan, even though both communities are now separated from their leader. Isolated from the charismatic force that animates the world, Qadian's Ahmadis turn to the routinized practices of bureaucracy to capture intimacy with the caliph from afar, to enchant their world, and to sacralize their lives. Bereft of their leader, they engage the labors of this system to cultivate and enable a relationship that is more intimate and immediate than even that which they share with their own parents. Their desire is for a society that reproduces itself from the top down, for what Marshall Sahlins has called a heroic polity, in which the life of the leader is the life of a group and in which history is "anthropomorphic" such that it might unfold around the single heroic individual.[32] Their challenge is that they must construct this bottom up.

It is impossible that the caliph does everything that his followers attribute to him. Even with the superhuman abilities he is supposed to possess as a result of divine favor, he is head of too vast an organization to ever be responsible for the micromanagement that his followers attribute to him. His power arises from the self-effacing enchantment of the bureaucracy. What is created out of Qadian's practices of bureaucratic self-erasure is nothing less than a utopian alternative to the Indian state. It is a system that redistributes resources fairly and is made fundamentally legible to its citizens because of their supposedly direct relationship to their caliph. In this sense, the utopian hopes of the Ahmadis can be compared to Anand Taneja's ethnography of petitions made by citizens of Delhi to the jinn (Muslim spirits) in the ruined fortification of Firoz Shah Kotla. These petitions seem to mix medieval notions of justice with modern bureaucratic practices, for they seek to capture a politics of alternative times that might be turned against a state that is both illegible to its citizens and determined to forget the city's prepartition Muslim past. Taneja's interlocutors petition the jinn through a language of rationalized bureaucracy: they leave multiple photocopies of their petitions throughout the ruins "as if they are applications sent to the different departments of a modern bureaucracy," and they attach their own addresses and photographs so as to identify themselves to the jinn as citizens of the state.[33] For Taneja, the justice expected of the jinn is linked to their ability to bear witness to the lives of people who petition them "in spite of the magical amnesia of the state."[34] In a similar fashion, the magical and enchanting bureaucratic practice of Qadian promises to recapture an intimacy forever lost at partition. It is also through the paper workings of Qadian's bureaucracy that an enchanted relationship might emerge, which bypasses the forgettings and illegibility of the modern state and replaces it with a system of perfect justice. Ultimately, this bureaucracy is responsible for the creation of an intimate relationship in which the voices of Ahmadis are witnessed by their divine leader, just as they come to witness the truth that he embodies.

The Threat of the Bureaucracy

While bureaucratic technologies make the intimate power of the caliph possible, they also produce uncertainties about that relationship. These uncertainties occur most notably when a need to maintain the caliph's infallibility comes into conflict with the Ahmadis' ethical commitment to witness his intimate power.

Fairly early on in my fieldwork, I decided to interview the head of an office (*daftar*) in Qadian who was a controversial character in the town and about whose work I had heard some people express misgivings. I arrived at his office unannounced, and before I could even open with pleasantries or small talk, he began to thrust a series of papers in front of my nose, exclaiming, "Look! Everything is done with the direction of Huzur. Huzur has approved everything." Possibly suspecting that I had heard criticism of the work of his team, he had launched a preemptive offensive, telling me that what he was doing was not the result of his own decisions but part of a bigger program, sanctioned and led by the caliph. To admit that the work of the office was a result of his own will would be to open it up to criticism, yet to position himself as a servant of the caliph was to make the actions of his office not of his own doing and thus beyond reasonable criticism. This, of course, was a defensive strategy, but it raises the question of what happens when things go wrong in a system in which everything is said to happen due to the will of an infallible leader.

People regularly criticized one another in Qadian. Relationships in offices turned sour, and controversial decisions aroused the ire of colleagues. In many cases conflicts in the Jama'at necessitated that bureaucratic mediation became visible. An example can help to explain this. In late 2011, a change was made to the timetable in the theological college in Qadian (the Jamia Ahmadiyya), which was responsible for training missionaries for the whole of India. Previously, classes had run from 8:00 A.M. to just before 2:00 P.M., at which time the call for *zuhr* prayers would be sounded, signaling the end of the working day. These were standard office hours for all of Qadian's many administrative departments. Under the new system, however, the college timetable was changed so that it no longer aligned with this system. Under the new rules, lessons ended sooner, a lunch break was included, and some lessons were shifted to the early afternoon. This change resulted in the same number of teaching hours being spread over a longer period in the day, and consequently, many staff and students felt that they had less free time in the afternoon. It was immediately apparent that the decision to make the change had been controversial, and the feelings of those I spoke to greatly influenced the way in which they described the decision-making process. People who approved of the changes were forthright in their assertions: "Huzur has instituted these changes." But those who did not like what was happening told a more complicated story: "Principal Sahib has sent a letter to Huzur saying that everybody agrees with the change, and therefore Huzur approved of the change," one member of the college told me, "but Principal Sahib didn't consult with anybody. What he must have meant is that everybody *will* approve." Those who wished to avoid conflict and embody the ethic of service to an even greater extent simply commented that their responsibility was to follow the system, not question it.

A few months later, another change was made in the college, this time to bring the syllabus in line with the supposedly tougher standards of the Ahmadis' theological college in Pakistan. This was a very controversial move, for while the Pakistani college can rely on the fact that all its students begin their studies with competency in Urdu, the Indian college has no such luxury. Indeed, the first year of college education had previously been set aside for language learning, as students coming from many parts of India (in particular, the south) usually knew little to no Urdu. Thus, there was a great deal of concern among certain sections of both staff and students at the college that coordinating the syllabus of the Indian college with the Pakistani one and thus introducing the Urdu works of Ghulam Ahmad in the first year would cause insurmountable problems for those students still learning Urdu. Ghulam Ahmad's Urdu works, especially those written early in his career, have a reputation even among native speakers of being extremely difficult to understand. Hence, the decision to introduce these Urdu texts was a source of consternation for some, and as in the previous example, those most vehemently against the change stressed the responsibility of the principal for making the decision.[35]

Once again, however, this decision came to be a flash point for different points of view. Some people agreed that a change had been necessary. They felt that standards at the Indian college fell short of what would be expected in the Pakistani college. Although the Indian and Pakistani colleges are the oldest, there are now Jamia Ahmadiyyas across the world, including in the United Kingdom, and many felt that the adoption of a single syllabus was a welcome move toward creating a global standard for the training of Ahmadi missionaries. One teacher at the college, feeling that the decision had been a positive move forward, boldly declared that the change had been a result of a direct order "from Huzur." Knowing as I did that there were rumors about the manner in which the decision had been taken, I questioned him: Was he actually sure that the decision came directly from the caliph? As soon as I began to ask the teacher about this, he admitted that he had no idea whether the final decision had been made by the caliph or the principal and had in fact not even been present at the meeting when it was announced.

These were minor conflicts, small disagreements of little consequence to the long-term history of the Jama'at. And yet they are also perfect examples of how the system operates in Qadian. Disputed events open up a tussle over responsibility; supporters of a decision will invoke the caliph's agency, while those who object must necessarily shine a light on the bureaucratic machinery behind the decision. In each case, the individuals involved remain committed to preserving both the caliph's sovereign right to make decisions and his infallibility in doing so. Ahmadi caliphs do not make mistakes; their link to Prophethood means that they are in constant communion with God. Ultimately, in cases where wrong decisions get made, this infallibility becomes irreconcilable with the caliph's ability to intimately control the minute details of life in his global following. In such a situation, only one thing can save his infallibility: it must be shown that he took a good decision on the basis of bad information; it must be shown that individuals in the system distorted his sovereign decision-making power by sending accidently inaccurate (or perhaps even deliberately misleading) reports to London. And such cases can be profoundly disquieting in Qadian, for they demand that the celebrated immediacy between caliph and follower be recognized as no more than a pious fiction. In place of this idealized relationship emerges a profusion of intermediaries who are said to be guilty of distorting the system. When this happens, bureaucrats in Qadian take the form of morally ambiguous brokers to the power of the caliph, for they are capable of both foregrounding the truth of the caliph in people's lives and distorting the system so that his distance is revealed. Thus, Qadian's Ahmadis are forced to confront the problem of faulty brokerage, which is strikingly reminiscent of the problems they encounter in dealing with secular bureaucracy. Jonathan Parry, for example, has shown how, in India more generally, failed attempts at corruption are often explained away by the hypothesis that corrupt brokers "eat" bribes before they have reached their real targets within a bureaucratic system. In both these larger discourses and in Qadian, an idea thus circulates that a direct and efficacious relationship between an individual and those in power might be distorted by the failure and dishonesty of intermediaries.[36] This equivalence is nonetheless deeply problematic in Qadian, where the Jama'at has always been dreamed of as something better than the Indian state, that is, as an administration without mediation that thus escapes the pitfalls of its worldly opposite.

Perhaps unsurprisingly, cases in which distortion was felt to have happened for personal gain—be it financial, social, or otherwise—could be spectacular for their ability to disrupt the running of the Jama'at bureaucracy. On one particularly memorable occasion, I was drinking tea with a group of Ahmadi men in Qadian, when one of them began to viciously attack the character of a senior official in the Jama'at in a manner deeply at odds with the usual polite way in which people spoke of each other in my presence. It was out and out the angriest tirade I ever heard in Qadian. There was a reason for this, however, for it soon emerged that my interlocutor felt that the recipient of his bile had written letters and reports to the caliph's office in London that attempted deliberately to mislead the decision-making process of the caliph for personal financial advantage. In writing these reports, the other man had opened himself up to the most vehement of criticism, for he was distorting a system ordained by God. What made my interlocutor so angry was, of course, the fact that this man had sought to manipulate the caliph and thus produce judgments in his own favor which could not be questioned by others.

A final danger of corrupt brokerage in Qadian was that it could distort the operation of justice within the system. When legal disputes arise between members of the community in Qadian, individuals do not go to the civil courts but, rather, take their issues before the community's sharia court. The caliph has in fact "totally restricted Ahmadis" from taking "any dispute of a routine nature before a worldly court" unless they are legally obliged to do so. Failure to abide by this ruling can lead to severe penalties.[37] Arguing that other court systems do not always ensure justice, my interlocutors were quick to point out the superiority of their system over that of other courts, for in the Ahmadi case, the caliph stands as the ultimate point of appeal. In other words, at an ideological level, the caliph's unmediated connection to his followers is understood to ensure justice. Anybody, I was told, could write directly to the caliph, whereas if there had been barriers between the individual and the caliph, inefficiencies would be produced, and people would be unable to take their case directly to him. This system is said to ensure that, irrespective of connections or power, everybody is treated fairly. I was given the hypothetical example of a woman, who if beaten by her husband, would be able to petition the caliph directly. No matter how well connected her husband was, she would thereby be ensured justice. The problem, of course, is that this is an idealized view. People manipulate the system, powerful voices can prevail, and justice is not always done. In cases where corrupt brokerage does distort justice in this way, the actual decisions taken by the caliph cannot be questioned: only the process that led to them may be interrogated.

In cases where the bureaucracy is seen to have caused injustice, a further danger exists for those who feel wronged: the caliph retains the sovereign right to expel anybody from his Jama'at. Just as all Ahmadis may enter the community only by taking bai'at from the caliph, so too does the caliph have the sole right to excommunicate them. The act of expulsion does not render somebody a non-Ahmadi, and indeed, I met expelled members who still regarded Mirza Ghulam Ahmad as the Promised Messiah. Rather, expulsion cuts the link between the follower and their caliph; it enforces a painful separation, denies them the right to donate money to the Jama'at, and isolates them from the administrative system through which they might find security in their own sense of being Muslim. It is an act of spiritual exile that severely limits a person's ability to fulfill their obligations to truth. That the infallible caliph might expel a person because of a corruption in the bureaucratic process exposes a horrible reality: that bureaucratic misdeeds can turn the caliph's intimacy with his followers from a relationship of justice into a relationship of arbitrary symbolic violence inflicted with impunity.[38] In such moments, it is clear that the Jama'at system, like any bureaucracy, can be productive of crushing acts of "indifference."[39]

The examples in this section are illustrative of the fact that there is a deep incompatibility between the caliph's infallibility and the unmediated relationship of justice that he is supposed to share with each individual Ahmadi. In daily life and bureaucratic practice in Qadian, things do go wrong, and without some kind of adjustment or acknowledgment of this fact, there is a danger that the caliph will appear to be either unjust or fallible. In such moments, if the caliph's infallibility is to be preserved, his unmediated relationship to his followers must be acknowledged as a creation of bureaucratic process. To save their caliph, Qadian's Ahmadis must thus admit to their distance from him and confront the reality that his presence within their lives is always mediated and rarely direct.[40]

A Duplicitous Proof

The Jama'at system parallels, overlaps, and fills perceived lacunae within local government bureaucracies. For Qadian's Ahmadis, comparisons between these systems are obvious and are frequently made. Administrative experience within the Indian state is seen as a boon for those who want to work within the Nizam-e-Jama'at. I knew of young men sacrificing time and money to try and pass the highly competitive and elite Indian Administrative Service (IAS) examinations, not to secure this most desired of government jobs for long-term personal financial security but so as to take skills learned in government administration back into the Jama'at upon their eventual retirement from the IAS. It is, nonetheless, usually the Jama'at that is seen to have something to teach the Indian state, for when it functions correctly with petitions heard and justice done, Qadian's enchanting system is seen as an exemplar of what worldly bureaucracies could become.

There is, however, a striking parallel between these systems that is less likely to give rise to hubris in Qadian—namely, the capacity of each system to dilute the authentic with that which is imitative or fake. In an analysis of the meanings behind the Hindi/Urdu word *sarkar*—which is commonly translated as "state" or "government"—the anthropologist Nayanika Mathur shows how one common implication of its adjectival form (*sarkari*) "is that of untrustworthiness; of being fake/fraudulent."[41] This means that such bureaucratic objects as sarkari documents and statistics are routinely categorized "as that-which-is-not-real."[42] A similar observation can be taken from Bhavani Raman's history of early colonial governance in South India. Raman argues that the British instituted vast bureaucratic writing practices as a way of managing trust across distance and ensuring accountability but that these writing practices nonetheless introduced both new forms of discretionary practice into rule and new kinds of anxiety over the duplicity of documents.[43] Paper technologies of attestation both authorized bureaucratic relationships and introduced a struggle to control the authenticity of written documents.[44] This was a problem for the East India Company (whose anxieties arose from racialized fears of "native" duplicity), as well as for Indians, who saw the colonial state as a space of deceit.[45] Raman's account thus introduces a question of how those same documentary techniques that could fix, codify, and authenticate also introduced new possibilities and worries about imitation and forgery. Raman's account draws on Veena Das's observation that when the state "institutes forms of governance through technologies of writing, it simultaneously institutes the possibility of forgery, imitation, and the mimetic performances of its power."[46]

A similar observation can be made regarding the Jama'at bureaucracy, in which the process of authenticating and enchanting people's relationship to the caliph introduces the danger of this relationship being counterfeit. This occurs due to the tension between my interlocutors' desire to make the caliph intimately responsible for everything, and their desire to preserve his infallibility. These parallel goals can only be balanced for so long, and the need to preserve the caliph's infallibility can ultimately result in his unmediated intimacy being exposed as an imitative creation of bureaucratic self-effacement. This would be less of a problem were it not for the fact that—as explored in the last chapter—it is through this relationship that my interlocutors seek to prove their Muslimness to the world. As such, Qadian's Ahmadis are placed in a curious position. Due to their long isolation from their caliph, they must of necessity rely on bureaucratic mediation if they are to demonstrate this relationship and verify their Muslimness to the world. In doing this, they have a chance to fulfill their obligation to respond to the truth of Ahmadiyyat. Yet this is a process that cannot be shorn of uncertainty, for the very means through which Qadian's Ahmadis seek to prove this relationship also make the relationship vulnerable to exposure as something that is constructed, inauthentic and forged. In other words, the bureaucracy of Qadian provides a way of fulfilling obligations to truth, but it also threatens to undermine what certainty it offers. What thus emerges from bureaucratic practice in Qadian is a *counterfeit proof* of Muslimness. As I will show in the coming chapters, a concern about the imitative nature of all evidence is in fact central to the ambivalences that characterize my interlocutors' attempts to demonstrate and prove their Muslimness. What I have here chosen to call *counterfeit proof* is a cause of serious moral concern in Qadian.

In the introduction to this book, I described how a narrow analytical concern with religious doubt might lead us to mistake doctrinal conviction for an untroubled relationship with truth. Doubt, I argued, is an obfuscating term, and when deployed analytically it is as likely to distort the relationships that people have to religious concepts as it is to illuminate them. What I hope to have described in this chapter is an anxiety over how to relate to truth that is in no way inconsistent with viscerally felt convictions about that truth. It is a form of religious uncertainty that is irreducible to what anthropologists have traditionally described as "doubt." In engaging in the various administrative practices described in this chapter, my Ahmadi interlocutors never came to question the veracity of their doctrine or the truth of their Muslim status. What they were confronted by, however, was the confounding problem of how to make that truth apparent within the world. We do not tend to think of bureaucratic labor—the writing of letters, the circulating of reports, the signing off of memos, the sending of faxes—as sites in which people might work through the anxieties, uncertainties, and ambiguities of their relationship to religious truth. In suggesting that Qadian's bureaucracy produces a counterfeit proof of Muslim belonging, I have thus sought to expand the domain in which we might study religious uncertainty; that is, I have shown how bureaucratic activities are processes through which Qadian's Ahmadis come up against the difficulties of proving their Muslimness. Indeed, I want to suggest that if anthropologists are to understand religious doubt beyond belief, then it is precisely from such unusual places that they must begin.

A FAILURE TO DOUBT?

Polemics and Sectarianism in Qadian

Ahmadis employed by the Jamaʿat in Qadian earned little money, for their work was seen as a personal sacrifice for the greater good of the religion. While Ahmadi missionaries were not allowed to pursue alternative sources of income, other workers—who were employees rather than devotees of the Jamaʿat—did often run side businesses and were frequently on the lookout for other opportunities by which they could supplement their household incomes. Sometimes, these opportunities would take my interlocutors out of Qadian, and it was while accompanying an Ahmadi worker on such an expedition that I found myself in a showroom in Batala, the nearest big city to Qadian.

My companion, a middle-aged Jamaʿat employee who originally came from outside of Punjab, knew a number of the men in the showroom from his own home state. They were all Sunni Muslims. We began a conversation with these men, at first open and friendly, but it did not take long for the conversation to turn to Islam. The other men knew that my companion was an Ahmadi and obviously saw his views as errant but not beyond correction, and they thus suggested that he read a specific book all about the finality of prophethood. Their intention was clearly to guide him to a Sunni view that Muhammad was the last of all prophets, that no prophethood is possible after Muhammad, and that, as a consequence, Mirza Ghulam Ahmad must be a false pretender. This is the major theological fault line between Ahmadis and other Muslims, and after just a few minutes in the showroom, we had arrived at it. The other men were nonetheless seemingly unprepared for what came next. My companion, undeterred, began to lay out his arguments in a swift, rapid, and coherent fashion. He explained in nontechnical terms how Muhammad was the seal of the prophets but that another servant of Muhammad could still bring a message.[1] Not only this, but he explained to them how Ghulam Ahmad's message had given rise to the richest, best organized Muslim community in the world. My companion was using the worldly success of the community as a theological proof of its divine favor.

As my companion delivered this defense of Ahmadiyyat, the other men in the showroom began to look uncomfortable. He finished his argument, and they remained silent. They did not appear convinced by what he had said, but they seemed to lack the ready-made arguments to respond. As much as they might have thought he was wrong, there was nothing they could do, in that moment, to respond. He had delivered a consummate performance that left no room for dissent.

I had been in Qadian many months when the above incident happened, and yet due to the lack of other Muslims in the local area, this was the first time that I saw for myself an event that is much mythologized and lionized in Qadian: the silencing of opponents through argument. I had come across such stories since I first arrived in Qadian. People would tell me about the arguments and proofs in favor of Ahmadiyyat: they would explain how the Promised Messiah or one of his caliphs had debated with opponents and put forward incontrovertible proof. And yet these stories rarely culminated with the proof itself but rather almost always finished at the moment when the opponents could no longer respond. As one interlocutor triumphantly explained after finishing such a story, "at this the opposition fell silent. There was nothing they could say in reply."

In the showroom in Batala, I had thus witnessed the enacting of a particular kind of idealized character. This character was the fearless Ahmadi polemicist, unafraid to enter the fray of debate and in complete command of the arguments and proofs of Ahmadiyyat. When stories are told of this celebrated figure, the emphasis is not just on winning an argument; it is on defeating opponents in such a final and total fashion that they are stupefied. What is most admired in Qadian is a strident defense of a position, the shoring up of a preexisting set of ideas, and the reinforcement of a sectarian identity.

This idealization of the routing of opponents is not uncommon in sectarian disputes between Muslim groups in South Asia. What makes Ahmadis interesting is that when they engage in polemics, they do so to advance a position that is frequently associated with a particular kind of modernity. They boast of their ability to silence opponents who suggest that jihad might be anything other than peaceful, and they tell stories of shutting the mouths of those who would suggest that Islam is incompatible with the secular nation-state or with science. And yet, if we take away the content of these arguments, we are faced with a question: How is the Ahmadi desire to unflinchingly defend a sectarian position different from that of their opponents? The Ahmadis may be espousing values that many

Western and Indian politicians approve of, but they do so through sectarian apologetics.

The Ahmadis may therefore not be as unlike their opponents as is often supposed. Yoginder Sikand has described how many of the sects that most vociferously oppose the Jama'at teach disputation as a science and prize the ability to rebut opponents in debate. He describes how, at Deoband and allied madrasas, "much of the literature produced by the madrasa is geared to the denunciation (*radd*) of ideological opponents, fellow Muslims as well as Christians and Arya Samajists."[2] Moreover, such seminaries as Deoband often hold weekly grand debates to train their students in disputation. During these occasions, students are divided into two groups: one representing Deobandi orthodoxy and another that of their opponents. The Deobandi viewpoint always prevails, but the debate gives students an opportunity to learn and practice the methods of defeating an opponent: "Rebutting other Muslim groups is thus regarded by many madrasa students and teachers as one of their principal tasks."[3] In such situations, the Ahmadis are unsurprisingly a prominent target of rebuttal.

This comparison raises the question of how much the Ahmadis might come to resemble a figure that darkly haunts their own discourse: the mullah. This is a word applied to local clerics in many parts of the Muslim world, sometimes given as a mark of respect. It can nonetheless also carry pejorative overtones of parochialism. For many of my Ahmadi interlocutors, the mullah represents an inability to reason, a failure to think, and a retreat into blind prejudice. But mullahism might also be thought of as an ever-present state of possibility: Naveeda Khan describes how, in Pakistan, the caricature of the mullah has become a specter that is both blamed for every problem and can be seen as a dangerous possibility that resides in all Muslims.[4] This figure of the mullah is a shadow that is always cast over the ulema—a possibility of decay that, as Khan shows, is continually manifested as object of comedy and fear. It is a fear of the Other in oneself.

Precisely because the Ahmadis are so unjustly persecuted by their coreligionists, many academics have taken to treating them as exceptions.[5] This exceptionality suits other Muslims who would exclude the Ahmadis from the mainstream but also suits the purposes of the Jama'at, which is ever ready to reaffirm its status as the one and only true Muslim sect. This chapter takes a quite different approach. I argue that to understand the intellectual practices of Ahmadis, we have to begin to see them as belonging to a wider culture of sectarian disputation. Ahmadi Muslims may be unusual for their theological views, but their celebration of a particular kind of polemical engagement with outsiders is part of an intra-religious culture of disputation. Indeed, Jonathan Parry has observed a very similar institutionalization of competitive disputation among Hindu priests in Varanasi: "Brahman culture is very much a culture of the spoken word, and a desire to dominate verbally, to render others speechless by the force of one's own speech and erudition, is a striking aspect of the ethos of the Benarasi Brahman. It is institutionalized in the *shastrarth*—a kind of formalized verbal battle over the interpretation of the texts."[6]

For many observers, ranging from the Western media to internal reformers, this culture of disputation—particularly when practiced by Muslims—has long been viewed as representing a very specific intellectual failure: a failure to doubt. The stereotype of the Muslim who doesn't doubt properly is, of course, common to many modernist critiques of the hard-liner, the fundamentalist, and the Islamist. It goes hand in hand with caricatures of the irrational believer, whose affective response to criticism does not allow them to engage in religion rationally.[7] Many anthropologists have argued against crude caricatures and have pointed out that even those involved in the defense of a sectarian identity must necessarily live lives that are characterized by fragmentation and ambivalences.[8] These anthropologists have, in other words, argued that caricatures of the non-doubting Muslim are simply wrong, because people everywhere do in fact doubt. In this chapter, however, I take a different approach. I show that any analysis that takes as its starting point the idea that epistemological doubt *should exist* within Qadian is premised on a fundamentally false assumption that the major modality through which the town's Ahmadis interact with doctrinal truth is one of belief. Rather, in Qadian, we find clerics who seek to practice doctrine, to discipline themselves to it, and to respond to its calls to be its witnesses. Theirs is by no means an uncomplicated relationship to doctrine, but it is not characterized by doubt. Through an examination of the ethics of sectarian disputation, I thus demonstrate how uncertainty might be rethought.[9]

Sectarians and Mullahism

By focusing on the role and function of debates and arguments within Muslim societies, anthropologists have in recent decades managed to overcome many of the problems that beset an earlier generation who found it difficult to reconcile an essentialized "Islam" with local practice. In various guises, an ethnographic focus on debate and contestation has enabled anthropologists both to understand the political importance of Islamic ritual and to understand the constructed nature of orthodoxy as a relation of power.[10] This said, there remains a lingering suspicion in much academic and popular literature that South Asian Muslims are not quite debating "properly." Sectarian engagements such as the one I began this chapter with are assumed to lead to dogmatism and fundamentalism, and questions about the vitality of the intellectual life of South Asian Muslims have tended to focus heavily on madrasas, or Islamic schools. These madrasas are criticized for their insularity, for banning publications representing alternative viewpoints, and for teaching their students only within the confines of one, narrow *maslak* (school of thought). Indeed, even those authors writing in defense of the madrasa tradition argue for the need for reform.[11] As a result, these madrasas and the intellectual tradition they uphold have often been characterized by the mainstream press in India and elsewhere as breeding grounds for terrorism.[12] In India, the madrasa is often defended as providing education free of cost to the poor, where either the state has failed or where anti-Muslim and anti-Urdu prejudice make state school education difficult for Muslim children. Yet such praise is usually mixed with a rational realization that the curricula used are incapable of creating students able to find employment or even deal with modern life in a globalizing world.[13] A further problem is that, as Ali Riaz points out, in a post-9/11 world, many observers have come to view the madrasa almost entirely through the lens of security, and thus media accounts often see the institution in ahistorical and decontextualized terms, despite its embeddedness within Muslim society.[14] Thus, images of repressed and intellectually stifled madrasa students are frequently repeated, without any real examination of the social processes that could conceivably produce such a situation.

The perceived ossification of the madrasas of South Asia is an extremely complex phenomenon, which has been argued to have a number of discrete causes. At the heart of much of the criticism of madrasas is their continued use of a syllabus, the *dars-i-nizami*, which traces its origins back to an eighteenth-century need to train administrators for the burgeoning Mughal state.[15] Although dominant until the end of the Mughal period, the dars-i-nizami ultimately became outmoded in 1837 when English replaced Persian as the official language of bureaucracy. A final death knell then sounded in 1844 when madrasa-educated men were effectively banned from entering government service. Nonetheless, this syllabus continues, in a modified form, to be the basis of much madrasa education in South Asia. This antiquated syllabus was an effective tool for most of its early life, but its continued use in the modern era has come to stand for the fossilization of Islamic learning in South Asia. As such, it has attracted much criticism for promoting insular and sectarian worldviews among its students. Various attempts to reform madrasa curricula have been undertaken since the latter half of the nineteenth century, but many of these reforms have themselves been accused of perpetuating the problem. The most famous such reform was the creation of the Deoband seminary, now one of South Asia's most significant centers of Islamic learning. Originally conceived as a reformist movement, Deoband is nowadays often caricatured as a bastion of unreflective narrow-mindedness. Even in the early years of its foundation, however, reform-minded ulema criticized Deoband for its supposedly backward-looking mentality. By the late nineteenth century, Muslims were under increased pressure from Christian missionaries, and yet in the words of one commentator, they spent their time debating internal issues that were so obscure they "could hardly warrant a controversy in a healthy society."[16]

This long history of reform and counterreform is saturated by an idea that South Asia's Muslims are too insular, and their sectarian identities too static. In India, much of the most fervent criticism of this intellectual tradition comes from Hindu nationalist politicians, who see madrasas as hotbeds of anti-Hindu propaganda. As Arshad Alam has argued, such critiques often misunderstand the true purpose of the argumentative discourse that takes place in madrasas. Members of various Muslim sects are usually concerned with the perpetuation of their own school of thinking through particular forms of stylized debating in which other schools of thought are systematically refuted. The Muslim Other as opposed to the Hindu Other is understood to be dangerous because of their close proximity, and thus it is through practices of polemical debating and refutation that the internal identity of groups comes to be structured.[17] In Pakistan, this is part of a broader social phenomenon that has been linked to the rise of a middle class: returning labor migrants from the Persian Gulf are drawn to the sense of belonging that a sectarian community can provide; they go to its mosque, partake in its fund-raising, and subscribe to its newsletter. In short, they enter into a social world in which the boundaries between their sect and others are constantly being drawn.[18] Such communities are frequently engaged in disputation with one another, but even when not, much of their doctrine is of a polemical nature, in that its truth is defined in contrast to the doctrines of other sects.

For internal reformers, of course, these sociological arguments are little consolation. Modern madrasa education thus continues to be criticized for institutional structures that make teachers unwilling to change and therefore produces a culture of "indoctrination" that aims to support, reproduce, and reinforce itself.[19] Students are seen as cocooned within this self-reinforcing system of ultimately useless knowledge, their capacity for free thought and individual will stifled. For many analysts, the link between this intellectual environment and the creation of the Taliban is obvious and self-evidentiary.[20] The picture that emerges out of this literature is thus one of a degenerated form of Muslim intellectual tradition. A belief in the preeminence of oral transmission is seen to have decayed into rote learning and indoctrination. A long-standing Islamic emphasis on the embodiment of texts under revered masters is now seen to have transformed into a condition of mullahism, where all that matters is the transmission of ossified knowledge.[21] Behind all these criticisms and concerns, however, lies another, even more basic assumption: that these are people who do not doubt properly. Behind every charge of intellectual ossification is the idea that South Asian Muslims live lives in which they do not question the boundaries of their sectarian identities. These criticisms are thus not just questions of intellectual practice but moral judgments. After all, what could be more "repugnant" about the fundamentalist than his or her inability to doubt?[22]

Anthropology has been at the forefront of challenging such ideas. Magnus Marsden takes on precisely these attitudes in his ethnography *Living Islam*, so as to defend and rehabilitate the intellectual practices of Muslims in Pakistan's North-West Frontier Province (now Khyber Pakhtunkhwa).[23] Through a detailed and evocative ethnographic account, Marsden shows that the people of Chitral live "mindful" and "intellectually vibrant" lives. These are people who are precisely aware of how to cultivate a healthy attitude of skepticism and doubt toward any totalizing or all-encompassing sectarian project. And yet, while Marsden's ethnography provides a much-needed reminder as to the diversity and heterogeneity of Muslim life in South Asia, it ultimately does not respond to the specific issue that I am raising here. This is because the intellectual vibrancy of Marsden's Chitrali interlocutors stems precisely from their spirited resistance to the increasing sectarianism of Pakistan's public discourse.[24]

To really understand sectarian polemics on their own terms requires a different approach. Describing South Asia's madrasa-educated ulema, Muhammad Qasim Zaman explores how many of their writings—for example, hadith commentaries—seem to make little intellectual contribution and instead merely recapitulate old ideas and debates. The notion that modern ulema lack any spirit of innovation is so pervasive, he argues, that we tend not to study them in comparison to their premodern counterparts, who are seen as genuinely intellectually pioneering. Zaman nonetheless argues that "intellectual significance" can be a poor measure of a tradition. Texts like hadith commentaries often reject innovation on purpose, instead being composed in order to preserve the "presence" or voice of revered teachers or to link scholars to one another's authority.[25] Thus, to begin to understand these forms of writing, we have to understand their purpose as creating or maintaining the relationships through which authority might be exercised.

This shift to a focus on the relational aspect of these texts can be further explored through the work of the anthropologists Michael Fischer and Mehdi Abedi, whose analysis of revolutionary discourse in Iran has argued against crude caricatures that see Islam as wholly prescriptive.[26] Fischer and Abedi examine sharia discourse in Iran to show that rather than just being seen as the imposition or enforcement of a rule, it must be understood as "an ethical discourse in the sense that it is always conducted in a communicative environment that assumes persuasive dialogue with others, that attempts to persuade those others to join one's own moral and political community."[27] This focus on the ethical is further evinced in Naveeda Khan's work, which resists the common idea that sectarian disputation in Pakistan need be thought of as a failure of consensus and instead reframes it as an inherently ethical process of becoming. She thus attempts to show that forms of disputation that do not sit easily with a liberal conscience should in fact be thought of in terms of striving for a better Islam.[28]

This literature can lead us to reassess the function and significance that modern-day practices of disputation and dialectical reasoning have for Muslims themselves.[29] For the faithful, the fact that polemicism is a major goal of many Muslim sects in South Asia is often explained by recourse to a hadith that predicted that there will be seventy-three sects but that only a single one of them will be the true Islam. Accordingly, a duty necessarily falls on the true sect to prove the others false.[30] What I have attempted to demonstrate here, however, is that ethical concerns to cultivate relationships with others—and even with one's self—often undergird discourses that might otherwise appear stagnant.[31] In the next section, I consider how this might apply to the valorization of polemic that I witnessed in Qadian.

The Origins of the Heroic Polemicist

To understand disputation in Qadian is to understand why a group of people who outwardly boast of their enthusiastic embrace of the modern world idolize a form of action that involves doggedly defending a sectarian position and crushing opposition through argument. For observers who have only ever encountered the Ahmadiyya Muslim Community through its claims to be "the most dynamic Muslim community in modern history," this may seem like an odd way of characterizing the Jama'at.[32] Criticisms of intellectual stagnation have, however, followed the Jama'at for decades, the most prominent of which was made by the poet-philosopher Muhammad Iqbal. Iqbal's comments, first published in Lahore in 1935, originated as a response to Jawaharlal Nehru's concerns about Muslim exclusion of the Ahmadis. Situating himself in a genealogy of modernist thought, Iqbal justified his concerns about the Ahmadis by accusing them of a dangerous conservatism: he saw Ahmadiyyat as dragging the masses back toward medieval mysticism. For Iqbal, Ahmadiyyat distracted people from the task of inner purification and placated them with a messianic figure whose function "is not to extricate the individual from an enervating present but to make him slavishly surrender his ego to its dictates."[33] Another (anonymous) critic of the Jama'at put this in far more direct language: "Ghulam Ahmad and his son [the second caliph] want robots and not men."[34]

Understanding polemical discourse in Qadian means fully dissecting this "slavish" relationship to authority. It means understanding the use of arguments in

Qadian as an ethical practice through which my interlocutors saw themselves to be imitating prophethood. To explain how this is so, we first have to appreciate the manner in which the life of the Promised Messiah, Mirza Ghulam Ahmad, is understood by Ahmadis to be a series of victorious encounters with opponents. My aim is to get away from a picture in which the single-minded defense of a sectarian position is understood only in a clichéd idiom of stony-faced hardness. Instead, I want to try and capture the joyous fashion in which my interlocutors celebrate disputation as the marker of an ethically refined life

It is by now a frequently stated truism that Punjab in the late nineteenth century was a place of dynamic religious change, characterized by an emerging public sphere centered on debates and arguments.[35] Mirza Ghulam Ahmad, of course, was a participant in this culture. A number of historians have written about this culture of debate, and many of them have made the sociological point that public argument and disputation in colonial Punjab helped to turn religion into a self-conscious ideology that could become the basis of group identity and loyalty.[36] This reading points to a truth about the public sphere in which Ghulam Ahmad operated, but it is perhaps limited in that it sees disputation only as a mechanism through which group identity is produced. But what if we start to think beyond functionalism, in order to consider the ways in which argumentation could be an ethical practice with goods internal to itself? What if we think, in other words, about the ethics of sectarian dispute? For Ahmadis, the notion that Mirza Ghulam Ahmad was born into an era of multireligious conflict is not a background fact: it is instead seen as crucial to the ethical mission of his prophethood.[37] Ahmadi sources place great emphasis upon the fact that Ghulam Ahmad's life was characterized by controversy, polemic, and public debates. Indeed, a biography by his son (the second caliph) reads as a long list of the various debates Ghulam Ahmad is reported to have been involved in and won.[38] In Ahmadi hagiography, what matters is that Ghulam Ahmad was able to inflict successive crushing defeats on all those who attempted to engage him in argument. In this way, Ahmadi hagiography of Ghulam Ahmad echoes medieval hagiographic works about Sufi saints in India, which often emphasized the latter's spiritual combat with Hindu yogis.[39] The difference is that Mirza Ghulam Ahmad's biographers do not ascribe fantastical miracles to him: rather, his rationality *is* the miracle of his prophethood. For his followers, the most important events in his life are thus neither extraordinary moments of divine intervention nor examples of practical action but rather moments of triumph in the deployment of proof using a mixture of reason (*'aql*) and revealed truth (*ilham*). That Ghulam Ahmad was born to an age of disputation has thus led to a particular privileging by Ahmadis of his argumentative work over other forms of deed and action—that is, a privileging of rational discourse and dialogue as a primary site of ethical action.

The title of Ghulam Ahmad's most important work, *Barahin-e-Ahmadiyya*, can be loosely translated as "the proofs of Islam." In this magnum opus, Ahmad claims to lay forth "300 incontrovertible rational arguments" in support of Islam.[40] He then reminds his readers that "the pitch darkness that has engulfed the world will only be dispelled when a vast number of proofs in support of Islam enlighten the world and the rays of its truth spread in all directions."[41] For contemporary Ahmadis, such sentences have a profound meaning. Ghulam Ahmad is said to have been granted a heavenly weapon to destroy falsehood: a set of proofs so powerful that even non-Ahmadi ulema steal his arguments to use for themselves without acknowledging the source.[42] For my interlocutors in Qadian, prophethood is not a distant, mystical station, and it does not gain its power from poetic ambiguity. Prophethood is a rational discourse; an ability to deliver detailed arguments in a logical fashion.

In Ahmadi accounts of Ghulam Ahmad's argumentative work, the Promised Messiah is thus often portrayed as a kind of investigative historian. A good example can be found in Ahmad's engagement with Sikhism. While much academic literature about the Ahmadis has focused on Ahmad's debates with Christian missionaries and Muslim and Hindu reformers, he also engaged Sikhism, a major religion in his native Punjab. For Qadian's present-day inhabitants, this is an important, although contentious, issue, for while they treasure Ahmad's arguments against Sikhs, they also recognize the potential that these discourses might have for upsetting their numerically superior neighbors. Ghulam Ahmad's major claim regarding Sikhism was that the founder of the religion, Guru Nanak, was in fact a Muslim saint (*wali*).[43] Jama'at accounts of how Ahmad came to construct this argument focus on his role as an empirical researcher uncovering evidence in the world. Thus, one important text describes how in 1895, Ahmad made a "great discovery" (*zabardast inkishaf*) regarding Guru Nanak.[44] Ghulam Ahmad claimed to have proved that Guru Nanak, although born in a Hindu household, was in fact a Muslim who went on hajj to Mecca, and whose cloak—preserved in the town of Dera Baba Nanak near Qadian—was inscribed with the *kalima tayyiba* (the Muslim confession of faith) as well as various other Qur'anic verses. In order to avoid dispute with neighboring Sikhs, Qadian's modern Ahmadis usually proclaim their respect for the guru, while privately visiting the shrine at Dera Baba Nanak to see the cloak and thus witness the empirical evidence through which their Promised Messiah triumphed over yet another religion. Although their love and admiration for Guru Nanak is therefore genuine, its sources are mostly glossed over in interactions with Sikh neighbors so as to enable ethical conversations between the groups.[45]

For many Ahmadis, the most significant, powerful, and all-conquering argument delivered by Ghulam Ahmad was his lengthy demonstration that Jesus escaped death by crucifixion and subsequently went to Kashmir in search of the lost tribes of Israel. First proposed in a systematic fashion in Ghulam Ahmad's treatise *Jesus in India*, this argument is seen decisively to prove the superiority of Ahmadi claims over both other Muslims and Christians, as well as to establish the necessary preconditions for Ghulam Ahmad to assume the rank of Promised Messiah.[46] *Jesus in India* draws on a range of evidence, both empirical and revelatory, and as I described in chapter 1, it represents the pinnacle of the idea of prophethood as enchanted rationality and critique. For modern-day Ahmadis, *Jesus in India* is celebrated for its concrete engagement with minute details and the sustained nature of its argument. One empirical detail from this book that Ahmadis in India place particular emphasis upon is Ghulam Ahmad's identification of a specific tomb in Srinagar, Kashmir, as the physical resting place of Jesus. For many, this is seen as the defining empirical proof of Ghulam Ahmad's thesis, which "decisively settled the question" of Jesus's death.[47] It is, however, one of the least elaborated-upon proofs in *Jesus in India*, receiving only a brief note from Mirza Ghulam Ahmad himself.[48] Later Ahmadi writers have therefore taken it upon themselves to continue the empirical verification of this archaeological proof. Further material evidence has thus been provided, for example, by a stone carving of a pair of feet found within the tomb, which Ahmadis claim show signs that Jesus survived the crucifixion.[49] Other members of the Jama'at would nonetheless like to take things further by testing the empirical evidence of Ahmad's thesis in a way that would make it falsifiable. Among other things, many Ahmadis I spoke with want the tomb in Srinagar to be opened up and subjected to scientific analysis. This, they hope, would prove once and for all that its inhabitant was born in the Levant and traveled to Kashmir in the first century. If this tomb is found not to be that of Jesus, such evidence, one interlocutor boldly declared, would signal the end of Ahmadiyyat, and he would therefore have to admit his mistake and renounce his acceptance of the Promised Messiah.

Perhaps what is admired most within *Jesus in India*, therefore, is the ability of Ghulam Ahmad's divine revelations (ilham) to be verified through empirical investigation. Other empirically verifiable revelations include Ghulam Ahmad's successful prediction of the death of a major opponent and his predictions about the future expansion of the Jama'at. These prophecies are important for present day Ahmadis precisely because of their supposedly empirically testable nature, and true to their word, many Ahmadis argue that an ambiguous prophecy (i.e., one that cannot be verified) is no prophecy at all.[50] For my interlocutors, Ghulam Ahmad's biography encapsulated prophethood and prophecy for a modern era. When I spoke to them about his life, they explicitly described his ability to engage opponents in debate as his major act of prophethood. Unlike other religious figures, he was held to be able to prove what he said about the divine through evidence provided in the material world. There was a sense in Qadian that this was how modern prophethood should be. As one very senior cleric in India told me, "this is the age of argument; claims alone will not suffice."

The caliph, who is the continuation of Ghulam Ahmad's prophethood and the "second manifestation" of his spiritual renewal, stands as the living representative of this legacy of proof. Caliphs have thus expanded and enhanced the Jama'at's repertoire of polemics. Mirza Mahmood Ahmad, the second caliph, penned an extensive commentary on the Qur'an, the *Tafsir-e-Kabir* (The great commentary), that is understood to be a masterful rebuttal of Christian and Orientalist attacks on the holy book of Islam. This commentary contains stories that my interlocutors would relay back to me, for example, of Christian missionaries being silenced in argument. The fourth caliph also significantly expanded the extent of Ahmadiyya proofs by introducing a new set of scientific concepts in support of Ghulam Ahmad's arguments.[51] Finally, it is the present caliph who ensures that Ghulam Ahmad's message remains pure and uncorrupted and who ensures that a correct interpretation of Islam is upheld within the Jama'at.[52]

The result of everything I have described up until now has been the creation of a profound moral sensibility around the ideal of the heroic polemicist. To defend Ahmadiyyat through fluent argumentation and to crush opposition so that it is silenced is an ideal form of ethical action in Qadian. It is a type of action modeled on the caliphs, who are themselves extensions of Mirza Ghulam Ahmad's prophethood. To successfully engage in polemics is thus to emulate the prophethood of Ahmad. But there is also a further point to be made here. Ahmadis do not see Ghulam Ahmad's prophethood as independent from Muhammad's prophethood. Rather, Ahmad is understood to have attained prophethood only through his intense love and devotion for Muhammad. Ghulam Ahmad thus brought neither a new religious law (a sharia) nor a new corpus of exemplary action that provides the foundations of what it means to live well in the form of a *sunnah*. The implication of this is straightforward: for Ahmadis, Mirza Ghulam Ahmad is the most perfect follower of Muhammad, and he thus provides a model for how they themselves should emulate Muhammad. Much has been written about the idealized relationship between a Muslim and the Prophet Muhammad. Saba Mahmood describes this relationship as predicated on an "assimilative" rather than "communicative or representational model," and she turns to Aristotle's notion of schesis to capture the "sense of embodied habitation and intimate proximity that imbues such a relation."[53] The emulation of the Prophet is thus a "labor of love" in which intimacy and desire bind the pious follower to Muhammad.[54] For Ahmadis who see Ghulam Ahmad as the reflection of Muhammad, being a heroic polemicist is a labor of love through which an exemplary Muslim selfhood might be attained. It is a public act through which my interlocutors cultivate and nurture their relationship to their caliph and demonstrate to the world that they can attain an Islamic perfection. When Ahmadis recite the arguments of their Promised Messiah, and when they engage in polemics with other Muslims, their own Muslimness is not just a product of the fact that they are espousing correct doctrine. Rather, their Muslim identity emerges out of their ability to appreciate, use, and deploy doctrine in a way that imitates prophetic action and demonstrates a relationship of obedience to their caliph.[55]

Sectarian disputes in South Asia frequently emerge out of the question of how Muslims should relate to the Prophet. It is because of their supposedly improper relationship to Muhammad—their failure to recognize him as the seal of the prophets—that Ahmadis are persecuted under blasphemy laws in Pakistan. A need to protect the Prophet might be said to constitute the "very ground of Muslim ontology" in South Asia, but precisely what this protection implies is a matter of constant debate and dispute.[56] Thus, the exact manner in which a Muslim should imitate the Prophet is one of the major fault lines running through the contested space of sectarian difference in South Asia. Debates abound about whether the Prophet is immanent in the world, whether it is possible for him to appear in dreams, and whether one should ecstatically love or only respect him. Believers are thus, as described by Naveeda Khan, often engaged in a "daily struggle" involving attempts to "ground this imitation in proper religious authority."[57] In this context, what is so interesting about Ahmadi polemics is that the act of arguing itself becomes an act of emulating prophethood. When they rigorously defend their Jama'at from accusations that it defames the Prophet, they are simultaneously demonstrating how to love him through imitation.

As a result of this idealized model of action, the dala'il (proofs/arguments/reasons) of Ghulam Ahmad have, in contemporary Qadian, come to represent a cache of perfectly formed arguments, in which individuals are expected to be well versed. At times, these arguments are explicitly treated as a kind of arsenal, as when they appear in a debater's handbook published by the Jama'at in India.[58] This manual guide to polemical debate contains numerous quotations from the Qur'an, hadith, and medieval Islamic scholars, in Urdu, Hindi, and English, arranged into three broad categories on which arguments with other Muslims center: the death of Jesus, the truth of the Promised Messiah, and the issue of the finality of prophethood. When I went to buy a copy of this manual in Qadian, the clerk in the Jama'at's bookstore insisted that I sit down to listen to a story about it. He recounted how he had been traveling on a long train journey when a mullah with a big beard sat down opposite him. The mullah began talking to the bookseller, and it quickly became clear that this mullah's intention was to be angry at the "Qadiani" in front of him. Rather than engage directly in debate (for, in his own words, he was a humble man) the bookseller simply gave a copy of the handbook to the mullah. For the entire two-day duration of the train journey, the mullah sat absorbed by the book and then finally turned to the bookseller and said, "Forgive me. I was wrong."

Not only were clerics exceptionally adroit at defending the faith through deploying ready-made polemics, but laypersons too would often entertain me with long discourses about the argumentative triumphs of Mirza Ghulam Ahmad and his caliphs. Such narratives would almost always culminate with a denouement in which Ahmadis silenced opponents. For my interlocutors, the potency of Ghulam Ahmad's arguments was a thing to marvel at, and they likewise expected me to join in this appreciation.[59] Such was the power of these arguments that they are seen to have world-changing properties. I was told, for example, that all modern Bibles have been altered as a result of Mirza Ghulam Ahmad's arguments. Predictions that were present in Bibles two hundred years ago are said to have been disproved by Ahmadiyyat, and Christians, afraid that their religion will be shown to be false, have removed those passages. Behind such stories, there was an absolute faith in the power of logical argument to persuade. In spite of the fact that logical conviction rarely seemed to play into the conversion of Ahmadis themselves, there was a persisting idea in Qadian that logical argument could and would produce a global conversion to Ahmadiyyat. Consequently, Qadian's Ahmadis held true to the explicit notion that they had an individual duty to tell others about the arguments of Islam. In India, private members of the Jama'at would spend their own money to self-publish books that recapitulated Ghulam Ahmad's arguments about Jesus dying in Kashmir, while lay members would do their best to engage fellow citizens in discourses whenever they could.[60]

In spite of my Ahmadi interlocutors' celebration of discourse and argument, however, there was rarely any theological debate in Qadian between Ahmadi clerics. During my time in the town, I was living with scholars; men who were the religious-intellectual elite of the Indian Jama'at. That is, men who had dedicated much of their lives to the pursuit of knowledge about their religion. And yet I witnessed neither disagreements over theological matters nor friendly and noncombative divergences of opinions. Once I realized this, I began to ask Qadian's clerics why they never seemed to differ with one another in religious matters, and why they never seemed to doubt received wisdom. Rather than tell me that I had misunderstood things, my interlocutors congratulated me on making this observation, for it was proof of their unity under the caliphate. The efficacy of the Jama'at system, they told me, was such that an internal debate never need become public. When differences arose, then judgment could be sought from a higher authority, leading all the way up to the caliph as the supreme guide, in order that final and correct interpretations of Islam could be propagated. This fact, of course, provided material for another proof in favor of Ahmadiyyat: where other Muslims are divided, the Ahmadis stand united.

The Ahmadiyya Jama'at has thus placed itself within an intellectual tradition with goals quite other to innovation. In Qadian, the model of the perfect public man is the debater, but he is not expected to innovate in argument or be original. Rather, this is a form of intellectual activity that involves cultivating a particular sensibility, understood to be a demonstration of Muslimness. It means emulating a prophetic mode of action and publicly demonstrating a disciplined obedience to the present-day incarnation of that prophethood: the caliph. For Qadian's Ahmadis, the idea of knowledge gained outside of a relationship of discipline is ludicrous. As such, during my fieldwork I was repeatedly asked who my guide was, the assumption being that my research could only be successful if undertaken beneath the tutelage of somebody who had already mastered the topic of my study. A similar attitude can be perceived in the fourth caliph's response to Iqbal's criticism that Ahmadiyyat represents the slavish following of a messiah that destroys any will to inner purification. The fourth caliph mocked the great poet, accusing him of being excessively inspired by Nietzsche. The very idea that Muslims might be able rationally to draw independent conclusions from scripture was, the fourth caliph argued, disproven by the lack of consensus between sects. Lamenting divisions with the Muslim world, he thus wrote: "What misery! Why can modern intellectuals not understand that the purification of a religious society is a task which the mere existence of a Perfect Book cannot perform?"[61] Knowledge should not be independently formulated but rather embodied through discipline.[62] As one very senior member of the Jama'at once warned me regarding my own thesis, "there are two types of student: those who try to be original and those who seek the truth." The two are not compatible.

Witnessing the Truth of Arguments

As the example that opened this chapter showed, small skirmishes between Ahmadis and other Muslims do occur and are in fact inevitable given the deep divisions and mutual prejudices that so often inform the relationship between the Jama'at and the wider Muslim world. Yet in spite of the absolute confidence that Ahmadis have in the power of their arguments, Ahmadi missionaries are banned from engaging in formal public debates with their opponents unless they have been given specific dispensation to do so by their caliph. Ahmadis fear that opponents, unable to counter the claims of Mirza Ghulam Ahmad through rational discourse, will resort to trickery and deceit to give the impression that they have beaten the Jama'at in argument.[63] Rather than engage in public debate, Ahmadi missionaries must therefore often express their disciplined relationship to the caliph by refusing to engage in polemics, and in such instances, obedience within the structure of the Jama'at becomes a proof of Ahmadiyyat, the potency of which opponents are said to be unable to deny. As I will show in chapter 5, the discipline of the Jama'at is contrasted with the disorder of its opponents to produce proof that Ahmadiyyat is the true Islam.

It is thus the case that Ahmadi polemics are often reserved for internal witnessing, while displays of organizational capacity become the medium through which the Jama'at advances its claims to truth within the wider world. That polemical arguments can only rarely be deployed in actual debate points toward an important fact, which is that they exist as much to be admired and witnessed as they do to be used. For my interlocutors, the distinguishing feature of being an Ahmadi is having recognized a truth that all other Muslims ignore. Like many other messianic groups, Christian as well as Muslim, Ahmadis understand themselves to have responded to a truth that the rest of the world stubbornly dismisses. Cultivating a responsiveness to truth—an ability to witness truth—is thus a major aspect of the moral lives of my Ahmadi interlocutors in Qadian.[64] Being a heroic polemicist is not just about the ability to recite arguments but also about making the self into a witness of those arguments. It is a practice that involves displaying truth to the world through the process of making the self susceptible and malleable to the potency of that truth.[65]

The truth of Ahmadiyyat is so potent because it is understood by Ahmadis to impose an obligation on the world to respond through the act of witnessing. This is evident in the fact that without exception, my interlocutors in Qadian understood natural disasters and humanitarian crises to occur because of the failure of nations to heed the coming of the Promised Messiah. For example, an Ahmadi missionary who thought much of himself and little of my research once asked me why I didn't change my topic of investigation, and he suggested a new question that would revolutionize my study. Why, he asked me, are those present-day countries (Palestine, Iraq, Iran, Afghanistan, Pakistan, and India) that Jesus passed through as he walked to Kashmir after surviving crucifixion in such bad political conditions now? The answer to this rhetorical question was obviously that these countries had failed to respond to the evidence of a prophet walking through their lands. As a result, they nowadays suffer from a divine punishment for their failure to heed an obvious truth. Terrible natural disasters—such as the 2005 earthquake in Pakistan—are reserved for those who have rejected the specific message of the Promised Messiah, but nations that never directly experienced his prophecy are nonetheless also seen to be vulnerable. When I was in Qadian in March 2011, an earthquake and tsunami hit Japan, making headlines across the world because of the immediate devastation it caused and because it precipitated a nuclear crisis in Fukushima Prefecture. The following week, during his Friday sermon on March 18, 2011, the caliph reflected on the causes of the Japanese earthquake.[66] He compared the earthquake to a string of other contemporary natural disasters, including an earthquake in Christchurch the previous month, flooding in Queensland, and storms in the United States. The caliph quoted, at length, a passage from Ghulam Ahmad's book *Haqiqat ul-wahi* (The truth of revelation) that builds on the Qur'an 17:15,[67] to say, "Had I not come, these calamities might have been delayed for a while, but with my coming the secret designs of God's wrath, that had long been hidden, have been manifested.'[68] Even a country like Japan, where the Jama'at is completely unknown, is thus vulnerable to divine wrath. This places an enormous responsibility on Ahmadis to make truth apparent, to present it to the world, and thus to give others an opportunity to witness that truth.

In practice, this need to demonstrate truth results in the continuous effort among my interlocutors to become living manifestations of a relationship of obedience to their caliph, be it through the cultivation of a polemical disposition or through their considered refusal to engage in formal debates without the permission of the caliph. In all cases, they attempt to make a relationship visible to the world so that it might become a potent truth to which other people could make themselves receptive in the act of witnessing. The importance of this relationship was apparent even in the caliph's explanation of what had happened in Fukushima. At the time of the caliph's sermon, global news sources were filled with information describing efforts in Fukushima to prevent a nuclear disaster, and plentiful information about the aftereffects of the earthquake was thus available from pretty much any news outlet in the world. The caliph nonetheless stressed the personal connection through which he had come to understand the situation in Japan, for he told his worldwide congregation that the Jama'at had teams on the ground in Japan, and that he had just received a fax from these Ahmadis who had informed him about relief efforts. This was an ideal image of devotion, in which local volunteers worked tirelessly to help humanity, while keeping tight their connection to the caliph, whose office could thus function as a nerve center for a developing global crisis.

Encompassing Modernity

The positivist nature of Ghulam Ahmad's prophethood means that for Ahmadis, there is no disjuncture between modern science and religion. Rather, the pursuit of scientific knowledge is understood as a religious act. In Qadian, as in the rest of the global Jama'at, both male and female children are encouraged to educational excellence in modern academic fields. Even for those students studying to become Ahmadi missionaries, what are seen as modern subjects like English and computing are taught alongside more traditional subjects, such as Arabic or *kalam* (theological discourses). The educational achievements of these students are explicitly understood as acts of devotion to the Jama'at and the caliph. As students are reminded in specially prepared pamphlets, it is the caliph's opinion that "worldly knowledge will also become religious knowledge" when it is learned for the correct reason.[69] For my Ahmadi interlocutors, there is no contradiction in the fact that the pursuit of science can be undertaken so as to craft a relationship of subordination and discipline to their caliph. Ahmadiyyat, they argue, conflicts not with science, but with those who see science and devotion as incommensurable.

On at least two occasions during my fieldwork in Qadian, I was told a story about the book *Revelation, Rationality, Knowledge and Truth* by the fourth caliph.[70] This book is widely admired by Ahmadis for its clear articulation of the idea that science and religion are compatible and intertwined with one another, so much so that the official publicity for the book describes it as "a book among books—perhaps the greatest literary achievement of this century." The story I was told went along these lines: shortly after the publication of this book, the Jama'at sent it to a huge number of scientists who are known for explicitly denying the notion that religion and science are compatible, among them the "new atheist" Richard Dawkins. Included with the book was a challenge: to disprove the arguments set forth by the fourth caliph. Despite the issuance of this challenge, however, not a single scientist responded. For my interlocutors who told this story, the reason for this was obvious: the atheist scientists had been unable to respond. When I first heard this story, I was not entirely convinced, and I therefore questioned one of the men who told it to me by suggesting that perhaps the scientists simply did not read the book. My interlocutor, however, was not to be persuaded. Scientists, he told me, relish the chance to acquire knowledge and therefore most probably did read it. The only logical explanation for the scientists' lack of response, he argued, was their complete helplessness in the face of the caliph's arguments. In making this argument, he drew upon the idea—common in Qadian—that the proofs of the Promised Messiah and his caliphs are so potent as to be able to render opponents incapable of response.

The idea that scientific practice should be about subordinating the self to a divine leader may seem counterintuitive to those brought up in a culture where science and religion are seen as incompatible, but it is a position that is by no means restricted to members of the Jama'at. Commentators have long noted that unlike many Christians, Muslims have historically been far less likely to feel that there is a conflict between their religion and modern knowledge. To borrow a phrase from Clifford Geertz, Islam is quite capable of becoming a "justification for modernity, without itself actually becoming modern. It promotes what it it- self, to speak metaphorically, can neither embrace nor understand."[71] It is thus perhaps unsurprising that, for my interlocutors, the proofs of Ahmadiyyat are seen to coexist in a relationship of mutual reinforcement with science. It is in this vein that the Jama'at celebrates one of its most famous members, the theoretical physicist Abdus Salam (1926–96), who in 1979 became the first Muslim of any denomination to receive a Nobel Prize in science. Salam is a model of achieve- ment for Ahmadi children around the world, but he is particularly admired for having managed to fuse faith and science.[72]

More unusual is the way in which the proofs of Ahmadiyyat are understood to silence opposition with devastating efficiency in other seemingly incommen- surable realms of judgment. A good example of this is how Ahmadi proofs are seen to shatter the legal discourses of the modern state and render judgments about rights null and void. In such instances, as the following instance shows, the proofs of Ahmadiyyat are understood not just to encompass the secular world but to supersede the mechanisms through which that world produces truth.

On October 20, 2010, a debate was held in the UK House of Commons about the treatment of Ahmadis in Pakistan and about how to deal with acts of intoler- ance in the United Kingdom.[73] The debate was instigated by the member of par- liament (MP) for Mitcham and Morden, the area of London that is home to the enormous Ahmadi mosque Baitul Futuh. She was compelled to ask for the de- bate, she explained, due to the murder of nearly one hundred Ahmadis in a ter- rorist attack in Lahore in May 2010. As might be expected, the debate centered on a series of key issues: human rights violations, discrimination, freedom of re- ligion, and tolerance. But the MPs present also seemed to imply that the persecu- tion of the Ahmadis was made ever more horrifying because the Ahmadis were a worthy reflection of the liberal values being expressed in the room. As the MP for Mitcham and Morden explained, the Ahmadis value inclusiveness, they are "peaceful," and they spurn "irrational interpretations of the Koran." In short, she concluded, "in Britain today, we regard such attributes as modern and tolerant."[74]

At the time of this debate, an Ahmadi journalist from Qadian was staying in London. A resident of Qadian since birth, he nonetheless spent significant peri- ods overseas, especially in the United Kingdom. While there, he wrote an article about the debate and filed it with a Punjabi-language newspaper back home in India. Many months later, when I had a conversation with the journalist about this article, he explained to me that the article had stated that the cause of the Ah- madis' persecution in Pakistan is their argument that Jesus survived crucifixion and died in Kashmir. For anybody familiar with the situation of the Ahmadis in Pakistan, this might seem like an odd statement. After all, opponents of the Jama'at usually state that their own reason for opposing Ahmadiyyat is that it violates the finality of Muhammad's prophethood. For Ahmadis, however, the journalist's argument makes perfect sense. As previously explained, Ahmadis understand Jesus's death in Kashmir to be the conclusive proof by which Mirza Gulam Ahmad established his own status as the Promised Messiah. For Ahmadis, this is the proof that renders Christianity and all other forms of Islam obsolete. Such is the clarity of Ghulam Ahmad's *Jesus in India* that most of my interlocutors felt certain that opponents in Pakistan knew it to be true, knew it could not be argued against, and thus continued to persecute Ahmadis because the Jama'at threatened their ability to make money by peddling a fraudulent religion to the masses.[75] This is why Ahmadis believe that their persecution is directly linked to their ability to substantiate their religion. As the journalist defiantly told me, "Jesus has died, and we have proved this."

The journalist explained that these statements about Jesus ended up enraging a group of ill-disposed Christians in Qadian. Even though the statements had been made only to explain Ahmadi persecution in Pakistan, the Christians lodged an FIR (First Information Report, an initial complaint) with the Indian police against the journalist. They did so under penal code 295a, which makes it an offense to deliberately or maliciously outrage religious sentiments.

The journalist's lawyer later explained to me that there was almost no legal basis for this complaint, yet it ended up in court and was of enough concern that the journalist's friends in the United Kingdom tried to persuade him to seek political asylum while he was still in London, as they felt that he would not receive a fair trial back in India. Unsure of what to do, the journalist managed to gain a meeting (*mulaqat*) with the caliph, and he was thus able to ask for his divine leader's advice. In such situations, the caliph's advice is much sought after, his opinions valued more highly than that of any lawyer, and his accessibility to his millions of followers (provided that they can physically get to his office in south London) is held up as proof of the beauty of the Jama'at system. During this meeting, the caliph told the journalist that the latter would certainly be granted bail. Heartened by this message, the journalist decided to return to India and fight his accusers in court, where he was indeed subsequently granted bail in December 2010. When I spoke to him about the matter nearly a year later in September 2011, the case was still ongoing. Still buoyed by the caliph's message, he exuded utter confidence that he would triumph, even if it took many years to make its way through the Indian courts.

While talking to me about the case, however, he did not once stress his legal advantage over his accusers. He could easily have done so. Indeed, this is precisely how his lawyer was apt to talk of the case: the Christian opponents were on slippery legal ground, for the newspaper article was never about them in the first place.

By contrast, the journalist spoke of Ahmadi arguments regarding Jesus as if they were court-admissible evidence, not just in their status as the doctrine of one particular community but as proofs that might be counted as evidence within the court. The Christian case was ridiculous, he told me, not because it rested on shaky legal grounds but because "we have proof that Jesus died." Thus, for the journalist, the legal case ceased to be a question of what can and cannot be said, of what counts as an insult and outrage, or of what counts as legitimate religious expression and instead became an adjudication of religious proof and evidence. The death of Jesus was for him an empirical issue that should be treated as such by a judge at his trial. As he explained it to me, whereas the Christians had no argument to prove what they believed about Jesus to be true, the Ahmadis would be able to decisively verify their claims in a court of law. By good fortune, this never proved necessary, for the case collapsed in the final few months of my fieldwork.

In Qadian, there is thus no sense that the arguments of Ahmadiyyat are subject only to a realm of religious judgment. Rather, they are seen to impose themselves in other domains, demand recognition, and, ultimately, shatter the rationalities through which judgments about truth might be made in those domains. In this regard, unlike the stereotyped figure of the mullah, the Ahmadis are not afraid of the outside world, and they do not retreat from it. Rather, they see it as a place of unlimited resources in which they might expand the potent and all-conquering arguments of their Promised Messiah. The modern world, far from being a place of doctrinal danger, is a landscape of opportunity in which Ahmadis might prove their devotion, subordination, and obedience to the caliph.

The Jama'at's expansion into the world is not, however, a one-sided embrace. As we saw in the above example, the Ahmadis are celebrated in Westminster as paragons of modern, tolerant citizenship. In India, they are frequently feted as "good" Muslims, the implicit comparison being to other Muslims whose loyalty to the Indian state is always under question by Hindu extremists. What is lost in this embrace is the fact that all those attributes that make the Ahmadis ideal and modern citizens—their rejection of violent jihad, their insistence on the scientific rationality of Islam, and their forceful praise of other communities' religious leaders—form the intellectual boundary of a sectarian identity, which they maintain for the decidedly illiberal goal of cultivating subservience to the caliph. In this respect, the Jama'at resembles another of India's dispersed minorities, who are also led by a leader in exile: Tibetan Buddhists. The anthropologist Michael Lempert has described how traditional forms of Tibetan monastic debate have been promoted through the Dalai Lama's modernizing leadership as markers of a critical and autonomous rationality that encapsulates both Buddhism and the enlightenment. Through this exercise of reason, Tibetan Buddhists in exile both garner outside (often Western) support and stave off accusations of "lamaism," a term that carries overtones of doctrinal inflexibility in a fashion not dissimilar to the term "mullahism." Lempert argues that this project nonetheless always remains a kind of "liberal mimicry" (albeit one that "cannot be reduced to pastiche, syncretism, or bricolage"), for underpinning Buddhist debating practices are also forms of discipline, inequality, and ritualized violence.[76] If, at times, the Ahmadis appear to be mimics or simulacra of modernity, it is worth remembering that for them, modernity—with its organizational modalities, its rules, and its bureaucratic and scientific rationalities—is only ever a pale imitation of Islam.

Doctrinal Doubt

As this chapter has shown, much liberal concern and anxiety over sectarian disputation among South Asian Muslims stems from the fact that these are people who have long been characterized as being insufficiently capable of doubting themselves in the correct fashion. Behind criticisms of ossification or parochialism are assumptions about an inability to be self-reflective and to entertain that cardinal value of the enlightenment: self-doubt. I have shown how, for Ahmadis in Qadian, many of these much-derided aspects of sectarian polemic are driven by a desire to craft a relationship of subordination to a divine leader. And yet such an argument still does not answer the nagging question of secular critics. We are brought, time and again, back to the questions: Surely these people sometimes doubt the things they are saying? Surely they sometimes question the sectarian version of the truth they are defending?

Perhaps we have been asking the wrong questions. Instead of asking, *Do they doubt?* we should have been asking, *But do they believe?* We have seen in this chapter that belief does not really encompass the kind of relationship that Qadian's Ahmadis cultivate to religious doctrine. Indeed, this fact is reflected in local language use. There are plenty of Urdu terms through which they could have described their ideas as beliefs, but by far the most common way of expressing a relationship to religious knowledge in Qadian was to use the verb "to understand" (*samajhna*). For Ahmadis in Qadian, religious doctrine was practiced so as to cultivate a relationship to the caliph. Truth was something to which people felt they owed a duty. In light of this, perhaps we need to set aside our concerns about people not doubting properly. If doctrine is not "believed" in, why should it be doubted, in the sense that people question its veracity or, furthermore, question their own ability to believe in it?

One important anthropological attempt to think about doubt beyond belief is Nils Bubandt's ethnography *The Empty Seashell*, which explores witchcraft among Buli-speaking inhabitants of the Indonesian island of Halmahera.[77]

Bubandt demonstrates how witchcraft has always been understood by anthropologists as a form of belief or a system of meaning that might have explanatory power for those who are faced by misfortune. Drawing on the work of Bruno Latour, Bubandt argues that this reading of witchcraft is a result of our "modern" need to believe in the belief of others.[78] If we can move beyond this need to read belief into the thoughts of others, Bubandt argues, we can begin to understand how Buli witchcraft is not a form of belief but instead a situation of unresolvable aporia. His informants live, he posits, in a situation of inescapable doubt, for the witches that they fear are undeniably real but also too contradictory and unknowable to be objects of belief. Witchcraft, in other words, is a "historical elaboration of an aporia, a constant collapse of meaning into institutionalized doubt."[79] I share with Bubandt a concern to "loosen doubt from its Cartesian moorings,"[80] but there is a fundamental difference between the situations that we are describing: Bubandt examines how the absence of belief might leave only doubt; I am suggesting that the absence of familiar forms of belief might also signal the absence of familiar forms of doubt.

This nonetheless leaves us with a further question of how to write about unfamiliar doubts. One place in which we might find inspiration in this regard is the rich anthropological literature on spirit possession. Take, for example, Michael Lambek's description of possession in Mayotte, which exists side by side with Islam. Lambek's interlocutors see both the truth of the Qur'an and the truth of spirits as indubitable, such that their differences cannot be resolved by logic. Lambek describes a situation in which a spirit (possessing one of this interlocutors) physically choked on liquidized Qur'an verses that it had swallowed as medicine. This was an extreme bodily reaction to the differences and contradictions between these traditions, for only through bodily ingestion or expulsion could spirit possession and Islam coexist and speak to one another.[81] Another example, described by Janet McIntosh, is the somatic manifestation of Giriama ambivalences toward a hegemonic Islam in coastal Kenya. Giriama are often deeply uneasy about the dominance of Islam, for which they see themselves as unfit, and they describe how they are tormented by Muslim spirits, which cause them to have somatic responses (including, once again, vomiting) to palm wine and bush rat, both of which are haram in Islam yet of great local importance. These are people who "carry with them an enduring ambivalence, such that their bodies enact an experience of hegemony which they decry or reject in speech."[82] Both of these example give us insights into the way in which ambivalences over indubitable religious projects might be manifested in ways that are not easily captured by an idea of epistemological doubt, for these are ambivalences that exist at a somatic level.

As long as we keep on assuming that there is a proper way to doubt, then we are going to keep on misinterpreting places like Qadian, where people do not accept a definition of modernity as a condition of self-doubt but instead enthusiastically claim that their truth embraces the world for all future. We have to begin to take seriously the joy with which individuals might inhabit and defend a particular subject position. We have to understand that religious uncertainty need not necessarily involve a questioning of truth or one's ability to know that truth. We have to realize that self-reflexivity comes in many different forms.

What, then, would doubt look like to a heroic polemicist in Qadian? The answer comes down to a question of what aspect of the polemicist's relationship to truth is problematized. Unlike in many philosophical formulations of doubt, the heroic polemicist is not concerned about his ability to ascertain truth; rather, he worries about his ability to authentically demonstrate that truth, and to fulfill his obligations to it. This is best illustrated with the example of a public question-and-answer session that I saw performed in Qadian. Most of the examples I have already given in this chapter occurred during one-on-one interactions between my interlocutors and me. During my time in Qadian, I nonetheless also witnessed a number of public spectacles that were designed as showcases for the heroic polemicists among the town's clergy. These events were frequently choreographed by the auxiliary organizations of the Jama'at and were usually quite formal in their presentation.[83] Although attendance was not mandatory, there was an expectation that all Ahmadi men would be present for such events unless they had a particularly good excuse for their absence.

The specific question-and-answer session that I am describing here contained a series of particularly polished and virtuoso displays of heroic polemicism.[84] In its very form, it was a deferential imitation of the caliphate, for it was unmistakably modeled on a series of question-and-answer sessions hosted by the late fourth caliph, which were filmed for MTA. In these MTA television productions, the fourth caliph is shown to answer questions confidently on a whole range of doctrinal issues, while also frequently shoring up his answers with digressions into issues pertaining to the secular world. His competent and fluid defenses of Ahmadiyyat during these televised discourses continue to be admired, rewatched, and discussed by Qadian's present-day Ahmadis.

The Qadian question-and-answer session faithfully replicated a number aspects of the fourth caliph's televised performances. Television cameras from the local MTA studio captured every aspect of the event, and the audience of local Ahmadis performed their part with aplomb, asking questions that specifically opened up and created opportunities for the panelists—a group of scholars—to deploy in public the most potent and undeniable of Mirza Ghulam Ahmad's arguments. The cumulative result was a spectacular display in which old arguments were meticulously rehearsed, answers originally proffered by caliphs or the Promised Messiah were repeated, and stories of opponents being silenced by the power of Ahmadi arguments were upheld as evidence of the truth of those arguments. Although the event was an open question-and-answer session, the questions asked came from neither a place of uncertainty about doctrine nor of doubt about beliefs. Rather, questions were posed as direct openings through which Ahmadi proofs could be further demonstrated. All in all, the session represented a communal achievement of the kind of idealized action that this chapter has sought to describe.

After the event, I was thus extremely surprised to hear several audience members jokingly dismiss the performances of the panelists. These audience members were faithful, devoted members of the Jama'at—undoubtedly admirers of the proofs and arguments that had just been showcased—and yet their patience had been tested in that evening's manner of delivery. It appeared that certain statements made during the question-and-answer session had simply been too insincere for them to bear. For these men, everything that had been said in the session had been doctrinally correct, and like others in Qadian, they themselves aspired to heroic acts of argumentation. Yet when I questioned them further, it turned out that they had found the session to be too excessively "acted," its demonstrations of proof almost hyperreal. Their accusation was not that the question-and-answer session had been a bad representation of Ahmadiyyat. Nor did they seem to think that the panelists had been poor exemplars of what I am here calling heroic polemicism. Rather, their mirth and mockery stemmed from the fact that this all-too-perfect performance had taken place during an event staged for personal aggrandizement. They were concerned about the self-importance of the panelists.

On its own, this example might seem unremarkable, but it must be read against more general concerns about moral failure in Qadian. As I have described in the previous chapters, many Ahmadis in Qadian see their separation from the caliph in 1947 as the start of a slow decline in the spiritual condition of the town. As a result of this, there is nowadays a real fear in Qadian that public displays of obedience to the caliph might mask private failures of devotion. Consequently, I was warned a number of times during my fieldwork not to assume that the actions of corrupt officials could in any way reflect the truth of the Jama'at. These officials were seen to use the Jama'at for personal gain and to abuse their positions of power within the hierarchy, all the time pretending to be faithful servants of the caliph. Allegations of deceit, corruption, and decline are, however, always mediated by another concern: the idea that the moral condition of other people is essentially unknowable. As one man teasingly told me, "I do not know what kind of person you are, but I have seen that you have adapted to live with us very quickly. So I suspect that inside, you are much like us." In other words, he could only *suspect* what he knew of me: he could never know it with certainty, for only God can have a pure knowledge of the spiritual state of other humans. This insistence on the moral opacity of others is foundational to much Islamic thought, and it is not co-incidentally crucial to the Ahmadis' critiques of the Pakistani state's claim to know their inner thoughts.[85] Within Qadian, it serves as a caution against gossip and speculation, but when approached seriously as a statement about the relationship between people and God, it introduces ambivalence into moral life.

Taken together with my interlocutors' conviction in their absolute ability to know truth, this emphasis on the moral opacity of others can help explain why an event such as the question-and-answer session could be generative of a particular kind of uncertainty. At issue is the question of what an authentic demonstration of truth might be and how it can be separated from its counterfeit. In the ritual performance of polemic heroism just described, how could an audience member distinguish an absolute demonstration of truth based on love for the caliph from an insincere demonstration performed only to bolster the demonstrator's status? As audience members, what truths were we witnessing if we could not know the moral state of those before us in the panel?

In other words, the uncertainty that clung to this question-and-answer session was not about the veracity of Mirza Ghulam Ahmad's message, and it was not a fear that the sectarian position occupied by the Jama'at might not be true. Nobody in Qadian ever expressed any doubts about the ability of their arguments to silence opponents in debate. Neither did my interlocutors suffer from a fear that they could not live up to the ideal of Ghulam Ahmad's message by successfully inhabiting the station of heroic polemicist. By all accounts, the question-and-answer session had been a brilliant success as a demonstration of Ahmadi polemic and as a recounting of the Jama'at's superiority over opponents. Rather, uncertainty emerged at a moment when the town as a whole seemed to successfully embody and enact an exemplary ideal. My fellow audience members were mocking the fact that what could have been an absolutely perfect demonstration of discipline to the caliph appeared more like an (almost faultless) imitation of that discipline, undertaken only to increase the personal status of the panelists. In other words, despite the fact that these audience members knew the proofs of Ahmadiyyat to be true, they could not trust that this demonstration was anything more than just a simulacrum. At stake was the status of the evidence being presented to the audience for witnessing. Was this question-and-answer session a proof of a deep and sincerely cultivated attitude of love toward the Promised Messiah and his caliphs? Or was it a polished simulacrum of that love in which the proofs of Ahmadiyyat were being deployed to aggrandize the individuals on stage? The line between these is blurred, ambiguous, and that evening, it proved to be a source of significant concern. In Qadian, a place separated from its caliph for so long, to act as an authentic heroic polemicist always seemed to run the risk of appearing a fake. Even as truth remained stable, its proof could be counterfeit.

The question-and-answer session was a good example of what I have been describing in this book as my interlocutors' uncertainty over how to evidence their Muslimness in the world. It is thus an example of what I have described as doubt beyond belief. A major argument of this chapter has been that in Qadian, theological arguments—particularly those designed to persuade others of the truth— were rarely treated simply as propositions in which to believe. Rather, such arguments were practiced to imitate prophethood and cultivate subordination and discipline. This meant that when Ahmadis studied, learned, and engaged with these discourses, the question that they asked themselves was not whether they had sufficient conviction in the arguments but whether their use of these arguments was successful in demonstrating an actual relationship with their caliph. That this might never be the case was a very real cause of uncertainty in Qadian.

PRAYER DUELS TO THE DEATH

The Mubahala

On June 3, 1988, the fourth caliph, Mirza Tahir Ahmad, announced a challenge that would dominate public discourse in the Jama'at for months and years to come. Tahir Ahmad had been in exile in London for over four years, and the continued premiership of General Zia ul-Haq in Pakistan meant that antagonism against the Ahmadis remained high. Surveying this situation, Tahir Ahmad announced that argument and debate between the Ahmadis and their opponents had arrived at an impasse. The Promised Messiah's demonstration of proofs—his *'ilm-e-kalam*—had been "so potent [*qavi*] and overpowering [*ghalib*]" that it had left the opponents of the Jama'at no option but to resort to wickedness and intimidation.[1] Having been utterly defeated in argument, the Jama'at's opponents had taken to spreading lies about the Promised Messiah. As such, Tahir Ahmad declared, "the time for understanding has passed."[2] Addressing his opponents directly, he announced that between the Ahmadis and their detractors "no matter of argument is left. When this condition is reached, there is nothing left to do but a mubahala."[3] In this manner, he challenged his opponents to a trial by ordeal: a spiritual duel that could result in death.

In the previous chapter, I showed how the proofs of Ahmadiyyat are thought to be imbued with such potent truth that they can only be denied by falsehood or hypocrisy. The Urdu term for this condition is *itmam-e-hujjat* (*itmam al-hujjah* in Arabic), literally meaning "the completion of truth" and describing a situation in which a prophetic message is so fully and logically realized that opponents cannot deny it. Ahmadis recognize this as being a feature of Muhammad's revelation but also see Mirza Ghulam Ahmad as having revived this condition of itmam-e-hujjat through his demonstration of proofs (*dala'il*) and arguments (*barahin*). In the present chapter, I look at what happens when the denials of opponents are thought to have reached such a level of obstinacy that only one option remains: a highly ritualized form of divine judgment by ordeal known as the mubahala.

At the time of Tahir Ahmad's mubahala challenge, Ahmadis in Pakistan were the object of all manner of scurrilous rumors, most of which persist in modified form to this day. Opponents would both criticize and insult Mirza Ghulam Ahmad and level a number of accusations at his contemporary followers. Among these accusations were the claims that Ahmadis were agents of the United States, that four hundred Ahmadis were fighting for the Israeli army, that four thousand Ahmadis were receiving guerrilla training in Germany, that the "Qadianis" have a God that is not that of the Qur'an, and that they believe in angels that are different from those in the Qur'an. It was furthermore rumored that the Jama'at was involved in plots to destroy Pakistan, that it had caused riots in Karachi, that it had a plan to kill five hundred ulema, and that a Qadiani military officer stole the plans for nuclear weapons from Pakistan and passed them to Israel.[4]

Against the background of these accusations, Tahir Ahmad proposed the mubahala as a functional method for adjudicating religious truth. It has been suggested that in a mubahala "the instigation or call to the ordeal is more important than the execution."[5] In this chapter, I extend this observation to show that it was through their failure as ritual events that mubahalas were expected to produce certainty and evidence. Every time a mubahala failed to produce a divine judgment, it demonstrated that unlike their opponents, the Ahmadis belonged to a global organization, which was able to sustain and prove religious truth because of its economic power, its technological expertise, and its disciplined unity under a single leader. I thus show that for my interlocutors, there was an indissoluble link between religious truth and the capacity to demonstrate that truth. The mubahala was an attempt by Tahir Ahmad to shift the question of the Ahmadis' Muslimness away from an indemonstrable quality of belief and toward verifiable social relations. In instigating the mubahala, Tahir Ahmad was calling on the global strength of the Jama'at as a witness to his Muslim identity.

This, of course, raises the question of what happens to those on the sidelines. What happens to those who feel that their link to this global truth-sustaining organization is tenuous? What happens, in other words, to Qadian?

Mirza Ghulam Ahmad and the Mubahala

The mubahala is first mentioned in the Qur'an. It is understood in both Sunni and Shi'a tradition to refer to an ordeal proposed by the Prophet Muhammad in

AD 632–33 against a group of Christians from Najran as a way of settling a dispute about the status and divinity of Jesus.[6] The challenge involved both groups coming together and calling for God's curse to fall on the false party. The Qur'an describes the call to mubahala as follows: "Now whoso disputes with thee concerning him, after what has come to thee of knowledge, say *to him*, 'Come, let us call our sons and your sons, and our women and your women, and our people and your people; then let us pray fervently and invoke the curse of Allāh on those who lie [*la'nata allahi 'ala al-kadhibin*]'" (Al 'Imran, 62).[7] Although the details of the Qur'anic mubahala are ambiguous, it has been much mythologized, particularly in Shi'a texts.[8] Throughout Islamic history, the mubahala appears to have been regarded more as a historical event than an actual model by which theological disputes might be settled. While mubahala ordeals may have been considered a theoretical possibility in various times and places, there are no academic histories of the practice, and references to mubahalas since the time of the Prophet are few and far between. In recent years, mubahala challenges appear to have gone viral on Indonesian social media, and one was even issued by the Islamic State (Daesh) as it sought to prove its legitimacy.[9] The practical question of how to conduct a mubahala nonetheless appears not to have been one that has been extensively elaborated on by jurists, a fact that has hampered its ritual enactment in the rare cases in which Muslims have resorted to it as a way of negotiating insurmountable religious differences.[10]

In contrast to this historical pattern, Mirza Ghulam Ahmad attempted to revive the mubahala as a practical and empirical method through which his supremacy over opponents could be established, and during his lifetime, he issued a number of mubahala challenges. There is some debate about whether any of Ghulam Ahmad's challenges ever actually achieved the status of being a bilaterally agreed-on mubahala, and it is certainly the case that his most high-profile challenges did not result in prayer duels taking place.[11] For the Ahmadis, possibly the most celebrated of Ghulam Ahmad's challenges was made not against an Indian opponent but in a transnational challenge against another charismatic religious leader, the Illinois-based John Alexander Dowie. Born in Scotland in 1847, Dowie had declared himself to be "Elijah the Reformer" and a prophet.[12] Mirza Ghulam Ahmad came across Dowie's writings and accused the latter of speaking of Muhammad in vile language and continually attacking Islam, such that in 1902 and again in 1903, "when his insolence had reached the limit," Ghulam Ahmad was compelled to send Dowie mubahala challenges in English.[13] Ghulam Ahmad also predicted Dowie's death irrespective of whether the latter accepted the mubahala challenge, a prediction that Ahmadi sources explicitly note was widely reprinted in the U.S. press.[14] Dowie's subsequent decline—during which he suffered paralysis, was exposed as a fornicator and embezzler, was denounced by his own disciples, and then fled to Mexico—was eagerly documented in the Ahmadis' English-language journal prior to Dowie's death in 1907.[15] The Ahmadi victory over Dowie was consolidated seventy-seven years later when an Ahmadi center was opened in Zion, Illinois, the planned city that Dowie himself had founded.[16] Ahmad's following had flourished where Dowie's had declined, although as scholarship has shown, Dowie's influence is still very much alive in Zionist movements in South Africa.[17]

Ghulam Ahmad issued another important challenge during an 1893 debate with a Muslim convert to Christianity, Abdullah Atham. During this debate, Ghulam Ahmad challenged Atham to a mubahala with a time limit of one year. When Atham refused to engage in a mubahala, Ghulam Ahmad predicted the party who had lied in the debate would be cast into hell within fifteen months.[18]Atham did not, in fact, die for over three years, which led Ghulam Ahmad to claim that the prophecy was true because Atham had secretly accepted Islam in his heart. Demonstrating his confidence in this new interpretation, Ghulam Ahmad then issued another mubahala, in which Atham was called on to swear that he had "not for a single moment stood in awe of Islam" and then supplicate God to strike him dead within one year should he be lying.[19]

The many mubahalas Ghulam Ahmad issued over his lifetime belonged to a larger group of challenges. These included challenges much like a mubahala, with strict rules to prevent prevarication, except that they did not require the invocation of a curse and thus asked participants only to supplicate God for a sign in favor of one party.[20] Ghulam Ahmad also proposed another challenge, similar to a mubahala yet not one, "because its benefit or harm is limited to me [Mirza Ghulam Ahmad] alone."[21] Other challenges were akin to mubahalas in that they required some form of ordeal or at least mortal risk through divine judgment but did not meet the full set of conditions that Ghulam Ahmad had elsewhere specified for the mubahala.[22] By contrast, other challenges did not require divine judgment but instead some form of impartial adjudication, and offered financial prizes from Ghulam Ahmad's own fortune.[23] Yet more challenges mixed financial compensation with the promise of divine signs.[24] To some extent, the mubahala was thus merely the most severe of all these challenges, in that it had the most drastic outcome, capable of affecting both sides. Yet the mubahala was unique in that it was understood to be a specific form of ordeal that had its roots within the Qur'an. The problem, of course, was that the Qur'an provided no specific instructions on how to perform the mubahala as a ritual.

The 1988 Mubahala Challenge

Such was the historical ambiguity about the mubahala ordeal that Mirza Tahir Ahmad's 1988 declaration was not just a mubahala challenge but also a definition of the ritual process involved. The Qur'anic verse is an ambiguous basis for ritual action. It details the most basic elements of the practice but does not specify the precise rules by which the mubahala, as a form of arbitration, might come to produce accurate, repeatable results. Much discursive work was thus required to turn it into a specific rule-governed form of activity. Tahir Ahmad's initial invocation of the mubahala was therefore split between two Friday sermons, during which he slowly established the conditions for the mubahala and made it clear that this was an act of last resort, before issuing an open challenge to anybody who dared accept.

Tahir Ahmad began his first sermon with a long discourse on the nature of the mubahala, in which explained to his followers that the mubahala had its origins in the above-quoted Qur'anic verse. He described the confrontation between the Prophet Muhammad and the Christians of Najran, and he stressed that Muhammad had made logical points that had silenced his opponents but that they had nonetheless continued to repeat foolish (*lachar*) allegations.[25] As a result of this situation, Tahir Ahmad argued that an impasse was reached, at which point Muhammad challenged the Christians to a mubahala. Both sides were to gather their people together and then invoke the curse of God on the lying faction with the Arabic words *la'nata allahi 'ala al-kadhibin*. This ordeal was clearly seen to potentially cause the death of the false party. The parallels between this situation and the situation facing the Jama'at in Pakistan in the 1980s would have been clear and obvious to his audience.

In fact, Tahir Ahmad's mubahala challenge was not a sudden and unexpected declaration but a cumulative result of efforts he had made to define the practice during the previous month of Ramadan.[26] During this period, Tahir Ahmad had referred to Ghulam Ahmad's works in order to extrapolate the three major conditions of the mubahala. The first was that only a person who believed him- or herself to have received revelation from God could issue a mubahala challenge; this is why Ghulam Ahmad was able to do so. The mubahala, he had explained, "is not issued on anyone's whims on the expectation that Allah will back the challenger: if it were so, such challenges would be flying about everywhere."[27] The second condition was that a mubahala can only be issued when debate has been exhausted. The third condition was that both sides must understand the other to be consciously and deliberately lying.

Throughout his first sermon on June 3, 1988, Tahir Ahmad was insistent in stating that the mubahala is not a routine activity. One cannot just challenge somebody over a minor mistake, for it must be that the person is lying, that they know their beliefs have no basis, and that they have no proof—in short, they must be somebody who slanders God. Moreover, they must continue to persist in refusing the complete and total proofs that are shown to them. Only when this has occurred and when there is no room left for debate—as was the case in Muhammad's interaction with the Christians from Najran—may a mubahala challenge be issued.

Tahir Ahmad further explained to his congregation that the curse (*la'nat*) invoked in a mubahala is not the same as a *l'an*, a mutual curse made by a husband and wife in a case of adultery where there are no other witnesses. What is specific about the mubahala as a form of cursing is that one side must claim to be from God and the other side must deny this claim.[28] This condition means that only some people are capable of calling a mubahala. A person cannot flippantly call for mubahalas without any reference to the Qur'an, and Tahir Ahmad maintained his right to ignore any challengers who did so. To be capable of engaging in a mubahala, a person should not only be sanctioned by God but should also be the representative of a *qaum*—a nation, community, or people. It was clear from the Qur'an, he argued, that the leaders of both parties must be representatives capable of calling on a huge group of people willing to risk everything by invoking God's curse on themselves should they be lying. A whole qaum must, in other words, risk their lives on the sincere claim that they are true and their opponents are liars. And thus it was clear right from the beginning that Mirza Tahir Ahmad, as the Ahmadi caliph, occupied the paradigmatic position from which to issue and accept challenges. To declare a mubahala, he was arguing, was to challenge an opponent to show that they, too, might be worthy of meeting such conditions.

Tahir Ahmad explained that he was not issuing a new challenge but instead resurrecting a mubahala challenge issued by Ghulam Ahmad in his 1907 book *Haqiqat ul-Wahi*. This challenge thus related specifically to the allegations that continued to be directed at Mirza Ghulam Ahmad. The challenge was addressed to all those who considered Ghulam Ahmad to be a liar (*kazab*). Be they Muslim or not, he invited them to participate in a written mubahala, which, he explained, had a set of specific conditions. Those who wished to accept the challenge had to publish their acceptance in several newspapers, in which they were obliged to state unambiguously that they swore by God that Mirza Ghulam Ahamd, who had claimed to be the Promised Messiah, was a liar whose revelations were fabricated and thus not the word of God. Additionally, they had then to state that they believed that Mirza Ghulam Ahamd was a slanderer, a liar, and the dajjal (Antichrist). The most important condition, however, was that having made these specific claims, the respondent would then have to invoke God's most severe punishment on himself should the claims be false.

The point that Tahir Ahmad was making in both his own words and in his quotation of Mirza Ghulam Ahmad's original challenge was that there are precise conditions to be met for both issuing and accepting a mubahala challenge. The mubahala must refer to specific issues of disagreement regarding which both parties declare the other to be a liar. Each party to the mubahala must also publish their acceptance to the utmost of their capacity in clear language and if possible even go on TV to declare that they are accepting the challenge.[29] What is more, each party must declare itself to be true, its opponent to be false, and call for the wrath of God to descend on whosoever is a liar. Such was the severity of this ordeal that Tahir Ahmad advised his opponents that they would be wise not to accept it. Just as the Christians of Najran had shown wisdom in the face of Muhammad's challenge and retreated, so too should the opponents of Ahmadiyyat.[30]

It was in the second of his two sermons, however, that Tahir Ahmad issued the specific mubahala challenge that became so important over the next few years. He began by once again recalling that, with the support of the government of Pakistan, the opponents of the Jama'at had broken all limits of decency in their persecution. He was now compelled to issue a mubahala challenge only because his opponents would not desist.[31] Tahir Ahmad explained that he did not wish to harm his opponents, yet all his efforts to make them understand had only resulted in an intensification of their antagonism. It was, he made quite clear, only because his opponents had transgressed all boundaries with their lies and slander that his mubahala challenge had become legitimate. His challenge was specifically directed to the *mukaffirin* and *mukazzabin*, or those who accused the Ahmadis of being disbelievers and liars. In other words, it was a challenge that was made against those who had described the Jama'at as false.

This sermon thus extended the mubahala revived in the previous week by including allegations made against the Jama'at, as well as those made solely against Ghulam Ahmad. Moreover, this mubahala was addressed to specific opponents who were accused of having fabricated accusations against the Jama'at, including the clerics Manzoor Chinioti and Muhammad Yusuf Ludhianvi, both famous for their antagonism toward Ahmadiyyat. Chinioti, for example, was alleged to have claimed that in Nigeria, Ghana, and Sierra Leone, Ahmadis were leaving the Jama'at in their thousands because they had realized that the *fitna* (sedition) of Ahmadiyyat and Israel are one and the same. Another named opponent, Hussain Ahmad, the then leader of the Jama'at-e-Islami, alleged that the "Qadianis" were the agents of the Jews, who wished to spread discord in Pakistan. It is important to note quite how often anti-Ahmadiyya propaganda is mixed into anti-Semitic ideas about a global Jewish conspiracy and how both forms of hatred revolve around a poisonous suggestion of deceit and deception.

Tahir Ahmad also addressed this challenge to the then president of Pakistan, General Zia ul-Haq, who had been directly responsible for an unprecedented increase in legal and governmental persecution of the Ahmadis during the 1980s.[32] This mubahala was, in other words, addressed to specific individuals, although all leaders of stature were invited to participate.

Having established over these two sermons the meaning, rules, and conventions of a mubahala, Tahir Ahmad finally issued an open mubahala challenge to the whole world, with particular reference to those named as having propagated the most heinous accusations and persecutions against the Jama'at. The challenge itself was long, and I provide only a summary of the main points as follows. The foremost issue of contention was whether Ghulam Ahmad was a prophet within the sharia of Muhammad. Tahir Ahmad then specified precisely what his opponents had to declare if they were to accept the challenge. They had to state that they believed that the Ahmadis were not just liars but that the Jama'at was tricking people into taking the path of fitna and disorder. Some of the statements Tahir Ahmad asked his opponents to swear to were fairly extreme, for example, "we believe that this Jama'at is the enemy of God, his Prophet, the nation, the homeland, and humanity."[33] Tahir Ahmad told his opponents that in order to accept the challenge they had to swear that the Ahmadis saw Ghulam Ahmad as greater than Muhammad, that the Ahmadis were agents of the Jews and the Christians, that the Ahmadis were responsible for all national disasters in Pakistan, that their sharia was different to that of Muslims—the list goes on. Most drastically, any signatory to this mubahala would have had to agree that the Ahmadis were deserving of violence, that their houses should be burned and their property stolen, and that they should be declared apostates whom it was fitting to kill.[34] Given that the challenge required both sides to then call on God to destroy the lying faction, these were huge claims to swear by.

The caliph announced that he would sign this challenge and that it would then be sent to the opponents. All those who were hostile to the Jama'at were invited to sign it, but, he cautioned, they should only accept on the condition that they then publicize their acceptance by every means possible. True to form, the Ahmadis published this open challenge extensively.[35]

Tahir Ahmad's mubahala challenge was thus no simple declaration. Tahir Ahmad was challenging his opponents to a trial by ordeal that would ideally end in death for the false party, but in doing so he was also performatively defining the felicity conditions by which the challenge and its acceptance might be uttered. He based the ordeal on Ghulam Ahmad's reading of an ambiguously recorded ritual in the Qur'an. Throughout these two sermons, however, he made a sustained argument that there were no ambiguities in the conditions of the ordeal. He detailed in precise language not only the general procedure to be followed but also the specific wording that his opponents must accept. Previous accounts of the Ahmadis have tended to give shorthand definitions for the mubahala, for example, that it "is used to signify a procedure in which two opponents in a debate invoke the curse of God upon the person who is wrong."[36] Such characterizations, however, suggest that the mubahala can be a fixed ritual independent of the discursive labor undertaken to define it. Tahir Ahmad's mubahala challenge showed that the act of issuing the mubahala was also an act of establishing its rules, conditions, and procedure.

Tahir Ahmad's mubahala challenge was thus also an act of exclusion, for the conditions that he enumerated meant that very few opponents would be able to accept the duel. To do so, they would have had to sincerely risk their lives on a set of allegations against the Jama'at that Tahir Ahmad himself had selected. Moreover, they would have had to meet a set of organizational and representational criteria that Tahir Ahmad alone was in a unique position to fulfill. Islamic ritual practice has often been characterized as something that is textually overdetermined, to the extent that it has only really become an object of anthropological study in the last few decades.[37] In comparison to this supposed overdetermination, the mubahala is particularly interesting because it is an Islamic ritual—mentioned in the Qur'an, no less—the rules of which have been historically under-elaborated. The kind of truth that it can evidence is therefore always being contested through acts of definition. As we shall see, the caliph's attempts to fix the conditions of the mubahala were not just statements about ritual practice, but more fundamentally, they were arguments about the kind of ethical relationship that should exist between an individual and society.

A Victorious Ordeal?

In spite of the publicity generated by Tahir Ahmad's 1988 challenge, few mubahalas actually occurred during the following months and years. Nonetheless, shortly after the challenge was issued, events transpired that Ahmadis interpret as clear signs that they were victorious in the mubahala. The first sign was the sudden reappearance, on July 10, 1988, of Maulana Aslam Qureshi, a Pakistani cleric who had actively campaigned against the Jama'at and who sometime previously had attacked a member of the khandan (family) of Mirza Ghulam Ahmad. His disappearance in 1983 was widely blamed on the Ahmadis, with a number of opponents, particularly the cleric Manzoor Chinioti, arguing that Tahir Ahmad was responsible for Qureshi's murder. Tahir Ahmad spent much of his inaugural address at the 1988 UK Jalsa Salana expounding on this wondrous sign, mocking Qureshi's transformation from violent criminal to a *maulana* (religious scholar), and explaining how he came to understand that the Pakistani government were complicit in the rumors that he, Tahir Ahmad, was responsible for Qureshi's alleged murder.[38]

The second and far more significant divine sign in favor of the Ahmadis was the sudden and unexplained death of President Zia ul-Haq, whose airplane exploded shortly after taking off from Bahawalpur, Punjab, on August 17, 1988. In his sermon the following day, Tahir Ahmad made absolutely clear that the death of General Zia was a result of the mubahala challenge.[39] This claim nonetheless violated one of the conditions that the caliph had himself worked so hard to define: that the mubahala "does not become operative unless the other party accepts it."[40] The reason that Tahir Ahmad was able to make this claim was that in a sermon the week before Zia's death, he had warned the president that any continuation of his oppression of the Ahmadis was tantamount to the acceptance of the mubahala challenge.[41] When I asked an Ahmadi cleric about this in Qadian, he argued that while it may not have been clear whether Zia's death was a direct result of the mubahala, it was unambiguously the case that the president had died due to God's wrath.

The third major sign of God's favor occurred when the leader of a rival sect, the Ahl-e-Hadith in Britain, Maulvi Mahmood Ahmad Mirpuri, was killed in a car crash on October 10, 1988, with his son and mother-in-law. Then, on the day of the funeral, approximately one hundred people crammed into his house, causing the floor to collapse into the cellar and injuring Mirpuri's wife. It is important to note that Mirpuri did not participate in the mubahala; in fact, he had been extremely active in writing against the Ahmadi mubahala and cautioning other Muslims against accepting it. An official Jama'at account claims that Mirpuri had actually challenged the caliph to a mubahala in 1985 but then dismissed the caliph's own 1988 challenge on the grounds that only a prophet could issue a mubahala.[42]

On the anniversary of the mubahala challenge, Tahir Ahmad used these three signs as evidence that the Jama'at had won the mubahala within its one-year time limit.[43] None of the above signs involved the bilateral completion of a mubahala, but instead, what each example was used to illustrate was the moral depravity of the opposition. The Qureshi example was both a vindication of the caliph and a demonstration of the hypocritical dishonesty of the opponents, particularly Manzoor Chinioti, who is reported to have sworn that if Aslam Qureshi were to be recovered, he would hang himself in public. The fact that he was still alive a year later showed him to be an utter liar: a man too dishonest to approach a mubahala sincerely. Moreover, reports emerged suggesting that Qureshi, who had initially claimed to be in Iran for the whole duration of his "abduction," had suddenly changed his story and claimed that he had, after all, been abducted. That he should do so was taken by the Ahmadis to be yet another demonstration of the fact that their opponents were unrepentant liars.[44] Likewise, the incident with General Zia ul-Haq only served to confirm his wickedness, while the incidents in Britain resulted from Mirpuri's continuous attempts to mislead the public.[45]

Throughout this period, there was a concern within Ahmadi reports to continue refining the precise conditions by which a mubahala might take place. Chief among these concerns was explaining the fact that the participants in a mubahala need not be gathered together in a single place for it to be valid. This was something that the caliph evidently felt his opponents were repeatedly misunderstanding. The Jama'at's press secretary in London issued a statement to the effect that opponents should first clarify their own understanding of the differences between a mubahala, a *munazara*, and a *mubahasa* (two forms of debate) before accepting the challenge.[46] The caliph himself issued a clarification that the opponents were only using the issue of the spatial location of the mubahala as a way of pretending to accept the challenge while actually fleeing from it. They would claim to have accepted a mubahala but would then call Tahir Ahmad to a specific place to perform it, thus demonstrating their lack of understanding of the procedure.[47] The caliph's efforts to establish procedure were thus juxtaposed against an assumption that the opponents were either incapable of understanding the subtleties of the mubahala or, more likely, that they were willfully playing with this divinely sanctioned process for personal gain.[48]

A year after the mubahala challenge, in June 1989, an interesting situation had therefore developed. The Ahmadis were claiming victory, despite the fact that none of the above events had resulted in the bilaterally recognized ritual performance of a mubahala. Nonetheless, throughout this period, the Jama'at continued to work hard to specify the precise conditions and rules of the mubahala. Moreover, Ahmadi discourse drew attention to the failure of opponents to meet these conditions, while framing the Jama'at's own victory in terms of a more general narrative of progress.

The Mubahala in Contemporary Qadian

When I was in Qadian, I would often hear stories about Tahir Ahmad's mubahala challenge, particularly in relation to the death of Zia ul-Haq, who many Ahmadis regarded as one of their major twentieth-century antagonists. After all, the mubahala was the most obvious empirical test through which Ahmadis could prove their Muslimness. In a town where the question of how to evidence religious truth was a major source of uncertainty, the mubahala seemed to promise to inscribe truth within the world in a way that no other activity could. During my fieldwork, I thus set out to investigate the history of the mubahala since 1988.

By early April 2012, I had spent several weeks in the Jama'at library in Qadian attempting to unearth documents relating to the various mubahalas that had been initiated, accepted, and refused since the fourth caliph issued his challenge in 1988. Details about the outcome of several mubahalas were proving elusive, in particular a mubahala that reputedly arose as a result of a challenge made on Palestinian TV on June 29, 2010, following a debate between the Amir of the Ahmadiyya Jama'at in Israel, Muhammad Sharif Odeh, and a rival cleric. There was a video of this on YouTube, yet little other information was available online.[49] The video shows a debate between the two men, which becomes increasingly hostile until the non-Ahmadi sheikh swears by God that the Ahmadis are agents of the Jews and of the British, at which point Odeh says he wants a mubahala, his opponent echoes the call, and both men invoke a curse on the liar. Knowing that there was an Ahmadi cleric who had spent many years as a missionary in Israel, had contacts there, and spoke fluent Arabic, I decided that he would be the best person to ask about the outcome of this televised mubahala challenge. On arriving at his office and asking him what he knew, however, I discovered that he was unconcerned by the result. Not only did he not know the date or the outcome of the challenge; he did seem to think it necessary to find out. Feeling slightly perplexed, I decided to try my luck elsewhere. I jumped on my bicycle and rode over to the office of *Badr*, the Jama'at's official newspaper in India, to ask the editors there if they had received any reports about the Palestinian mubahala. The response I got was again the same; they neither knew about the mubahala, nor did they seem to think it was important to find out anything more about the result. This was puzzling. I knew that my interlocutors cared deeply about demonstrating the truth of Ahmadiyyat. They would regularly narrate stories of the triumph of the Jama'at over its opponents, and indeed, one such story that was often held up as a definitive proof of Ahmadiyyat was the death of Zia ul-Haq. They nonetheless seemed to be unconcerned about the history of modern-day mubahalas and the opportunities these presented for witnessing the truth of the Jama'at. In a town in which nothing matters more than making Muslimness demonstrable, a question thus has to be asked: *why?*

While I was in the office of *Badr*, one of the staff members took an interest in my research and asked me about the other mubahalas I was investigating. In response, I showed him a transcript of the fourth caliph's inaugural address at the Jama'at's 1999 Annual Gathering in the United Kingdom.[50] In this speech, delivered on July 30, 1999, Tahir Ahmad had mentioned a mubahala that had occurred sometime previously in Karachi. He had described how two Ahmadi missionaries had been caught in the trap of an opponent, who had invited them to a debate (mubahasa) with the prior motive of suddenly springing a mubahala challenge on them. These two guileless (*bhole bhale*) missionaries not only accepted the mubahala challenge but even went so far as to challenge the opponent on behalf of their divine leader. The fourth caliph was evidently not pleased that this mubahala had taken place, for he had previously declared that mubahalas should cease. He explained that the missionaries had had no right to issue a challenge on his behalf, but he nonetheless accepted the challenge because they were devoted Ahmadis. Tahir Ahmad then listed the accusations of the opponent so that it might be conclusively proven just from the mubahala itself that the opponent was a liar: among the more far-fetched accusations was the claim of the opponent that the Ahmadis believed that by going to Qadian once a year all one's sins might be washed away, something that, if true, would constitute an unacceptable innovation reminiscent of Hindu practices. Throughout this speech, Tahir Ahmad had been extremely careful not to mention the name of this opponent, and additionally, he had explained that the reason he asked his followers to desist from mubahalas was so that he might conduct mubahalas only with the universally recognized representatives of a nation (qaum), not with just anybody who might want to challenge him. In responding without naming his opponent, Tahir Ahmad was demonstrating their difference in rank so as to leave his audience in no doubt that the important issue at stake was the continued growth, success, and development of the Jamaʻat, not the challenge of some nobody cleric from Karachi. Who, after all, did this challenger represent? If he had no followers, after his defeat who would witness the victory of Ahmadiyyat (and, by implication, convert)?

Unsurprisingly, the nameless opponent appears not to have shared Tahir Ahmad's view. A quick search reveals that his name is Illias Suttar, and that on Facebook he presents himself as "Allama Illias Suttar Mubahila Winner." For Suttar, the result of the mubahala was quite clear: shortly after accepting the challenge, Tahir Ahmad had fallen ill, and then his health steadily deteriorated until he died on April 19, 2003. Suttar, meanwhile, claims to have remained healthy to this day.

The *Badr* staffer and I discussed this speech for a while, before I asked whether he knew the outcome of the 1999 mubahala. Given that it was a one-year challenge, I had already looked at the records of the UK Jalsa Salana 2000, but I found no reference to any Ahmadi victory. My interlocutor's reply was very clear: it was not necessary for us to find a direct reference to the result of the mubahala. Just as he and his colleagues had earlier appeared entirely unconcerned by the outcome of the Palestinian mubahala, he was now advising me that even searching for the outcome of this mubahala, which had been accepted by the fourth caliph in front of an audience of thousands, was not necessary. When I told him that there was a man from Karachi, Illias Suttar, who claimed to have won this mubahala, he replied that such a victory was simply not possible. Despite having never heard the name Illias Suttar before, the *Badr* staffer was absolutely convinced that

Suttar would have faced public disgrace or dishonor since the mubahala. Indeed, he hinted that Mirza Tahir Ahmad's acceptance of the mubahala in front of so many people might have been Suttar's moment of dishonor, for Suttar's ridiculous claims were aired in front of a global television audience, thus exposing him as a buffoon. My interlocutor was simply not concerned to address Suttar's claims that he had won the mubahala. Indeed, his lack of interest in the mubahala echoed the caliph's dismissal of Suttar, namely, that he was a nobody whose lowly status was incomparable to the global spread of Ahmadiyyat.

Perhaps unsurprisingly, the *Badr* staffer's dismissal of the need to find out the result of the mubahala was couched in a simultaneous concern to elucidate the rules of the practice. The important question, he explained, was about the capacity of each side to fulfill the conditions of the mubahala. We must, he told me, study the precise conditions of the mubahala. Exactly what was it, he asked, that each opponent prayed? Did they pray for their death in the eventuality that they were wrong? Or did they pray only for a curse (la'nat) or perhaps only dishonor on the liar? And then there is the matter of whether the claims of each side were published and whether each side disseminated its acceptance of the mubahala widely. Likewise, another interlocutor, who was not coincidentally a lawyer, had previously advised me not to bother searching for historical incidents of mubahalas. I would be better off, he argued, clarifying the precise conditions necessary for a person to issue a mubahala challenge. Against whom and under what circumstances might this particular form of imprecation be practiced? It was the rules and not the results of mubahalas that seemed to excite my interlocutors in Qadian.

In explaining the rules that governed the mubahala, the *Badr* staffer juxtaposed Illias Suttar's inability to satisfy the mubahala's conditions with the continued global success of the Jama'at. We must, he said, understand all the mubahalas together in relation to the rise of the Jama'at and the failures of its opponents. As we discussed this, I asked for his help in interpreting some of the more difficult passages in the caliph's speech, which he began to do, before suddenly digressing to tell me about a completely unrelated proof of Ahmadiyyat over Christianity. Had I heard the story, he asked, about the debate between a Christian missionary and an Ahmadi on the topic of the Trinity? He then told the story as follows: A Christian missionary told an Ahmadi that his Oriental (*mashriqi*) mind could not comprehend the Trinity. The Ahmadi missionary, unsure of how to respond, took this challenge to the first caliph, who replied as follows: Jesus was also an Oriental, so how was he supposed to understand the Trinity? The missionary then returned to the Christian and relayed this argument, and the Christian unsurprisingly fell into a stunned silence. This digression—a sudden intrusion of potent proof into our discussion of the mubahala—signaled quite clearly that my interlocutor saw the details of the results of this particular mubahala as only a small and rather unimportant part of a more general story about the Jama'at's ability to conquer the world through truth.

Later that day, after I left the *Badr* office, I finished translating the caliph's speech, and I realized that it was structured by the same logic as my interlocutor's discourse. Tahir Ahmad's final point had been to argue that regardless of mubahala challenges, the Jama'at would continue in its advancement while its opponents would be accursed. This occurred in the context of what was evidently, at the end of the millennium, a period of intense conviction among Ahmadis that their sect was growing exponentially. Three weeks before publishing the above-mentioned speech, *Badr* had printed a sermon from March 26, 1999, in which Tahir Ahmad had expressed absolute certainty that within a year, ten million people would join the Jama'at.[51] Likewise, an article from January 1999 noted that the caliph had reported the extraordinary progress of the Jama'at in India such that within the first four months of the year, there had been 253,283 converts, over twice the figure for the first four months of the previous year.[52] Given that even today, there are unlikely to be more than 200,000 Ahmadis in India and that Indian conversion figures for 2008–09 and 2009–10 were 2,417 and 2,761 respectively, the 1999 figure is presumably fanciful.[53] At the time that the Illias Suttar affair occurred, there was quite clearly a mood of optimism among Ahmadis regarding the swelling of their ranks.

It was growth and development on a global scale that made the Ahmadis paradigmatically suited to meeting the conditions of the mubahala in a way that could never be the case for Suttar. In asking questions about the procedure, method, and rules of the mubahala, my interlocutors were establishing the criteria by which the success of the Jama'at could be witnessed. Moreover, their concern with the legalistic aspects of the mubahala was no mere pedantry but rather an attempt to give definition to the structures and relationships through which their own Muslim identity could be known. This was about belonging to a community with a single leader, acting with unity and discipline, having the capacity to broadcast a message on a mass scale, and being globally significant.

The Almost-Mubahala of Bangalore

The fact that my interlocutors showed little interest in the results of mubahalas is extremely important, for the mubahala rarely signals truth through divine adjudication. Even the death of Zia ul-Haq is an ambiguous example of a mubahala working as a ritual process, and as described above, people in Qadian were happy to admit this. What really mattered to them was that his death was divine punishment for his persecution of the Jama'at. In the rest of this chapter, I will focus on two examples of mubahalas that occurred in India to show that it was precisely in moments of ritual failure that these mubahalas were most effective as mechanisms for the evidencing of a true Muslim identity. I will explore this question by looking at one mubahala that never quite occurred and one mubahala that took place yet produced no result.

In October 1997, a Deobandi cleric in Bangalore, Maulana Shoaibullah Miftahi, published a series of articles in two Urdu newspapers. In response, one of Bangalore's Ahmadis, Muhamad Azmatullah Qureshi, sent a series of replies to these newspapers, but they refused to publish them.[54] As a result, his responses were first published individually in Qadian's newspaper, *Badr*, and then as a pamphlet.[55] In this pamphlet, Qureshi attacked Miftahi by deploying long quotations accompanied by a combative commentary that openly derided Miftahi's poor scholarship. Much of Qureshi's pamphlet was devoted to highlighting Miftahi's misquotations of Mirza Ghulam Ahmad. He argued that Miftahi had lied so as to catch the public in a trap and thus turn them away from the Jama'at. By taking Ghulam Ahmad's prophecies but then "cutting and slashing" them, Miftahi was said to have exposed only his own depravity and the extremes he would go to mislead the populace.[56] One example of this ("Maulana Miftahi's great lie") was Miftahi's use of Ghulam Ahmad's own writings to argue that Ghulam Ahmad had declared that Qadian was mentioned in the Qur'an.[57] This was not an original argument, and opponents of the Jama'at often make this claim to argue that Ghulam Ahmad had poor knowledge of the Qur'an and that he was introducing innovations into Islam.

Qureshi responded to this "great lie" by arguing that Ghulam Ahmad's statement about Qadian had to be contextualized. It originally came as part of a longer passage from Ghulam Ahmad's book *Izala-e-Auham*. Qureshi argued that in its proper context, Ghulam Ahmad's statement referred to a *kashf*, or revelatory vision, in which Ghulam Ahmad saw the name of Qadian in the Qur'an. On this basis, Qureshi concluded that Miftahi was willfully trying to mislead the public by pretending that a vision is the truth.[58] Having made this point, Qureshi concluded his pamphlet by encouraging Miftahi to accept a mubahala and place the issue in the court of God, for "what advantage is there in misleading the public?"[59] A note was placed at the end of the text informing Miftahi that a copy of the mubahala challenge had been sent to him, which Miftahi was asked to sign and return. Copies of this pamphlet were then distributed in Bangalore.[60]

Following this challenge, both sides launched a series of allegations and refutations, with the Ahmadis printing open letters in response to articles by Miftahi and his associates. As part of this exchange, in a May 1999 issue of *Badr*, Inam Ghori, who is nowadays chief secretary of the Indian Jama'at, wrote three open letters in response to articles that had appeared after the distribution of the muba-hala challenge in Bangalore. These letters were often sardonic in tone and mocking of the allegations the opponents had leveled against Ahmadiyyat. Yet a serious theme ran through them, which was a concern to understand the conditions under which a mubahala might take place. The first letter responded to a chal-lenge by an ally of Miftahi, who appeared to have challenged the Ahmadis to a debate on their own satellite TV channel on the topic of the "truth and falsity of Mirza Ghulam Ahmad Qadiani."[61] Ghori's response was to demonstrate not only that his opponents were duplicitous but moreover that they had failed to meet the basic conditions by which to engage in the debate that they themselves had proposed. The main reason for this, he explained, was that the opponents still adhered to the common Sunni doctrine that Jesus survived the crucifixion, is cur-rently alive in the heavens, and will return at the end of days. If they held this doctrine, they could not believe in the coming of a second messiah who was dif-ferent from Jesus. Ghori's logic was thus that there was no point in these oppo-nents debating the merits of Mirza Ghulam Ahmad's character, for even if they found Ghulam Ahmad to be upstanding, they could not accept him as a messiah. Ahmadis, on the other hand believe that Jesus died of natural causes in Kashmir and are thus in a position where they can and do accept the logical possibility of the coming of a second messiah. Expanding on this theme, Ghori declared that before the opponents debate the character of Ghulam Ahmad, they should therefore first attend to the issue of Jesus's death. Regarding Jesus's death, Ghori reminded his opponents that Ghulam Ahmad himself issued several challenges with monetary prizes that remain unclaimed to this day. The first challenge was issued in Ghulam Ahmad's book *Izala-e-Auham*. Ghulam Ahmad offered one thousand rupees in cash to anybody who could disprove his interpretation of the word *tawaffa* in the Qur'an, which he took to refer to Jesus's death. This challenge remained open, its prize ready for collection by whoever could fulfill its conditions. The second challenge was much the same; in the book *Kitab ul-Bariyah*, Ghulam Ahmad had offered twenty thousand rupees to anybody who could provide a hadith that substantiates the mainstream Sunni belief that Jesus has ascended to heaven alive, where he awaits his eventual return. Ghori then listed one further prize challenge, offered by Mirza Tahir Ahmad to all Muslims in his concluding address to Qadian's 1994 Jalsa Salana, of ten million rupees. This third prize was evidently a self-conscious farce, a satire of mainstream Muslim doctrine concerning the coming messiah. Playing on the fact that most Muslims believe that Jesus is alive in the heavens and awaiting his descent to earth once more at the end of times, Tahir Ahmad challenged them: if the ulema can get together and in any way bring Jesus down from the sky, he would give each and every one of them ten million rupees!

The point of this letter was thus not just to show that the opponents were in-capable of winning a debate against the Ahamdis; it mocked their inability even to arrive at the conditions that would enable such a debate to occur. The next two letters dealt more explicitly with the mubahala but from the same angle; the op-ponents were morally incapable of meeting the conditions whereby judgment could be striven for.

The second open letter was addressed directly to Miftahi, in reply to an article that Miftahi had published a few weeks earlier.[62] Ghori noted that Miftahi made reference to the supposed acceptance of the mubahala by the Pakistani opponent Manzoor Chinioti. Ghori proceeded to demonstrate how Chinioti's actions in 1988 made a mockery of the mubahala he claimed to have accepted. Just as Chin-ioti's evasions were farcical, Miftahi was shown to have delegitimized his own participation in the mubahala by following Chinioti. Miftahi was merely evading and prevaricating (lait-o-la'al), and what's more, he had a history of doing so. Ghori's advice was clear: cease this prevarication, and "in accordance with the con-ditions laid down in the mubahala challenge," affix your signature to it and publish it! Miftahi was thus shown to have failed completely to demonstrate the solem-nity required for the mubahala to begin functioning as a form of arbitration. In a third and final letter, Ghori worked further to expose the lawless nature of his opponents. These were people who would sooner conduct jihad against the Ah-madis than hold a mubahala with them—precisely the kind of attitude that had led to the "law of the jungle" in Pakistan.[63] Ghori wished to leave us in no doubt that his opponents were incapable of engaging with conditions, rules, and laws.

This whole affair came to a rather abrupt end a month later, when an open letter appeared in Badr, addressed to he who had "fled the mubahala by excuses and ruses": Miftahi.[64] Hidden away on page 10, this article followed the Ahmadi convention of quietly dismissing opponents as if their challenge was barely worthy of mention. The letter, written by the head of the Jama'at in Karnataka, Muham-mad Shafiullah, was an indictment of Miftahi. Miftahi, Shafiullah claimed, was never serious in his acceptance of the mubahala but instead used it as an excuse for the generation of cheap publicity. Indeed, there was evidence that he never even understood this mubahala to be a mubahala. Miftahi had claimed that Mirza Ghulam Ahmad was the dajjal (Antichrist) and that Muslims therefore need not hold mubahalas with Ahmadis. Shafiullah chided Miftahi: Did he not consider himself to be a Muslim? Or was the mubahala a joke to him?

A more important question remained, however, of what the conditions might be for holding a mubahala. Shafiullah reminded Miftahi that the fourth caliph, Mirza Tahir Ahmad, had tens of millions of followers in over 150 countries. That is, people willing to give their lives for him. And yet Miftahi still thought that he had the right to call Tahir Ahmad to Bangalore. Miftahi was not even the representative of Bangalore's Muslims, Shafiullah reminded him, let alone India's or the world's. First he should establish his own station; only then should he call Tahir Ahmad to his city. Shafiullah thus argued that only one way remained for Miftahi to partake in the mubahala: he had to sign his name on a printed copy of the mubahala declaration, along with the specific curse *la'nata allahi 'ala al-kadhibin* (the curse of Allah on those who lie). He then had to publish this acceptance in a newspaper or promote it by any means possible. Most importantly, he had to desist from his habit of accepting the mubahala while simultaneously declaring it unlawful. The article was clear: Miftahi had to recognize his lowly status, cease presuming to call Tahir Ahmad to mubahalas, and realize that the mubahala is only possible when one approaches it sincerely rather than as an opportunity to increase one's own status.

With this letter, *Badr*'s reporting of the affair ceased. After two years of increasing rhetoric and back-and-forth polemics, the matter was, at least for the Ahmadis, concluded. In spite of protestations from both sides that they were either willing to accept or already had accepted the challenge, the mubahala never occurred. Instead, a whole series of legalistic questions had proliferated. It is nonetheless questionable whether the Ahmadis ever actually intended for this confrontation to culminate in a mubahala. Indeed, it was precisely because of the fact that the mubahala didn't happen that the desired goal of finding an opponent wanting was achieved. This mubahala was a ritual that generated meaning not because it produced the desired result but because time and again it failed to do so. So long as the opponents were incapable of meeting the criteria, the ritual could not be performed. The mubahala thus ceased to be a divine trial by ordeal and became a competition about which side had the resources both to define the conditions of the practice and then completely satisfy those conditions.

Throughout this entire long process, the Ahmadis' careful attention to the conditions of the mubahala challenge served to narrow the question of who was Muslim into a set of clear and empirically verifiable parameters. Who had the economic resources to publish their acceptance of the challenge across a wide range of media? Who had the ability to legitimize their participation in the mubahala by publicly broadcasting their participation to every corner of the world via satellite television? Who, in other words, had the social resources to turn their own participation into something that could be legitimized through public scrutiny? That the opponents could not do this was of course due to their lack of lawfulness, unity, order, discipline, and obedience beneath a universal leader. The broader question at play was who could make their Muslimness into something that could be empirically demonstrated.

The Kodiyathoor Mubahala

Possibly the first face-to-face mubahala to take place after Tahir Ahmad's 1988 open challenge occurred in South India, in the village of Kodiyathoor, Kerala, on May 28, 1989.[65] Forty Ahmadis and forty opponents performed this mubahala. The opponents were members of the Anjuman Isha'at-e-Islam, a group whose main purpose appears to have been organized opposition to the Ahmadis.[66] The mubahala was reputedly witnessed by seven to ten thousand people and was reported by a number of news outlets. It appeared that the ritual conditions of the ordeal had been met. Yet, within the six-month timeframe that the two sides agreed on, no discernable victory conditions had been met. Nobody had died.

I visited Kodiyathoor in July 2011, accompanied by the missionary stationed there and a few other young Ahmadis. They all agreed that the Jama'at had won the mubahala, and to prove this point, they jokingly pointed to the rude health of the youngest of their number, who had been a baby in 1989 when his parents took him to participate in the mubahala. If the Ahmadis had lost, would this young man have survived? A problem nonetheless remained, for with no definitive divine sign to point to, how could they really say that there had been an Ahmadi victory? They suggested that discord within the Sunni community of Calicut following the mubahala could possibly have been a sign of the opponents' defeat in the mubahala, yet they admitted that the evidence for this was far from conclusive. To function as a clear sign of divine arbitration, a mubahala ideally demands a death.

My interlocutors thus proposed a reason for the lack of a definitive result. While the Ahmadis had enacted the conditions of the mubahala correctly, the opponents had acted in such a way that they avoided the full wrath of God. A mubahala can only work, the local Ahmadi missionary told me, if both sides are absolutely sincere in their prayers, and while this was the case for the Ahmadis, it cannot be said for their opponents. Later, one of my companions showed me a Kannada-language account of the mubahala, which, he argued, showed that while both sides invoked the Arabic curse *la'nata allahi 'ala al-kadhibin*, only the Ahmadis added in the vernacular a plea that should they be false, they should be punished by God.[67] Translating the text, my companion explained that the opponents had merely prayed that they be cursed, not punished, if found false.

This interpretation was supported by *Badr*'s official Urdu version of events. The newspaper provided a detailed account of how the conditions of the engagement were decided on.[68] This process involved a significant amount of discussion, which resulted in a set of rules that both sides agreed on. Both sides agreed that they would print thousands of copies of a joint statement. Additionally, they agreed to share responsibility for erecting the stage to host the mubahala. It was agreed that the mubahala would include women and children and that the mubahala would take place at a precise time and date in a specific location in Kodiyathoor. The entire list of conditions was then printed and sent to newspapers. In spite of this apparent cooperation, however, *Badr*'s description stressed the fact that the opponents were disobliging. To begin with, rather than accepting a written mubahala—as had been proposed by the caliph—the opponents insisted on it being face-to-face. Then, they said that they were not willing to do a mubahala with reference to the set of beliefs and allegations outlined by Tahir Ahmad but would instead only hold a mubahala centering on the issue of Mirza Ghulam Ahmad's prophethood. In each case, contrasted with these objections, the Ahmadis were shown to be a model of order, for they calmly accepted their opponents' demands, only after first having sought permission to do so from their caliph. In fact, the Ahmadis only participated in this mubahala as a result of the special permission of the caliph.[69]

During the mubahala itself, the Ahmadis were reported to have prayed that Mirza Ghulam Ahmad was a prophet within the sharia of Muhammad, that he had received true revelations (ilham and *wahi*), that the denial of his prophethood is tantamount to the denial of any prophet and therefore punishable by God, and that prophethood is possible within the sharia of Muhammad. After stating this, the Ahmadis beseeched God to deliver severe punishment on them should they be lying, along with the Arabic imprecation *la'nata allahi 'ala al-kadhibi*. Should they be truthful, however, they asked that God have mercy on them and show a sign by which their truth might be known.

By contrast, the opponents were said to have stated that they believed that Mirza Ghulam Ahmad was not from God, that he was not a rasul (a prophet), and that he was not an *ummiti nabi* (a prophet within Muhammad's umma) or a *ghair tashr'i nabi* (a prophet without a sharia). Moreover, they stated that to deny Ghulam Ahmad did not doom a person. As my companion had reported, however, at this point the Sunni faction were said to have only beseeched God to curse them should they be lying. They did not, in other words, ask for a harsh punishment of death. Nonetheless, after both sets of prayers had taken place, a joint prayer was issued, which called on God to ruin the liars, thus somewhat complicating the neat narrative that the Ahmadis would later construct.

Even though Ahmadi accounts display skepticism about the sincerity of the opponents, the mubahala was presented in Ahmadi sources as a ritually complete performance. The newspaper *Badr*, for example, makes repeated reference to the huge crowds who witnessed it, to the joint statements of conditions that were issued to the media, and to the media presence at the event itself, which even led to the story being carried in the United States. All of these facts implied that the mubahala had been successfully executed. Yet as in the previous examples, Ahmadi accounts of the event glorified the Jama'at as the side most fully able to engage with the criteria of the mubahala. Even though a legitimate mubahala took place and even though both sides agreed beforehand on the conditions, the Ahmadis were able to fulfill these conditions in a more effective fashion than their opponents. The Ahmadis wept due to the sincerity of their supplications to God, they called for the most awful punishment on themselves should they be wrong, and in their manner of deciding on the conditions, they behaved in an exemplary fashion that demonstrated their absolute obedience to and unity under a single leader. In other words, they were able to exceed the bare minimum conditions because of their unique and virtuous form of social organization.

A similar series of events occurred in the United Kingdom in 1988, when the leader of the British Jama'at Ahl-e-Sunnat (Barelvi) accepted Tahir Ahmad's mubahala challenge on the condition that both sides assembled in their own mosques at the same time on December 22. The official Jama'at history of this event argues that although a mubahala did take place, the opponents failed to satisfy fully its conditions by first, engaging in "chicanery" and second, invoking the curse of God only on the Ahmadis, not on themselves. The Ahmadis, by contrast, prayed to God that he punish them should they be found to be lying.[70]

The Kodiyathoor mubahala, which at the time of its occurrence was described with anticipation as an "unprecedented event in the history of Islam," ended quietly with no obvious winner.[71] Yet, as with the example from Bangalore, this mubahala came to prove Muslimness precisely because it failed to function as an ordeal of adjudication. What was at stake was each side's ability to fulfill the conditions of the mubahala. The Ahmadis did just that, for as the present-day missionary in Kodiyathoor reminisced, the Ahmadis were victorious on that day because they prayed sincerely and, even so, no damnation befell them. The mubahala thus became a question of whether either side was composed of the kinds of people who were morally capable of qualifying for adjudication due to personal integrity and organizational structure. The opponents were shown to be wanting because they were incapable—morally, materially, and organizationally—of partaking in the ritual process of the mubahala in such a way that it could function.

By the same logic, an otherwise indisputable victory over an opponent who lacked the qualities of being a social equal to the caliph could never really count as a significant proof. One such instance occurred in the late 1980s in a Sri Lankan village, where a maulvi had been agitating against the Ahmadis for some time.[72] After the maulvi accepted the caliph's 1988 mubahala challenge, he met an unpleasant end, which involved his own followers beating him with *lathis* (heavy sticks) and launched a vicious attack on his house. The maulvi had a heart attack and died on his way to the hospital. This would appear to vindicate the Jama'at and to be a clear demonstration via divine judgment of the truth of Ahmadiyyat, yet this victory is not mentioned in the Jamaʿat's official history of the mubahala and is, as far as I can tell, completely forgotten.[73] This was a maulvi in a tiny village, who we can only assume had no ability to publicize his acceptance of the challenge beyond his immediate vicinity. This was a man whose status made him incapable of fully meeting the conditions of the mubahala: he lacked precisely those virtues of globality, unity, and media reach that make the Ahmadis so capable of participating in these challenges.

Ultimately, this raises an interesting question as to whether, from the perspective of the Jamaʿat, a ritually fulfilled mubahala is actually possible. No opponent could ever meet the conditions of Tahir Ahmad's mubahala challenge, because the conditions of the mubahala effectively state that to be eligible, opponents must be just like Ahamdis, and their leaders must be just like the caliph. The consequence of this is that the actual outcome of any given mubahala usually remains unimportant, for it is in the failure of the ritual that the evidence of Muslimness is produced. The ideal and virtuous Muslim selfhood that my interlocutors strive for cannot be achieved in isolation. It is dependent on membership of a global Jamaʿat that operates in a systematic fashion, is united under a single leader, and has the capacity to project its message through media. These features of the Jamaʿat are both the signs and the conditions of its truth.

In the essay *Pain and Truth in Medieval Christian Ritual*, Talal Asad defines the ordeal as a form of ritual that regulates conflict between social equals. It does not in any way resolve disagreement, for no party involved feels themselves to be in any doubt about truth and guilt. Rather, the aim of the ordeal is "to provide rules for producing an unequivocal outcome on which a clear decision about social relations can be made."[74] If we treat the mubahala as an ordeal in this sense, we see an interesting situation emerge. The mubahala, as Tahir Ahmad defined it in his 1988 sermons, is supposed to provide a clear ruling about which side is correct in a conflict that has reached a definitive impasse. Yet, as we have seen in these examples, mubahalas almost always fails to do that, while paradoxically still producing evidence. This is because the work of the mubahala occurs at the level of performatively enacting its rules, in short, its felicity conditions.[75] As in Asad's definition of ordeals, the mubahala is in all senses understood to be a ritual that can only work when fought between two equals—that is, between two agents who belong to comparable social organizations. In Ahmadi discourse, performatively enacting the rules of the mubahala thus becomes a way of denying the social and moral equality of opponents. The fact that the mubahala fails time and again to evidence truth on the bodies of its participants is thus key to how it does produce meaning. To paraphrase Evans-Pritchard on Zande oracles, the fact that the mubahala doesn't work when it is interfered with (by the deficiencies of the op-ponent) shows how accurate it might be when the correct conditions are met.[76] The fact that the ritual doesn't work prompts a series of questions about why this should be so, which culminate in the Ahmadis' opponents being found wanting. The failure of the ritual is ultimately always a result of their failure to be worthy participants.

Tahir Ahmad's mubahala challenge has to be understood in light of the strug-gles that Ahmadis faced in establishing the truth of their Muslim identity in Pak-istan in the late 1980s. As the anthropologist Asad Ahmed has shown, from the 1970s onward, Pakistani courts drew on a liberal legal discourse that emphasized belief as the criterion of religious belonging in order to exclude Ahmadis from the legal definition of Islam.[77] The Ahmadis nonetheless continued to use sharia law—which emphasized observable acts and practice—to argue that their per-formance of Islamic ritual made them Muslims.[78] This tension between "legal" and "ontic" identity was only resolved after Zia ul-Haq's introduction of Ordi-nance 20 in 1984, which created the framework for Ahmadis to be understood as imposters or frauds. With the passing of this ordinance, the Pakistani state could criminalize Ahmadis for acting as Muslims because it claimed to know that their beliefs were not those of Muslims, even though they acted like Muslims. There is thus a forgotten liberal genealogy—with its emphasis on personal belief and conviction—behind the legal exclusion and persecution of the Ahmadis in Paki-stan.[79] This liberal framing of identity as belief made Ahmadi Muslimness inde-monstrable: What possible form of persuasion could the Ahmadis employ if the state declared that it could know their minds and that it could thus know their non-Muslim identity?

It is in fact possible to read Tahir Ahmad's instigation of the mubahala as a mockery of the Pakistani state's claim to be able to know the inner thoughts and beliefs of the Ahmadis. In an essay titled *Epistemology and Tragedy*, Stanley Cavell has argued that the trials by ordeal inflicted on early modern European women accused of witchcraft emerged from the "horror that proposes our lack of cer-tain access to other minds." Unlike the material world, human beings can never be knowable and "open to ocular proof," and this unknowability is what gives way to the "madness and bewitchment of inquisitors."[80] If we take seriously this idea that trials by ordeal are rituals designed to produce an inner truth about a person, we can begin to see how Tahir Ahmad's decision to instigate an ordeal *in order to let it fail* might be seen as a cutting rejoinder to those who claimed to have certain access to the minds of his followers.[81] For Tahir Ahmad, the failure of the ordeal was a productive failure, for it was a failure that demonstrated the falsity of taking belief as a criterion of religious identity. This failure thus opened the door for him to make an argument for religious identity being relational. By challenging his opponents to a prayer duel to the death, Tahir Ahmad was thus pointing toward a way in which the Muslimness of Ahmadis could be discerned, known, and verified. Namely, he was pointing toward the notion that this Muslimness might be evidenced through the relationships that Ahmadis cultivated to one another and to him. The ritual failure of the mubahala might thus be read as an argument that Muslimness really could be proved, that it really could be made falsifiable, and that the medium for doing so is the social structure of the Jama'at itself. In the preceding chapters, I have argued that a central source of religious uncertainty for Ahmadis is the essentially unanswerable nature of the question: *how do you prove that you're Muslim?* As long as Muslimness is seen a deep inner quality of a person, then of course it will remain the kind of truth that simply cannot be evidenced in a falsifiable manner. The failed rituals that I have described in this chapter should be seen as one attempt by the fourth caliph and his followers to overcome their problems with evidence and to inhabit a form of Muslimness that could be manifested in the material world.

It is worth comparing the Islam envisioned in Tahir Ahmad's mubahala challenge with the ethereal idea of Islam that Faisal Devji argues forms the basis of the Pakistani state.[82] In short, Devji argues that the state of Pakistan was not founded on an idea of ethnicity or territory or even the linkages between the two, but instead on an abstract idea of Islam. This gave birth to a form of nationalism in which religion was not a supplement to geography but rather an alternative.[83] As such, nationality was not debated through the question of geography but the question of who was Muslim.[84] For Devji, the ethereal nature of this Islam has made it "uniquely vulnerable to disruption" a fact which explains the threat that Ahmadis are seen to pose to the Pakistani polity.[85] Devji's argument is deliberately provocative and by no means universally accepted,[86] but read alongside the history of Tahir Ahmad's mubahala challenge, it produces an interesting idea: that in issuing his call to mubahala, Tahir Ahmad may well have been challenging the foundations of the Pakistani state. For Ahmadis, the ritual failure of mubahala ordeals makes Islam demonstrable and visible in a very material fashion: it makes Muslimness into something that is discernible and provable. The caliph's mubahala was thus deeply antagonistic to the fragile and disembodied idea of Islam that Devji argues underpins the Pakistani nation.

In contemporary Qadian, the relational understanding of Muslim identity that is revealed in these mubahala challenges creates opportunities for a triumphalist narrative about belonging to the only community through which a truly Muslim identity can be empirically demonstrated. It provides a way of envisioning a Muslim identity that can be proved without any doubt. But it also introduces a danger, for if Muslim identity is fundamentally premised on the quality of connections a person has with their community, what becomes of their Muslimness when those connections are fragile? As we have seen, Qadian's residents do not just fear that they will not be able to prove their Muslimness; they also fear that their own post-partition separation from the global Jama'at (and in particular from the caliph) has left them in a perilous state of spiritual decline. The next chapter considers this problem in greater detail and shows how Qadian's Ahmadis' tenuous relationship to the broader global Jama'at both threatens their religious being and creates opportunities for the witnessing of religious truth.

TELEVISING ISLAM

The Aesthetics of the Caliphate

Distinctions between the inner and outer have been extensively elaborated on within various traditions of Islamic thought. The most well-known such distinction is that between an apparent surface meaning (*zahir*) and an esoteric and unseen truth (*batin*), with the latter term having been much developed in Sufi thought. The historian Michael Cook has shown how scholarly discussion about forbidding wrong in medieval Islamic texts reveals a complex distinction between the public (which could be interdicted) and the hidden, which was best left undisturbed. For the medieval scholars described by Cook, there was no inherently private domain, but rather the private was defined by the fact that it was not public knowledge.[1] Shahab Ahmed has noted that the distinction in Muslim thought between the public, or seen, and the private, or unseen, has often been important in enabling "the spatial separation of contradictory norms."[2] Ahmed describes an ideal separation between a public space of conformity and a private space (which might better be thought of as a restricted public) in which people's training and education enabled them to explore complexities and contradictions. This spatial distinction maps onto the linguistic pairing—found in languages from Arabic to Urdu—of the terms *khas* and *am* to refer respectively to the private, high and elect, and the public, low and common.[3]

This hierarchical ranking between inner spirituality and common public existence is present in discourse in Qadian. Ahmadis celebrate the mystical aspects of Mirza Ghulam Ahmad's work in such books as *The Philosophy of the Teachings of Islam* (*Islami Usul ki Falasafi*), and they are in awe of the esoteric revelations (*wahi*) that he received from God.[4] Through his writings and his preaching,

Ghulam Ahmad is understood to have reinvigorated humankind's spiritual link to God. For the Ahmadis of Qadian, Ghulam Ahmad showed that we can all have a connection to a God who is in constant communication with his creation. Indeed, they claim to belong to the only Muslim sect for whom God is truly *living*. Revelatory dreams are both a constant feature of life and deeply private and moving experiences. On multiple occasions, Ahmadis in Qadian told me that all that really matters is our own private relationship to God. This is something that nobody else can judge, and in comparison to it, all matters of the public and material world are inconsequential. Real spirituality—like that said to be possessed by the elderly derwesh of Qadian—can be opaque and even invisible from the outside, for those who have truly found God are humble and self-effacing. Theirs is the virtue of *taqwa* (piety), an awareness and even fear of God in everything that one does. They know that it is only God's judgment that counts. And yet even though these esoteric aspects of Mirza Ghulam Ahmad's reform are so highly valued, to be able to dwell on them at length is a luxury in which few Ahmadis may indulge, for most members of the Jama'at are faced by a more pressing problem of how to make their Muslimness legible at the level of the surface and in the realm of the public. Claims by opponents that Ahmadis hide their secret non-Muslimness behind a deceitful exterior mean that every public interaction is potentially a situation in which Ahmadis might have to demonstrate an exemplary Muslimness. Moreover, this need to be exemplary falls on every single member of the Jama'at, for, as we have already seen, the greatest proof that Ahmadis have of their Muslim identity is their unity as a community under the caliphate. It is through displays of discipline and strength as a Jama'at that they seek to inscribe on the world evidence of the fact that they have met their obligations to truth.

Since 1994, the meaning of exemplary display in Qadian has subtly changed due to the enormous impact of the Jama'at's satellite television network, MTA. As consumers of this network, Ahmadis have been provided new ways of seeing and hearing their caliph and thus of witnessing his message. "There is now a personal relationship [with the caliph] through MTA," one Jama'at employee told me, before comparing this new relationship to the pre-MTA days, when sermons were available only on cassette, and people would go to the extreme and costly measure of trying to cultivate a bond with their caliph by listening to his sermons live via international phone calls. Even more fundamentally, however, MTA has created a situation in which every Ahmadi man can potentially be held up to the world as an instance of exemplary discipline. (Adult Ahmadi women are rarely featured on MTA due to the demands of modesty.) This is because—although the majority of programming is produced in studios—a sizeable part of the schedule comes from the filming of community events in which Ahmadis are participants. MTA studios now exist across the world, including one in Qadian, and although this studio was small compared to studios in London and Pakistan, it was none-theless responsible for producing programs that could be broadcast across the world, as well as documentaries about major Jama'at events in India. Furthermore, the studio was increasingly involved in documenting every community event in Qadian, even those not destined for broadcast. As such, even though the studio employed only a few young men, the town's entire Muslim population shared the burden of producing programs, for it was their behavior that the cameras would capture and turn into representations of the truth of Ahmadiyyat. In this way, residents of Qadian can switch on the TV to find their behavior being presented to the whole world as a documented proof of Ahmadiyyat. They can thus become the truth to which both they and others must respond. In other words, they can witness their own idealized images as evidence of the truth of Ahmadiyyat.

In this chapter, I will first examine the aesthetic ideal through which Ahmadis attempt to display their Muslimness, both in everyday life in Qadian and when they find themselves under the gaze of the camera. I will then explore several examples—the most important one being an encounter between Ahmadis and protesting opponents in Delhi—to ask precisely what it is that Ahmadis see when they witness their own image in Jama'at-produced media. I then bring the discussion back to the question of doubt in Qadian. I ask what happens when Qadian's Ahmadis are presented to the world as "proof" of something even though they might feel their actions to be imitative of genuine exemplarity. What happens, in other words, when they are called on to witness truth in their own "counterfeit proof"?

A Universal Aesthetic

The particular aesthetic through which Ahmadis attempt to turn the surfaces of their lives into proof of an authentic Muslim identity is best introduced through an example of its policing within Qadian.

At the historic center of Qadian lies the *dar ul-masih* (abode of the messiah), a large walled complex built around the original family home of Mirza Ghulam Ahmad. In the last few decades, the dar ul-masih has been extensively restored and altered, to turn it into a center in waiting for global Ahmadiyyat. It contains the white minaret of Qadian and two historically significant mosques in which Ghulam Ahmad prayed and received revelation. One of these mosques has in the last decade been extended so that it can accommodate thousands of worshipers during such occasions as the Ahmadis' Annual Gathering (Jalsa Salana). The dar ul-masih also contains a tiny room, the *bait ul-du'a* (room of prayer), which Mirza Ghulam Ahmad constructed for private contemplation and supplication. It is in this private space that Ahmadis visiting from all over the world hope to be able to offer their prayers. The symbolic and historical importance of the dar ul-masih means that the Jama'at maintains strict security over who may enter the compound, for Ahmadis live with the ever-present fear that the dar ul-masih could become the target of a terror attack. Visitors therefore have to identify and register themselves, and the compound is closely guarded, both by young Ahmadi men and armed police. One afternoon in late March 2012, I was talking to these men by the gate of the dar ul-masih, when one of the Ahmadis on duty noticed that two individuals who looked typically Muslim—they wore tight white skullcaps and had long beards—had emerged from one of the mosques in the dar ul-masih. The Ahmadi guard, vigilant about the possibility of a security breach, walked over to another member of the Jama'at who seemed to be with the two outsiders and inquired firmly but respectfully as to their identity. The bearded men were, it turned out, Ahmadis. They were *maulims*—low-ranked clerics—from a rural part of India, and they were dressed as was normal for Muslims from their local area. The threat was shown to be illusory.

At one level, this example tells us much about the social distinctions within the Indian Jama'at. A semiurban aspirant middle class, which controls the administration of the Jama'at, is separated by a cultural gulf from more recently converted rural Ahmadi populations, who often come from more deprived socioeconomic backgrounds and lower castes.[5] These are people who, in the words of one Ahmadi, have converted without even knowing "who our prophet is."[6] There was, however, an additional layer to the guard's anxiety. The two visitors standing in the dar ul-masih were incongruous because they looked too obviously Muslim in the wrong way: they were not cultivating the aesthetic of the global Jama'at. This aesthetic involves a preference for particular kinds of hat—in particular the *qaraqul*, or Jinnah cap, which has distinct associations with elite Muslim identity—over the skullcaps often favored by Indian Muslims.[7] Ahmadi men mostly keep their beards short and neatly trimmed, and they are quick to mock Indian ulema who sport long beards or those who dye their beards orange with henna in supposed imitation of the Prophet. In Indian cities, most Ahmadi men favor a dress code of shirts and pants, in such a way that they are not immediately identifiable as Muslim. In Qadian itself, however, many Ahmadi men choose to wear a loose cotton *shalwar kameez* of a type more commonly seen in Pakistan, while Ahmadi women are never seen outside without a burqa. Certain Punjabi aesthetic signifiers are also highly valued. The caliph is always photographed wearing a white and gold turban, a practice shared by some very old members of the Jama'at and by Ahmadi missionaries on their graduation day.

Bodily aesthetics in Qadian are therefore best understood as a desire to avoid association with backward forms of Islam and to craft a unique aesthetic of the

FIGURE 3.   Students from Qadian's theological college walk into Qadian on the day of their graduation. They are sporting white and gold turbans similar to that always worn by the caliph.

caliphate. Qadian's Ahmadis reject aesthetic markers that they associate with what they see as the illiteracy, extremism, and mullahism of India's Muslims. Unsurprisingly, given their own pariah status, the Ahmadis have little sense of fellow feeling toward these Muslims. They argue that the relative poverty of Indian Muslims is due to this group's own failure to heed the Promised Messiah, and they ascribe political, economic, and ecological problems within the broader Muslim world to the same thing. At times, this results in political views that would make many other Muslims uncomfortable. During a discussion about global politics, for example, one Ahmadi man told me that God had deprived the Palestinians of their land because they were engaged in violence and did not follow the Qur'an. He thus argued that God gave the land to the Jews who were "less *polluted*" (he used the English word). At times, this antipathy to the Muslim mainstream leads Ahmadis to justify and even endorse Euro-American and Indian expressions of Islamophobia. They would often claim that non-Muslims were right to distrust Muslim populations, for these populations were hotbeds of terrorism. Perhaps predictably, white European converts to Ahmadiyyat were some of the most vociferous proponents of these arguments, feeling perhaps that their own newly found Muslim identity gave them a license to criticize the religion as a whole. For example, one European convert, when reflecting on popular fear of Muslims in Europe, told me, "Well, I can understand why they [other Europeans] feel that way, looking at other Muslims. I, too, feel that way."

Personal aesthetics are thus one aspect of a broader attempt by Ahmadis to differentiate themselves from what they see as a corrupt and failed Muslim civilization. Ahmadis, after all, see themselves as the only true followers of the Promised Messiah sent to reform Islam. In this sense, Ahmadis pride themselves on confounding misconceptions, on being unlike other Muslims—in short, on being exceptional. Occasionally, academics have highlighted this exceptionality to confound generalizations about Muslims. I think, for example, of a study of the Lahori Ahmadis in Nazi Germany, which argued that "their actions in saving the life of their formerly Jewish co-religionist call into question the claim that Muslims shared the Nazis' deep-rooted antisemitism."[8]

The aesthetic impulse of Ahmadi life is not so much about being modern as it is about being universal (*'alimgir*), an aspiration that is common among reform-minded Muslims.[9] This aesthetic involves an aspiration to escape a South Asian Islam that Ahmadis argue is dominated by ignorant mullahs and thus to achieve a global way of being. It is about creating an image that might be witnessed in any context by any person as a sign of truth. Nowhere is this clearer than in the construction of the caliph's image by MTA. On MTA, the caliph is seen to tirelessly repeat the same message of love, peace, and discipline over and over again. During one of the ethnographic examples that I describe later in this chapter, the live broadcast of one of the caliph's speeches was preceded by a short excerpt from a press conference in which the caliph took questions from journalists.[10] The clip of the press conference had been edited such that the questions asked by the journalists were erased: only the caliph's voice remained, his message universal in such a way that it was not tied to the questions of any specific person. In this way, the caliph's voice is understood to sonorously reach the corners of the earth, carrying a moral message of universal truth that goes beyond any local understanding.[11]

The desire to achieve a universal aesthetic means that the Jama'at must frequently leave aside its own historical specificities, local particularities, and theological nuances. Thus, Ahmadis rarely acknowledge the ways in which their institution of the caliphate is deeply embedded within a broader history of South Asian (and more specifically Punjabi) cultural practices. They will, therefore, admit of no comparison between their caliph and the Punjab's Sufi saints. In India, where speaking to a broad audience can involve switching from vernacular languages into English, translation is frequently the moment when aspects of Ahmadi thought that do not fit a sanitized image of universal love must be jettisoned. A similar process occurs in Euro-American contexts when the Ahmadis seek to present themselves as a universal solution to Islam (by definition, understood as a problem). When the Jama'at constructs its universal image of discipline, the message of Mirza Ghulam Ahmad is frequently rendered in a very singular fashion, as a rediscovery that the true nature of Islam is a plea for peace. Much of what makes Mirza Ghulam Ahmad a compelling historical character is erased: gone is his liberal use of metaphor, his willingness to use fiery language against his opponents, or, for example, his ability to antagonize Christian missionaries by teasingly suggesting that Jesus as depicted in the Bible was a drunkard.[12]

A result of this desire for a universal aesthetic is that the practices described in this chapter might seem quite different from and even irreconcilable with the vitriolic polemics that I described in the previous two chapters. Old sparring partners from Mirza Ghulam Ahmad's era—for example, Hindu reformists from the Arya Samaj—are now invited to attend and give speeches at the Ahmadis' Annual Gatherings in Qadian. On the surface, Ahmadi polemics and Ahmadi aesthetics therefore represent quite contradictory modes of being. Both, however, are attempts to produce the same outcome, which is a visible and demonstrable relationship of devotion to the caliph that might become an object of regard for the world. Moreover, the production of this universal aesthetic is as much a mode of sectarian disputation as the actual polemics in which Ahmadis engage, for in being exemplary, Ahmadis are creating a proof of Muslimness that might be explicitly compared to the image of other Muslims.

Exhibiting Discipline

To understand how the Ahmadis' cultivation of a universal aesthetic functions as an argumentative discourse, it is worth considering the example of an encounter between Ahmadis and hostile opponents in India.

In late September 2011, the Jama'at curated an exhibition about the Qur'an in New Delhi. It was a meticulously planned event held in the exclusive and expensive Constitution Club of India, which is frequented by numerous politicians and parliamentarians. Most of those involved in organizing the exhibition were from Qadian, and I traveled to Delhi by train with a large group of Ahmadi missionaries and students. In the twenty-four hours before the exhibition began, these men worked without pause to assemble a visually stunning display that was the result of months of planning by the Jama'at in Qadian and Delhi. High-quality glossy posters explaining various principles of the Qur'an were attached to display stands that lined the entire room, while specially made wooden display cases were erected in the center of the room, and within them, hidden LED lighting strips were used to illuminate copies of every single one of the Jama'at's many Qur'an translations.

FIGURE 4. Inside the Qur'an exhibition, an Ahmadi cameraman takes photos.

To the side, a television played a documentary the Jamaʿat had created for the event. Integral to this was an MTA camera crew, which documented both the event and its reception.

The exhibition was completely in English and sought to present Islam to a cosmopolitan, wealthy, and influential audience. It was an argument, sustained through the visual beauty of its material presentation, for Islam as the end point of modernity. For most Ahmadis, the idea that Islam is compatible with modernity is too simplistic. Rather, they see Ahmadiyyat as providing a way for modernity to culminate in Islam. In its physicality, its beauty, and its shining, glossy exteriority, the exhibition thrust itself on viewers as a testament to truth. Although most organizers of the exhibition had come from Qadian, little reference was made to the town. This was perhaps no accident, for Qadian as an ambivalent place of origin was insufficiently global to carry the message that the Ahmadis wished to convey through this exhibition.

In preparation for the exhibition, one hundred thousand text messages were sent out to Delhi residents inviting them to attend, and particular groups were also targeted with publicity. Among these were journalism students, who I was told would be "shaping the opinions of tomorrow." Such people, one Ahmadi in attendance argued, would almost certainly have "misconceptions" about the Qur'an; the idea was to convince them of its beauty and relevance. The exhibition did not explicitly reflect on the difference between Ahmadiyyat and other groups; rather, it aimed to present Islam as a solution to global problems.

Almost immediately, however, the Qur'an exhibition became the subject of a dispute between the Ahmadis and Delhi's substantial non-Ahmadi Muslim population. For the Ahmadis present, this marked the moment when the exhibition transformed into a battle between atavistic localism and Islam as a modern success story of global growth and encompassment.

The exhibition came to the attention of a broad Muslim public on Friday, September 23, when the *shahi* imam—often regarded as the de facto leader of Muslim opinion in Old Delhi—denounced it in his sermon. A group of Muslims soon gathered outside the Qur'an exhibition, waving placards and shouting slogans. The scene was tense but thus far nonviolent. The protesters claimed that in displaying the Qur'an, the Ahmadis were dishonestly representing themselves as the voice of Islam and thus misleading people into thinking that they were Muslims. This was, of course, a variation on the old prejudice that Ahmadis seek to deceive others into thinking that they are Muslims. It was a claim driven forward by the same logic that has led to Ahmadis being criminalized for "posing" as Muslims in Pakistan.[13] Not only was the Ahmadis' propriety in representing Islam questioned, but some protesters even doubted the appropriateness of displaying the Qur'an in any fashion, claiming, "The Holy Qur'an is not a thing to be exhibited." When I showed a video of this to several trainee missionaries that evening, they laughed openly at such an argument. "They are worried only because they will lose their income," one trainee contended, referring to the idea that once the Jama'at gains ascendency and removes all misconceptions, the mullahs will no longer be able to peddle fraudulent theology for money.

Soon, television camera crews arrived at the exhibition, and the various protesters, although still few, spoke over one another and clamored to speak in the microphones proffered in their direction. In response, the Ahmadis comported themselves quite differently. They stood back from the protest, either remaining inside the building or, when necessary, venturing out to form a perimeter. They did not speak to journalists, and despite the protesters' attempts to engage them, they held back from either name-calling or entering into debate. Moreover, they drew comparisons between their ordered behavior inside the exhibition and the protesting rabble outside. An important change had thus occurred, for the systematized behavior of the Ahmadis in attendance, rather than the exhibition, had become the primary object on display.

The protests slowly began to intensify while remaining nonviolent, and I moved to the opponents' side to take pictures and record what they were saying.

FIGURE 5.   Protesters line up outside the Qur'an exhibition, waving placards that read: "Stop meddling with Islam," "Ahmedias are not Muslims," "Don't deceit [sic] the innocents by using the name of Islam and the Qur'an," and "Freedoms of religion doesn't mean to deceit [sic] the nation." It is important to note that these placards together carry the message that Ahmadis dishonestly present themselves as Muslims in order to fool an unsuspecting outside world into accepting them as such.

As I was talking to one of the protesters, however, an older Ahmadi gentleman grabbed me by the arm and steered me inside.

"Come this way," he said.

"But I was talking to that man there!"

"I know. Come this way."

It was an order, not a request, for I had broken rank and upset the running of the system.

The personnel at the exhibition consisted of a number of Ahmadi clerics and nearly thirty final-year students from the theological college in Qadian, but as events unfolded, none of them moved forward to speak to the waiting journalists or engage with the protesters. The reason for this was simple: "We do not have permission." Only one group of Ahmadis did cross this line: the MTA cameramen, who silently documented the incoherence of the opposition while also training their cameras on the TV news crews who were in turn filming the crowd. It was a representation of a representation, a witnessing of the fact that this event was about to receive nationwide coverage.

It was only when an official spokesman from the Jama'at came forward to give a statement that the Ahmadis finally engaged the waiting news reporters. The spokesman delivered a speech in which he recited the *kalima* ("There is no god but God, and Muhammad is his messenger"), confirmed that the Ahmadis consider themselves Muslims, stressed their doctrine of peace, underlined that they are law-abiding citizens, and made the point that the exhibition was going ahead with permission from the authorities. His message was straightforward: we are doing this in a correct, orderly fashion, and our doing so has direction and coherence. As this statement was read out, a group of Ahmadis stood around their official spokesman. They spoke only to join in with his recitation of the kalima and to unite in intoning, "Sall Allahu 'alay-hi wa-sallam" (Peace be upon him) after the name of the Prophet Muhammad.

As the spokesman turned to go, however, there was a brief moment when the Ahmadi group and its opponents found themselves face-to-face. To my side, several protesters began talking among themselves about whether the Ahmadis believe in the nabi (the Prophet Muhammad). Like most Muslims, they evidently had little familiarity with Mirza Ghulam Ahmad's notion of prophethood, which rests on fine distinctions that might easily be lost in the middle of a heated protest. A young Ahmadi missionary in training, unable to resist, turned to them and said, "We do believe in the Prophet."

"And after him?"

"There is no prophet."[14]

Then another student interjected, "Muhammad is the last law-bearing prophet."

At this point, a senior missionary looked over with concern and, understanding that a discussion was about to flare up, began to usher the young students physically back in. "Don't debate! In accordance with our system!" he told them.

Then, turning to the protester, he said, "It's over, sir."

Once again, there was a worry that breaking ranks could lead to confrontation and violence. The many young Ahmadi students were particularly problematic, since their zeal was liable to become "hot." As one man explained: "If we engage, then things will get hot. Then we will fight." Juvenile fervor has historically resulted in confrontation between Ahmadis and non-Ahmadis, for example, in 1974, when clashes between youths led to Pakistan-wide riots and killings of Ahmadis. Reading the Ahmadi reaction as a mere fear of violence, however, misses how Ahmadis understood their studied nonengagement with the opponents to be a presentation of truth. The protesters, they told me, did not need to be argued with, because they were demonstrating their own falsity through their raucous and uncoordinated protest. By contrast, the Jamaʿat's superiority was seen as evidently knowable from this comparison. Display thus became part of a broader competitive polemics through which the Ahmadis engaged their opponents. This was a setting in which Ahmadis refused to be drawn into the kind of argumentative discourse that I described in chapters 3 and 4: instead, they sought an aesthetic triumph over their opponents.

The next day, Saturday, police with riot gear came to guard the exhibition. Fearing a major communal incident, they asked that all physical copies of the Qur'an be taken off the display stands in case one were to be knocked over and land on the floor, which could potentially spark a riot. Protesters were forced off the property on which the exhibition was being held, and although the exhibition was technically still open, it felt like it was under lockdown. That afternoon, the shahi imam himself arrived to inspect the exhibition. He swept into the exhibition hall, where he seemed particularly annoyed by the Ahmadis' Qur'an documentary playing on a TV and demanded that it be switched off. At this point, the protesters agreed that if the exhibition were closed, they would return home. The police appeared to view this as the easiest compromise, and the exhibition was shut down: it had not even lasted the weekend.

In spite of this premature closure, my interlocutors were universally happy with the outcome and convinced that the exhibition had been a success. Following the protests, a number of major Indian newspapers—including the *Times of India* and the *Hindu*—featured articles about the exhibition, and these were widely hailed as allowing the public to see for themselves the truth of the Jamaʿat.[15] "They have given us publicity worth 1 *lakh* [100,000 rupees]!" was how one Ahmadi summarized the occasion, thus highlighting the fact that the protesters had unwillingly aided the spread of the Ahmadis' message. In the days and weeks that followed, Ahmadis shared and looked back at images and recordings of the exhibition as proof of their triumph over their opponents. As one interlocutor explained to me when I returned to Qadian, "Now that you have seen the opposition, you can really begin to understand why we are true." They saw their own display of unity, cohesion, and discipline as signs of Ahmadiyyat's indubitable truth, and it was a sign that had been witnessed across India.

Doubting Exemplarity in Qadian

Back in Qadian, the Qur'an exhibition was quite clearly viewed as a splendid demonstration of Ahmadi Muslimness. Through their projection of a universal aesthetic of unity and discipline, the small group of Ahmadis who had traveled down from Qadian for the exhibition were understood to have proved an exemplary Muslimness in contradistinction to the disorder of their opponents. The opponents, as is so often the case, had drawn on a language of deceit and duplicity to accuse the Ahmadis of appropriating and imitating Islam. The Ahmadis felt themselves to have risen above such discourse to inscribe Muslimness in the world through an undeniable portrayal of the relationships that bound them to one another and to their caliph.

Demonstrations of exemplarity in Qadian are, however, rarely so unequivocal, as the following example can help to elucidate. During the final week of my fieldwork in Qadian, several Ahmadi missionaries asked me to prepare an educational speech for the young boys of their area, in which they wanted me to explain my academic work and to describe some of my findings. The speech was to be given in one of the smaller mosques of Qadian, in a northern neighborhood of the town. On the day of the event, just as we were preparing to begin the program, word arrived that the Jama'at authorities in the center of town had not granted permission for the event and that I would therefore not be able to speak. The organizers had initially secured permission at the neighborhood level to hold an educational gathering (*tarbiyyati ijlas*) in a mosque, but they had not specified that I, a foreigner, would be speaking. By this time, I had been resident in Qadian for almost a year and a half, and yet even so, permission for me to speak in public had to be sought directly from the chief secretary of the Jama'at in India. As a result, my presentation had to be canceled. The local boys had nonetheless already assembled in the mosque, and thus a missionary was summoned at short notice to give an edifying talk. He began by addressing the room about the failed program: "It is a shame we cannot hear Nick speak, but it is best this way." Why this should be so, he continued, was because "in this way, we are following the system, and the system is good." Having spoken for a little while, he then addressed me directly. I may have seen weaknesses and sins while I lived in Qadian, he said, but I should remember that the residents of Qadian are only humans; I cannot judge Ahmadiyyat by them. Instead, I must carry out my research on what the Promised Messiah wrote and according to what his caliphs have said.

The message given in this speech was complex, not least because it aimed to do two very different things: instruct a group of young boys in their moral duty to a system and warn an outsider about where to look for truth. As a result, this short speech also revealed in clear detail a perennial source of tension in Qadian. On the one hand, the missionary was helping the boys to understand that in obeying the system, they were being exemplary Ahmadis. The fact that permission had not been given meant that our plans had been disrupted and we had gathered together for nothing, but as the missionary pointed out, not doing what one wants in order to obey the system is a far more important act. This performative act of telling the boys to follow the system was therefore also aimed at me. The very fact that they were all obeying the system while listening in disciplined silence to a missionary exhort the virtues of the system was itself a perfect demonstration of their fidelity to the Jama'at. On the other hand, even as he and the boys put on this exemplary display of discipline, the missionary warned me not to look at the system in Qadian for signs of truth, for it was full of human failings. This was, in other words, a very clear example of what I have described in the previous chapters as a counterfeit proof. It was a demonstration of Muslimness that nonetheless carried the potential to undermine itself. As a proof, it was suspended between evidence and a simulacrum of evidence.

In many ways, counterfeit proof is an unavoidable fact of life in Qadian. As we have seen in the previous chapters, the town's separation from the caliphate means that all too often Qadian's Ahmadis' attempts to inscribe Muslimness in the world are underwritten with uncertainties about what it means to authentically do so. In Qadian, surfaces seem to be unavoidably problematic. In this way, the aspiration to cultivate an exemplary exterior in Qadian is very different from that described, for example, by Saba Mahmood in *Politics of Piety*. Mahmood challenges the conventional assumption that bodily surfaces are "superficial particularities through which more profound cultural meanings find expression."[16] She thus demonstrates that for her interlocutors—members of a women's mosque movement in Cairo—exterior self-representations need not just be the manifestation of interior dispositions but can be disciplinary practices through which a virtuous interior selfhood is achieved. For Mahmood's interlocutors, visible piety is thus both the expression of aspired-to norms and the medium through which such norms are cultivated. As in Mahmood's ethnography, it is undeniably the case that in Qadian, the practice of exterior piety is a means through which an inner pious subjecthood is cultivated. Yet an important distinction remains, which is that in Qadian surfaces are also explicitly evaluated for their ability to prove Ahmadiyya Muslimness. Qadian's Ahmadis are less concerned with the correspondence between inner piety and outward display as they are concerned with the merit of those displays in evidencing more abstract truths. In other words, the question is not so much how surfaces reflect or discipline the self but whether they are an effective fulfillment of one's obligations to truth.

The example of the Qur'an exhibition shows us how important it is that the Ahmadis are able to demonstrate the Muslimness of Ahmadiyyat through their actions in a way that is not duplicitous. What I aim to show in the rest of this chapter is that while fears of imitativeness may constitute the uncertainties that structure people's attempts to evidence truth in Qadian, the global media reach of the Jama'at—and in particular the television network MTA—can provide Ahmadis in Qadian with a sense of surety in their Muslimness that is otherwise hard to achieve. For Qadian's Ahmadis, the true blessing of MTA must be understood as its ability to transmute their counterfeit proof into a form of evidence that cannot be denied.

Witnessing Representational Ability

To understand how the Jama'at's global media reach is able to transform counterfeit proof in this way, it is worth returning to the story of the Qur'an exhibition. Several months after the exhibition, when the initial jubilation about its press coverage had died down, I visited the MTA studio in Qadian to find out what was happening to all the footage that they had recorded from the event. The studio workers, it turned out, were producing a documentary about the exhibition. Their plan, however, was to focus on the exhibition itself rather than the fracas that it caused, and thus they aimed to show the opposition in only a few still shots without sound. One reason they gave for this was their desire to avoid fanning the flames of dispute, and yet there was something more fundamental at stake, for they explained that the aim of the documentary was to focus on the success of the exhibition, the achievements of the Jama'at, and, most importantly, the ability of the Jama'at's voice (*awaz*) to reach the population of India.

As we chatted about this, something that I had previously overlooked became apparent in how Qadian's Ahmadis saw truth to emerge out of the events of the exhibition. The exhibition had generated multiple forms of media—newspaper articles, TV reports, self-made documentaries—about the Jama'at. Such materials were seen to make the truth of the Jama'at tangible and knowable, but this was not just because of their obvious value as depictions or records of disciplined behavior. Rather, as the MTA workers implied, these images were valued precisely for their ability to be disseminated. What mattered was not just that these images showed the Jama'at as it should be—it was that they were backed by institutional and organizational capacities to be replicated, reproduced, and broadcast across a vast area. MTA too produced a representational capacity that could itself become an object of contemplation. In a sense, what therefore mattered was the mechanical reproduction of an endlessly exemplary surface. As such, there was an ambiguity as to where, exactly, my interlocutors identified the proof of their Muslimness. At one level, the exemplary surfaces themselves functioned as proof. These were, after all, potent forms of communication that could have powerful effects on those who witnessed them. At another level, however, the proof of these images lay in their dispersal. In other words, the exemplary surface began to function as evidence precisely through its reproduction and through its being endlessly witnessed.

It is worth illustrating this with several more examples. Let us consider the Ahmadiyya Peace Symposia, a form of public outreach instituted in the twenty-first century by the fifth and current caliph, Mirza Masroor Ahmad.[17] These symposia are staged to promote interfaith dialogue and improve the image of Islam among non-Muslim populations. The original Peace Symposium was held in London, where it has now become an annual event. This London symposium now provides the occasion for another innovation of the present caliph: the presentation of the Ahmadiyya Muslim Peace Prize. The London symposium has been emulated elsewhere, and I attended Peace Symposia in both London and Delhi. In both locations, the symposia followed a common pattern. A platform was provided for a number of guest speakers—including other faith leaders and, ideally, politicians—to affirm the importance of religious understanding and harmony.[18] This celebration of harmony was made possible precisely by the deployment of terms that were effective because their content was neither questioned nor deconstructed.[19] Many of the Ahmadis I spoke to understood these Peace Symposia to have a great impact on the world, and in Qadian I was frequently asked whether I had attended the symposia in London. The Peace Symposia are, in other words, the paradigmatic institutions through which contemporary Ahmadis attempt to speak to a broad non-Muslim demographic and impress on that audience the fact that their version of Islam is a universal and peaceful solution to an otherwise broken faith.

It was only after attending several of these symposia that I began to realize that they had a greater meaning for Ahmadis than was contained within their stated goal of affirming the need for peace. This is best illustrated with an example from the Indian Peace Symposium in Delhi. Before any of the guest speakers took the stage, a video was played, showing scenes from the London symposium, in particular recordings of British Members of Parliament speaking positively about the Jama'at. The aim behind this video was clear: the audience at the symposium in Delhi was being given the opportunity to witness powerful politicians in another democracy witness the truth of the Jama'at. And in seeing this, what was required of the audience in Delhi was that they too recognize the truth that this pointed toward. As I watched this video, I became aware of the fact that the success of the event was achieved not just through the conversation about peace that it fostered but also through the way in which it highlighted the ability of the Jama'at to produce a message at a global scale and to have that message witnessed by powerful individuals.

Similar concerns underpin the Jama'at's reporting of the caliph's global tours. A much celebrated event that occurred shortly after I concluded my fieldwork in Qadian was an address given by the caliph on Capitol Hill in Washington, DC, on June 27, 2012. The *Review of Religions*, the official English-language mouth-piece of the Jama'at, described this occasion in extensive detail. In introducing this event, the *Review* referred to U.S. tours by previous caliphs, all of which, it pointed out, received "prominent" coverage in U.S. newspapers.[20] The speech on Capitol Hill, however, was of even greater importance, for the location of the speech was far more prestigious than that of any previous event. The *Review*'s cov-erage of the event stressed over and again the high profile of the people who at-tended, for example, the Speaker of the House of Representatives, Nancy Pelosi. It then detailed how the 140 attendees, including 30 members of Congress, had received the transcendental message of the caliph and that they "were overheard describing the address as 'profoundly deep,' 'thoughtful,' 'powerful,' 'earnest,' 'pure gospel' and 'a sorely needed message from a humble Muslim leader.'"[21] Powerful people, in other words, were shown to be receptive to the word of the caliph, and they were in attendance not to interact with him but to absorb what he chose to tell them. Throughout this narrative, what mattered was that the au-dience received the message of the caliph in an unproblematic fashion.[22] The au-dience were praised for attending the session even though they had affairs of state to see to, and the *Review*'s Ahmadi reporter noted with approval that some members of the audience even took notes as the caliph talked.

Several pages after these comments, the *Review* printed a photo in which the caliph was shown meeting dignitaries. In this photo, the caliph is shown sur-rounded by the monumental architecture and aesthetics of U.S. federal power, and around and behind him a crowd gathers.[23] The photo, however, appears an odd choice for publication in a magazine, for at first glance, its composition is messy. The caliph is just a tiny figure in the middle of the scene. On both left-hand and right-hand borders, the arms of members of the public holding cameras intrude into the photo. Indeed, this is not a picture of the caliph; this is a picture of the caliph having his picture taken from multiple angles by multiple individuals. This is not, in other words, a poorly taken photo but rather a deliberate attempt to create a record of other people spontaneously recording the caliph's visit. Immediately below the photo, the article states: "We witnessed foreign diplomats and leading luminaries assemble in line just to catch a glimpse of Khalifatul Masih V[(aba)] [the caliph]. We witnessed droves of American onlookers, young and old, overcome by the allure of Khalifatul Masih V[(aba)], flash photographs of him as he stood in the center of the U.S. Congressional visitor's center."[24] The same point is then echoed by another article in the *Review*, which describes how onlookers, who had no knowledge of the caliph's identity, were nonetheless so impressed by his "magnetic personality" that they were compelled to take pho-tos of him.[25] Moreover, the broadcast of this event meant that, "through the power of Muslim Television Ahmadiyya, now the entire world—and not just those present in the Rayburn Gold Room on June 27, 2012—witnessed this transformative event."[26]

An identical style of reporting was used to describe a similar address given by the caliph to the European Parliament. Writing in the *Review of Religions*, a senior cleric from the United Kingdom described how the caliph's speech "concluded to applause which transcended mere ceremonial clapping—the address had visibly impacted the listeners in a profound manner."[27] For yet another Ahmadi witness, the caliph's message was special because it transcended mere rhetoric by virtue of being substantiated by the "practical model established by the members of the Ahmadiyya Community worldwide."[28]

These short examples again underline the fact that for Ahmadis, proof of their Muslimness can be found in their organizational ability to communicate and broadcast proof. In the examples just quoted, Ahmadis were being encouraged to witness the fact that their caliph's message was being witnessed by the great and the powerful. The truth of the message was demonstrated by the fact that it could be broadcast and known throughout the world. Ahmadis and non-Ahmadis alike were being enjoined to witness the enormous technological, economic, and social capacity of the Jama'at to demonstrate truth. Emilio Spadola has written about how, for Muslim revivalists in Morocco, the calling of others to Islam (through *da'wa*) "explicitly foregrounds the *force* of communication, and in so doing defines Muslim subjects and societies as communications' material effects."[29] What we have to appreciate in the case of Qadian is quite how much my interlocutors value the *force* of their communications. After all, in a fashion similar to that described by Spadola, the communication is seen to place an obligation on members of a society to respond. It thus has a potent ability to reform that society and to render it a "material effect" of the Ahmadiyya message. Perhaps most importantly, however, this forcefulness of communication can enable Qadian's Ahmadis to feel certainty in their own responses to truth. To illustrate this, I turn to a grand public event in Qadian in which the whole town was called on to witness its own exemplary image on MTA.

Becoming One's Own Exemplar

For 'Eid al-Adha, 2011, celebrated on November 7, a large group of worshippers gathered in Qadian. The weather was mild, and so 'Eid prayers were held outside on Qadian's *jalsa gah*, a field to the south of the main town that once a year hosts the Jalsa Salana (Annual Gathering) and the rest of the year is used for playing cricket and football. Not everybody at the 'Eid prayers was a resident of Qadian or even a longtime Ahmadi. Some were only recent converts to Ahmadiyyat. Others were laborers who worked in Punjab but originally hailed from other states such as Uttar Pradesh or Bihar. Somewhat vindicating the Ahmadi claim that many common Muslims have no cause for disagreement with Ahmadiyyat, these laborers appeared to have no issue with the fact that their 'Eid prayer was being led by an Ahmadi imam, for in terms of the ritual observance in prayers, Ahmadi practice is largely indistinguishable from that of many other Sunni Muslims in the subcontinent. Before the commencement of the 'Eid prayers, a respected and senior Ahmadi cleric made a long announcement to the assembled crowd, describing exactly how they should conduct themselves during the prayers and explaining that the 'Eid prayer would be followed immediately by a sermon that was an integral part of the ritual. This particular prayer is said only once a year, and the cleric was thus anticipating that many of the outsiders in the congregation would not know what to do. The cleric also stressed the importance of listening to the caliph's live televised sermon, which would be broadcast later in the day due to the time difference between Qadian and London. Yet in spite of this admonition, after the 'Eid prayers were said, a very large portion of the congregation rose and started to leave the field. The man next to me looked on in disbelief and said, "You see, that is the problem with new converts. They do not know that the sermon is a part of prayers."

Nearly two months later, another huge gathering occurred on the same patch of open ground: the 2011 Jalsa Salana. These annual gatherings are celebrated by Qadian's residents for their intensely spiritual (*ruhani*) and affective qualities. This is partly because of a spatial reconfiguration of the town creating new intimacies among people who were previously strangers. For most of the year, private and public space in Qadian is structured by the distinction between discrete household units and public male space, but at jalsa time this distinction ceases to operate as the old family homes of Qadian are flooded with guests (sometimes as many as two dozen) from across the subcontinent. At this time the spatial fabric of the town is suddenly demarcated into gendered zones, with barriers in the road creating a partition between which men and women might walk. With the household no longer the site of intimacy during this short period, relationships between people of the same gender who were previously strangers can be intense and nonhierarchical to a degree never normally possible. Qadian thus takes on an alternative experiential dimension for those who attend the yearly jalsa. Yet the affective qualities of the jalsa are also created by the carefully managed displays of discipline, which are both produced and witnessed as testament to the truth by Ahmadis in attendance. It is not just the local Qadian leadership who encourage exemplary behavior; a general guide for worldwide jalsa etiquette lists how the correct ordered form of the event is to be achieved, including the instruction

to "try to portray the true and beautiful image of the Jamaat to outsiders, especially our neighbors."[30] One goal of the jalsas is therefore the creation of an exemplary image of harmony and coherence, the witnessing of which produces a
feeling of intense spirituality and intoxication both for those in attendance and
those watching the events on MTA. Where else in the world, several people asked
me, could you find such a large group of people behaving so peacefully? When
Ahmadis described the jalsa as spiritual, one of the major things they were describing was thus their continued systematic and disciplined behavior even as
normal social relations were being inverted.

In Qadian, however, where the population always fear that their relationship
to the caliph might be just a little too tenuous, such displays of discipline were
not always easily achieved. The 2011 Jalsa Salana provided an example of this. After
three days of talks, prayers, and addresses, the jalsa was set to end with a speech
by the caliph, broadcast live on MTA from London and addressed directly to the
gathering at Qadian. During this speech, live footage from Qadian was also to be
mixed into the video stream and shown across the world on MTA. Before this
session began, however, the chief secretary of the Indian Jama'at gave a final
roundup, during which he offered thanks to various government authorities that
had allowed the jalsa to take place and commented on the positive signs of spirituality he had seen during the jalsa. He then discussed the nature of the Jalsa Salana.
It was, he told us, a worldwide gathering, a global jalsa, because people across the
world were simultaneously watching and experiencing it via MTA. This event was
made global by its visual representation on screen. Because of this, however, the
chief secretary chose this moment to give a special warning to the crowd regarding the immanent live broadcast from Qadian. Do not react, he instructed the
crowd, when you see your face on the screen. And behave yourselves for the entire duration of the live recording. Crucially, nobody was to be seen leaving the
arena during the caliph's speech, for such an act of indiscipline would be seen on
MTA by people around the world.

At this point the chief secretary recounted an anecdote, a favorite of his that I
had heard at least once before. He recalled the events described immediately above,
when many new converts and non-Ahmadis came to Qadian for 'Eid but, because
their tarbiyyat (cultivation/upbringing) was weak, left before the sermon was finished. He then compared this to a Jama'at function he had attended in Kerala,
where the Ahmadis are often held up as being the most devoted and disciplined
in India. At the end of the function in Kerala, the chief secretary explained, he
had had to quickly rush out, and when he shortly returned to the function room,
he fully expected that everybody would be leaving. But instead, all the attendees
were sitting exactly where he had left them, waiting for him to give them permission to go. These were people, he explained to the jalsa audience, who truly un-

derstood the system, people who displayed the tarbiyyat (cultivation/upbringing) appropriate to a community led by a caliph.

In giving this speech, the chief secretary was thus instructing the entire gathering, comprising thousands of people, on how to be disciplined in front of a camera so that such discipline could be known across the globe. This was an image designed to have a profound impact on its audience, which would include those seated in Qadian, watching themselves watch the caliph. And yet, as the chief secretary's speech indicated, it was also quite clear that Qadian's proclivity for indiscipline had the potential to ruin this exemplary image. There was a real worry that Qadian would be unable to produce a public proof of its unity under the caliphate.

After the chief secretary's preparatory talk, the caliph's speech began, with cameras rolling in both India and the United Kingdom. That year, the Jama'at had decided not to pay the expensive fees for a live satellite broadcast from India. Instead, the Qadian video feed was streamed to the London studios via the internet and then mixed into the footage from the London mosque where the caliph was giving his speech. The combined footage was subsequently broadcast across the world live on MTA. The speech was addressed directly at those in the Qadian jalsa, who watched it on a giant screen at one edge of the field. The live footage from Qadian was not only mixed into the footage from London, however, for a TV screen in the mosque in London where the caliph was giving his speech also showed the internet stream from Qadian. As a result of this setup, a loop was created, albeit one with significant lag, in which the cameras in Qadian filmed the faithful watching themselves being filmed on the screen. An endless cycle of being seen and seeing was created, a mise en abyme in which they observed themselves observing. Cameras in Qadian took footage of Ahmadis watching the big screen there. This footage was then broadcast on a screen in the mosque in London. A camera picked this up as part of the broader image of the mosque in London, and thus the image of Qadian seeing and being seen was once more projected on the big screen in Qadian, only for the process to begin again. This was an occasion for the performance of the globality of the Jama'at, not just because it was an event shared between disparate locations but because the cycle of witnessing and presenting a self to be witnessed became linked across transnational boundaries. The global nature of the Jama'at ceased to be a discursive construct and was instead produced in a materially tangible fashion.

A custom in the jalsa is the shouting of n'are (call-and-response slogans). These usually begin with a loud cry of "N'are takbir!" to which the congregation respond, "Allahu akbar!" before getting more complex to include such n'are as Jalsa Salana Qadian! or even Insaniyat! (Humanity!) followed by a rousing Zindabad! (Long live!) This can occasionally get out of hand, as zealous Ahmadis jump up and shout

FIGURE 6. Ahmadis in the Jalsa Salana watch their caliph on a big screen.

out slogans at the slightest mention of the Jamaʿat's success. As a result, nʿare are nowadays, like every aspect of the jalsa, subject to official control. In the example at hand, the nʿare were a shared product of London and Qadian, originating in one place and being answered in another. In Qadian, the vast congregation thus both produced and witnessed an undeniable demonstration of their membership in a global community that was unified beneath the caliph.

The only problem was that in Qadian itself, this was a counterfeit proof. This performance was not simply a spontaneous display erupting out of loving devotion to the caliph. (That is not to imply that many of Qadian's Ahmadis did not feel loving devotion.) Rather, it was an enforced surface, for following the chief secretary's admonition, young men had begun to patrol the aisles of the jalsa gah, ordering congregation members to stay in their places and, on occasion, physically ensuring that this order was followed. There was to be no loitering in the aisles, and everybody was barred from leaving while the caliph gave his speech. This was an enforced surface, an imitation of the authentic display of unity that everybody in Qadian knew was the key to proving their connection to the caliph. To audiences outside of Qadian, the broadcast of the jalsa could be viewed as no more than a beautiful surface: an exemplary proof of Ahmadiyyat. For those within the town, however, the broadcast's disjuncture from Qadian as they knew it was potentially quite obvious.

I nonetheless want to argue that in this moment, Qadian's Ahmadis were able to achieve a certainty that overrode their normal uncertainties about inscribing truth. And, in a slightly paradoxical way, the disjuncture between the absolute proof of the broadcast and the ordinary anxieties of Qadian was in fact key to that certainty, for the disjuncture made apparent the whole set of relationships through which the Jama'at inscribed truth as success. For those inside the arena, it was what the camera captured only in passing that enabled them to see every-thing.[31] What my interlocutors saw in this moment was the power of their Jama'at to show themselves to themselves as disciplined bearers of proof. They saw that they belonged to a global movement that had the enormous representational ca-pacity to override their local struggles with truth and in doing so sustain a proof of them as perfect Muslims. These exemplary images thus did much more than represent something; through their disjunctures and fractures, they evoked the power of the Jama'at to have things seen. In this cycle of witnessing the self wit-ness, what became apparent was the capacity of the Jama'at *as an organization* to enable everybody to fulfill their obligations to witness truth. The global system of media capture and distribution thus allowed Qadian, as a place of ambiguous exemplarity, to become a shining beacon of the Jama'at's theological triumph over opponents. For a moment, Qadian's residents saw the proof of their Muslim iden-tity rendered static and certain in a way that was normally never the case.

Ahmadi uses of the camera bear similarities to cases encountered by ethnog-raphers of other religious movements. Simon Coleman, for example, describes a comparable process in which charismatic Christians taped their sermons.[32] In doing this, they created a situation in which the audience for self-presentation was not just the Other but also the self. Coleman describes how the camera, in capturing and commoditizing worship, enabled ordinary participants to be turned into "iconic objects of contemplation."[33] "Personal experience," he continues, "becomes collective representation, and, moreover, one that can be reconsumed by individuals as they buy and watch a service in which they have taken part."[34] The manner in which Coleman's interlocutors reconsumed their own image is nonetheless different from what I am describing here. In the case explored by Coleman, words and images were understood as Maussian gifts that expanded the charismatic agency of their creators.[35] In his account, words and images may have been externalized from persons, yet they were also understood to be inalien-able from their creators.[36] Coleman thus shows how the gifting of words could lead to an expansion of charismatic agency through an externalization of the self toward "an unbounded, potentially global, sphere of influence."[37] In contrast, I want to suggest, the alienability of exemplary representations in Qadian—the fact that a disjuncture could be recognized between the images and their creators—was key to their ability to stabilize truth and thus ultimately communicate meaning back to those who had created them. What mattered in Qadian was that the global Jama'at could take an image of my interlocutors, strip it of its imitative qualities, its uncertainties, and its inauthenticities, and then return it to them to be witnessed as a pure and indubitable statement of their Muslimness.

In this way, my interlocutors could be certain—if only for a moment—of their ability to respond to the enormous obligations of truth. Moreover, they knew that the reason they could do so was because they belonged to the one global community capable of enforcing this truth upon them.

Representational Capacity

My argument is that in Qadian, witnessing the representational capacity of the Jama'at offers a way to find certainty beyond the doubts and anxieties that a person might feel regarding their attempts to demonstrate truth. Indeed, it would appear that this is a move that can be traced back to the theology of Mirza Ghulam Ahmad. A good example of this concerns the white minaret of Qadian. Clad in marble and soaring above every other building in the vicinity, Qadian's minaret is the indisputable landmark of the town. Its image is also used as an important symbol in the global Jama'at, appearing on the Ahmadiyya flag and in numerous publications. The use of a simplified image of the minaret is particularly associated with the media broadcast of Mirza Ghulam Ahmad's message. For example, the silhouette of the minaret appears as the T in the MTA logo, and it is occasionally depicted like a radio mast, with concentric waves emitting from its tip. For Ahmadis, this tower is an important symbol of Ghulam Ahmad's prophethood, for it corresponds to a hadith of the Prophet Muhammad that the messiah will descend near a white minaret in the eastern part of Damascus. While Qadian is obviously far from Syria, Ahmadis nonetheless argue that the hadith is true because Qadian lies directly to the east of Damascus. It is, in other words, a sign of the coming of the messiah, hence its formal name, *minarat ul-masih*, the minaret of the messiah.

As a physical proof of prophecy, however, the minaret is quite an ambiguous object. A fact seldom acknowledged in Qadian was that the minaret did not exist at the time of Mirza Ghulam Ahmad's birth. Rather, it was commissioned during his lifetime, finished many years after his death, and clad in white marble only decades after this.[38] The minaret might thus appear to be a failed prophecy, built after the event that it was supposed to be a feature of and then completed late. Indeed, several interlocutors even acknowledged to me that they found this theo-

FIGURE 7. The white minaret, a landmark in Qadian, and the symbol of the international Jamaʻat.

logically problematic. In other words, for quite a few Ahmadis today, the white minaret is something of a counterfeit proof, for it demonstrates Mirza Ghulam Ahmad's prophethood but does so in a way that introduces ambiguity.

The official Jamaʻat position on the minaret, however, is that its meaning in the hadith is metaphorical. That the Promised Messiah did not descend next to an already existing minaret in a literal fashion is, they argue, of no consequence. Mirza Ghulam Ahmad—in his own 1900 explanation for why he did not descend next to an already existing minaret—reframed the minaret as a metaphor for the lofty dissemination of his message, much as light might spread from a high place. For Ahmad, this was a matter of technological advancements that would allow his message to travel in the world. He thus informed his readership that "the railways, telegraph, steamships, excellent postal services, easy modes of travel and tourism and other such means have been established to fulfill the prophecy that the message of the Messiah will illuminate every corner like lightning."[39] Mirza Ghulam Ahmad thus rejected a literal reading of the hadith in favor of a metaphorical interpretation that focused on expansion through technologies of communication and contact. In other words, Ghulam Ahmad resolved the ambiguity created by the fact that he built the minaret he was prophesied to descend next to by turning it into a metaphor for the *representational capacity* that his message would gain through the use of new technology. He then went ahead and built it anyway.

In this way the minaret now stands as testament to the ability of the Jamaʻat to literally and materially fulfill prophecy, that is, to create the evidence for divine truths. As such, we might consider the minaret to be a symbol of the Jamaʻat's ability to overcome ambiguity through sacrifice, perseverance, and industry. This is an erasure of uncertainty through worldly expansion. The minaret no longer symbolizes only prophecy but also the enormous representation capacity of the Jamaʻat to evidence its own truth.

In a similar way, Qadian's Ahmadis could look at idealized images of themselves on MTA and see the worldly, material success of their Jamaʻat substantiated as a capacity (economic and technical) to momentarily make the surfaces of their lives into unambiguous proofs of Muslimness. They thus understood that they belonged to a transnational organization that enabled them to fulfill their obligation to both produce and bear witness to the successes and triumphs of Islam—even if it was only for the duration of the broadcast.

In a very different context, Lisa Wedeen has described how a politics of "as if" sustained power in Hafez al-Assad's Syria.[40] This was a personality cult in which public dissimulation underlined the power of the regime precisely because it made everyone aware that this regime could compel anybody to say things that nobody believed.[41] In the same way, the public performance I described in the previous section was powerful precisely because it was an enforced performance of Muslimness that made everybody aware of the authority of the Jamaʻat. The tension behind the images made the relations of power that had produced them ever more apparent and obvious. That these exemplary images were unlike the counterfeit proofs of everyday life in Qadian made the truth that they produced more potent. They were difficult to produce, and as we saw in the ethnographic examples, they required economic resources, organizational capacity, and technological expertise, all of which, when multiplied on a global scale, were understood to manifest the Jamaʻat's worldly success. In the example of the Qadian Jalsa Salana, the congregation were consuming an image of the Jamaʻat's vast organizational capacity to sustain their identity as Muslims who could both demonstrate and witness the truth without complication.

In academic accounts of the Jamaʻat, there have been few mentions of the importance that Ahmadis attach to the aesthetics of Muslimness. Partly, this is because of the emphasis of much previous research on Mirza Ghulam Ahmad's inheritance of esoteric ideas from Sufism.[42] The Ahmadiyya Jama'at can also appear to be austere and even antiaesthetic in its institutional outlook. For example, when I interviewed an architect responsible for many of the Jama'at's new mosques, he told me that his religious duty was to create buildings that were functional and lawful—preferably domestic in inspiration—rather than imposing or strikingly beautiful. Likewise, Qadian's Ahmadis are unusual among their Punjabi neighbors for holding weddings that seem to lack all qualities of ostentatious display. As I have shown in this chapter, however, Ahmadis are intensely concerned with the surfaces of life, and their decisions to keep mosques unadorned and weddings simple are two small examples of how they hope to cultivate an exemplary and universal aesthetic of the caliphate.

As the example of the Qur'an exhibition showed, everything is at stake in the Ahmadis' public demonstration of Muslimness, for they are faced by opponents who claim to be able to see within them duplicity and deception. Anthropologists have long recognized that there are ethical and analytical challenges posed by the study of the self-representations of persecuted minority groups such as the Ahmadiyya community. This difficulty lies in understanding what Andrew Shryock describes as the "off stage": the hidden spaces of the group where "the explicitly public is made, even staged, before it is shown."[43] Writing about Arab Americans—another group that faces intense pressure to represent itself in a particular public fashion—Shryock demonstrates how ethnography can capture intimacies behind the making of official discourses in a way that is embarrassing for his interlocutors. Indeed, to even acknowledge the possibility of artifice in minority groups' self-representations can dangerously destabilize their ability to make political claims.[44] In some ways, the situation in Qadian might be seen to echo such difficulties: to speak of the construction of exemplary Muslimness in the town might be seen to damage the authenticity of that identity. Indeed, anthropological theory—particularly that drawing on ideas of cultural intimacy—has tended to view tensions between the public self-representations of communities and the private worlds they inhabit as productive of both self-awareness and political vulnerability.[45] The case of the Ahmadis nonetheless demonstrates how disjunctures between official self-presentations and messy private lives might in fact be highly productive of certainty. For my interlocutors, the fact that their communal self-representations are in some sense "unreal" does not lead to an embarrassing admission of inauthenticity but rather points to a far more beautiful truth: that they belong to a system that has the authority to stamp the evidence of truth upon them.

The important point to be made is that Qadian's Ahmadis do not see Muslimness as something that they can achieve alone: in Qadian, the ethical project of being a Muslim must necessarily be undertaken within the relations that compromise the system. Efforts to cultivate an exemplary aesthetic while separated from the system lead to that aesthetic being a poor counterfeit of an authentic proof of Muslimness. Thus, if we want to understand why the "artificiality" of community self-representations can be a source of hope and possibility for Ahmadis (rather than solely being a source of embarrassment or shame), we have to shift our focus away from the acting self toward an idea of the self being acted on. This is a turn of phrase that I take directly from Amira Mittermaier, who explores the importance of dream-visions to the ethical lives of Muslims in Egypt.[46] As I have sought to do here, Mittermaier emphasizes the importance of witnessing in Islamic ethics, arguing that for her interlocutors, seeing and witnessing imply "overcoming the self."[47] She further contends that, as anthropologists, we should become attuned to how, for many Muslim subjects, "being acted upon . . . does not *erase* the subject." Instead, it "*constitutes* her or him as a moral being and witness."[48] In Mittermaier's own fieldwork, this can be observed in the fact that while her interlocutors might engage in practices to invite dreams, they are ultimately acted upon by dreams in ways that they cannot control. After all, one cannot decide to dream. Mittermaier thus describes a religious subjectivity characterized by an openness to being acted on: this is a mode of being that, she argues, exceeds tropes of self-cultivation.[49]

In much the same way, there are limits in Qadian to what might be achieved by the subject acting alone. People cultivate their ability to evidence exemplary Muslimness, and yet even so, the veracity of their demonstrations always remains an open question. What the example of the Jalsa Salana showed was that for these Ahmadis, the attainment of an unproblematic display of Muslimness meant an openness to being acting on: an openness to allowing the global system to impress an indubitable Muslimness on them, even if it could only do so for the few moments of the transnational broadcast. The Jalsa Salana broadcast gave Ahmadis in Qadian a chance to witness the fact that even if they were never able to demonstrate their Muslimness with absolute certainty by themselves, they existed on the periphery of a global system that held open the promise to one day make them Muslim in a way that could not be denied. The broadcast did not solve their problems with counterfeit proof, but it did provide them with vision of what an uncomplicated relationship to truth might look like.

Conclusion

THE PROBLEM WITH PROOF

On March 24, 2016, a day before Good Friday, a Muslim shopkeeper in Glasgow was stabbed to death. While initial rumors indicated that the killing was an act of white supremacy, the Scottish police were quick to correct misunderstandings by issuing a statement that this was a "religiously prejudiced" crime.[1] The shopkeeper, Asad Shah, had been an Ahmadi, and his killer was a fellow Muslim.

The murderer, Tanveer Ahmed, had driven to Glasgow from the Yorkshire town of Bradford on the day of the attack, with the intention of confronting Shah. CCTV footage showed the two engaging in an intense discussion, before the killer produced a knife and repeatedly stabbed Shah before chasing him out of the shop, stamping on his head, and finally killing him in the street.[2] Tanveer Ahmed then sat down at a nearby bus stop and waited for the police so that he could claim responsibility for the murder. We can only assume that Tanveer Ahmed had always hoped for a public trial in which he would plead guilty under worldly law but innocent before God.

Almost as soon as details about the murder emerged, media reports began to indicate that Shah had been killed because he was an Ahmadi. Newspapers published features about the Ahmadiyya Muslim Community, explaining their doctrine and outlining the daily slights and insults that Ahmadis in the United Kingdom face from other Muslims of predominantly South Asian descent.[3] Many reports attempted to explain to their British readership how a seemingly arcane schism between South Asian sects continued to incite hatred between Muslims living in the United Kingdom: one national newspaper described this sectarianism as having "been bubbling under the surface for centuries."[4] Indeed, throughout

169

Tanveer Ahmed's trial, conviction, and jailing, UK newspapers covered the story as primarily a matter of anti-Ahmadi hatred.[5] This was a story of imported sectarianism, which nonetheless made perfect narrative sense in a British city known for its own history of sectarian rivalry.[6]

Exactly one week after the murder, the caliph concluded his weekly sermon on MTA—addressed to the global Jama'at—with a mention of Shah's death.[7] In no uncertain terms, the caliph declared that Shah's death was a martyr's death. Yet this statement also carried a hint of ambiguity: the caliph acknowledged that Shah had sometimes suffered from psychological problems (*nafsiati bimari*) and that some people had had the mistaken impression that Shah had left the Jama'at. This, the caliph stated, was categorically untrue. Shah was a martyr, he had been a regular participant in Jama'at activities, and the head (*amir*) of the local community had confirmed that Shah's connection to the caliphate was strong. The caliph's sermon thus set a precedent for Ahmadis to see Shah's death as an unequivocal case of martyrdom: the first death in the United Kingdom to conclusively prove the truth of Ahmadiyyat. For my interlocutors, opposition is a visible, demonstrable, and material proof of Ahmadiyyat, and there can be no greater proof of divine favor than a martyr's death. As I wrote in the introduction to this book, an interlocutor in Qadian once told me, "Inshallah, there will be opposition [in Europe]." With the death of Shah, this opposition appeared to have arrived. Yet it was clear that the caliph's statement had been an attempt to fix a narrative and to establish the undisputable nature of Shah's martyrdom against a complex backdrop.

Quite why the caliph felt it necessary to do this became obvious during the trial, when a rather more multifaceted story emerged in which Shah's membership in the Ahmadiyya Muslim Community was only one of the motivating factors in his death. Shah had been a prolific user of the video-sharing website YouTube, and in a number of videos uploaded to the site, he had proclaimed himself to be a prophet.[8] At the time of my writing this, Shah's YouTube channel is still online, and its videos—mostly shot while he was at work in his shop—paint a picture of a gentle yet naïve character, with a professed love for humankind.[9] Shah's claim to be a prophet, however, appears to have so incensed Tanveer Ahmed that it drove him to murder. In a statement released through his lawyer, Tanveer Ahmed stated that he killed Shah "for one reason. . . . Asad Shah disrespected the messenger of Islam the Prophet Muhammad peace be upon him. Mr Shah claimed to be a Prophet."[10]

By killing a man who had declared himself to be a prophet via YouTube, Tanveer Ahmed felt that he was defending the Prophet Muhammad. In doing this, Ahmed placed himself in a line of men who have committed similar acts and are today revered by some in Pakistan. The first figure that he consciously modeled himself on was Ilm ud-Din, who is considered a national hero and holy warrior (*ghazi*) by many in Pakistan, for in 1929, Ilm ud-Din was hanged by the British for killing the Hindu publisher of a book, *Rangila Rasul*, which had attacked the Prophet and incensed Muslim opinion.[11] The other figure on which Ahmed consciously modeled himself was Mumtaz Qadri, a police bodyguard who killed the Pakistani governor of Punjab, Salman Taseer, in 2011.[12] Ahmed is not alone in his idolization of Qadri; there was huge popular support for Qadri in Pakistan.[13] Qadri claimed to have killed Taseer because the governor had publicly campaigned against Pakistan's blasphemy laws (the same laws that are used to persecute the Ahmadis), which many in Pakistan see as protecting their Prophet from attack. Like Qadri, Tanveer Ahmed was a member of the group Dawat-e-Islami, and again, like Qadri, Ahmed committed murder and then surrendered to the security services.[14]

Tanveer Ahmed's actions were thus embedded within a very specific history of policing Islam by violently defending the integrity of the Prophet.[15] Coordinated anti-Ahmadi actions are often expressed in terms of this defense of the Prophet, for Ahmadi acceptance of Mirza Ghulam Ahmad is understood by opponents to be an insult to Muhammad. Asad Shah's murder was nonetheless about more than just his membership in the Jama'at, for he had made an announcement of personal prophethood. In this way Asad Shah's murder points toward one of the central vulnerabilities within the official theology of the Jama'at.

As we have seen, Mirza Ghulam Ahmad's justification of his own prophethood required him to conceptualize prophecy as a continuous state of possibility.[16] For the vast majority of Muslims, the fact that Muhammad is described in the Qur'an as the seal of the prophets means that he is the final prophet in both a spiritual and temporal sense. For Ghulam Ahmad and his followers, however, it means that Muhammad is the highest of all prophets, the final prophet to deliver a new set of divine laws to earth, and the gateway through which future, lesser forms of prophecy might be achieved. Ghulam Ahmad thus argued that his own prophethood was a result of his devotion and faultless love of Muhammad. While this theological argument enabled Ghulam Ahmad to declare himself a prophet, it introduced a vulnerability to Ahmadi claims, for once the door to prophethood has been opened in this way, it must forever be left ajar. Ahmadis cannot, in other words, deny the theoretical possibility of yet more prophets coming after Ghulam Ahmad. As a result, officially unrecognized claims to divine revelation have periodically erupted within the Jama'at. A number of splinter groups have emerged that claim to resurrect the original message of the Promised Messiah and thus challenge the authority of the caliph. Prominent among these are Abdul Ghaffar Janbah's Germany-based Jama'at Ahmadiyya Islah Pasand, a group that calls itself the "Green Ahmadiyyat," and the Jama'at ul Sahih al-Islam of Mauritius led by the caliph Munir Ahmad Azim. The last of these groups has even issued mubahalas as a way of challenging the main Jama'at-e-Ahmadiyya.[17] What these claimants overwhelmingly share is a desire to reaffirm Ghulam Ahmad's prophet-hood while challenging the legitimacy of the caliph. Their ability to gain followers rests on the fact that there do exist disaffected Ahmadis who want to get rid of what they see as a corrupt hierarchy and instead return to a pure relationship only with God. Such a view, of course, is highly corrosive to the kinds of ethical activity that I have described in this book. I have shown that, since the reign of the second caliph in the early twentieth century, the public demonstration of the caliphate has come to dominate the Ahmadis' attempts to prove their Muslim identity on a world stage. Given the innate vulnerability of the caliphate in the light of the Ahmadis' own prophetology, the Ahmadis, much like their opponents, must therefore rigorously police the boundary of the finality of prophethood. Asad Shah's martyrdom proved no exception to this.

Newspaper reports in the months after Shah's death bear clear traces of the way in which the British Ahmadiyya Jama'at's open and professional engagement with journalists helped shape a narrative. In newspapers, throughout the trial the complexities of the case were smoothed over, giving way to a simple story of anti-Ahmadi sentiment among the United Kingdom's Muslim population: the story of a community under siege.[18] The Ahmadiyya Muslim Community in the United Kingdom had evidently seized on this moment as a way of highlighting their global persecution and of promoting their goals of interfaith anti-extremism. A few weeks after Shah's death, the Jama'at paid for the logo "United Against Ex-tremism" to be placed on the sides of buses in the Scottish cities of Glasgow, Ed-inburgh, and Dundee. A number of faith communities were invited to the launch of this initiative, but while Christian, Sikh, and Jewish groups attended, other Mus-lim groups failed to make an appearance. This apparent rejection of the Ahma-dis' interfaith activities was reported in such a way that the Ahmadis emerged as progressive and their opponents as stuck in a sectarian past.[19]

The community politics behind these efforts to establish a narrative were for the most part hidden from public view, but they were described in quite vivid terms at the end of an article in *The Guardian* newspaper. Shah's family were said to have been unhappy about the Ahmadiyya Muslim Community's "use of the murder to highlight the broader conflicts with orthodox Muslim thinking," and an unnamed source claimed that the murder had become a "political football."[20] A terse statement issued through the Shah family lawyer simply stated that others had no permission to speak on behalf of the victim.

That Asad Shah was a member of the Jama'at was inseparable from his murder. To say that he was killed for being an Ahmadi, however, is to simplify. Tanveer Ahmed was, it seems, motivated by a particular historical sense of defending the

Prophet's honor, and Shah's supposed transgression in this regard equally threatened the Ahmadiyya Jama'at's own theological and conceptual boundaries. Asad Shah was the first Ahmadi martyr on British soil; his was a sacrifice that should have unambiguously demonstrated the truth of Ahmadiyyat. And yet this was not the case, for there was an ambiguity in Shah's death that Ahmadis had to work against if they wanted to see truth in his sacrifice. Shah's death both helped to define a visible Ahmadi public united under a caliph, while simultaneously constituting a challenge to the caliphate. Asad Shah's rambling but ultimately benevolent YouTube videos had, quite unwittingly, exposed a theological weak point of the Jama'at: its inability to restrict prophethood to the caliphate.

For the Jama'at, Asad Shah represented a problematic proof. At one level he was no more than an imitation of an Ahmadi prophet: a copy of what other Muslims already considered to be a counterfeit. And yet his death produced a representational opportunity for the Jama'at to spread its message through national and international media. This meant that he was upheld as a martyr whose sacrifice proved Ahmadiyyat, even if his life had undermined the truth that his death had created.

Toward an Anthropology of Doubt

I began this conclusion with the story of Asad Shah's murder because it provides a vivid image of the kinds of anxiety and uncertainty that I encountered in Qadian. Moreover, it demonstrates the need for a richer anthropological approach to the religious anxieties that my interlocutors both hold and are held by.[21]

In many ways, there has never been a better time to question how we understand religious doubt. Across the discipline, anthropologists have begun to reassess both uncertainty and doubt, to think of them not just as negative states but as the productive conditions for the emergence of new social forms and even certainties. If previously, anthropologists were concerned to document the processes through which specific kinds of local certainty were produced, the discipline is now increasingly turning to consider how, in the words of François Berthomé, Julien Bonhomme, and Grégory Delaplace, "uncertainty is not always reducible to accidental misunderstandings, but can also be a constitutive or 'built-in' element of various social settings."[22] Indeed, as a social resource that can be productive of relationships, uncertainty may even be cultivated.[23] Such ideas echo the concerns of anthropologists—such as Limor Samimian-Darash, Paul Rabinow, and Frédéric Keck—who are interested in how new forms of governmentality are emerging around the management of uncertainty as an object that cannot be calculated but must necessarily be anticipated.[24]

This disciplinary interest in uncertainty is helping to align anthropological theory with something that has long been a staple of Western philosophy and theology: the idea that uncertainty is a necessary precondition to knowledge.[25] For example, in a monograph exploring the fragility of conviction in post-Soviet Kyrgyzstan, Mathijs Pelkmans draws on a metaphor of "pulsation" to show that "conviction thrives in contexts of instability" and that "the potency of ideology is rooted in its fragility."[26] Certitude, Pelkmans argues, is often reliant on its opposite. Other anthropologists have made similar arguments for the co-constitution of doubt and belief in religion, for example, an article by Hatsuki Aishima and Armando Salvatore on Islam, or Matthew Engelke and Anna Strhan on Christianity.[27] Several anthropologists have even begun to think about the ways in which doubt might be essential to the production of anthropological knowledge. Thus, Rane Willerslev and Christian Suhr call for a Kierkegaardian anthropology that involves the methodological "letting go" of the tension between certainty and doubt. Doing so, they argue, will enable our discipline to be pushed forward by moments of "existential anxiety" that "produce the form of doubt that is essential if one is to open oneself to new knowledge."[28]

This general anthropological turn to uncertainty has in large part been a reaction against earlier anthropological work that privileged the explicit and unequivocal statements made by informants at the expense of their harder-to-assess expressions of doubt or uncertainty.[29] The result of this methodological focus on statements made with certainty was that for much of our discipline's history, ethnographers produced coherent and neat accounts of social worlds that many nowadays find to be simply unreal. As a result, many anthropologists have quite rightly begun to focus more explicitly on the ambiguous and inchoate aspects of people's social lives. Nowhere is this trend toward including uncertainty in our ethnographic accounts more obvious than in the anthropological study of Islam. Indeed, there has been a huge explosion in anthropological attempts to understand the fractured and uncertain ways in which many Muslims experience religious faith, the ways in which they negotiate multiple competing claims to religious authority, and the confusions that they might feel regarding their religious identities. A good introduction to this literature (which also places it in comparative perspective with ethnographies of Christianity) can be found in David Kloos and Daan Beeker's volume *Straying from the Straight Path*, while other contributions have been made by Benjamin Soares and Filippo Osella, and Lara Deeb and Mona Harb.[30] A particularly influential example of this literature was Samuli Schielke's much referenced critique of Saba Mahmood's approach to the study of an Islamic piety movement.[31] With its taut analysis of Egyptian women's efforts to live beneath a totalizing ethics of self-subordination, Mahmood's pioneering ethnography *Politics of Piety* inspired much anthropological debate about the nature and limits of freedom within ethical self-cultivation.[32] Nonetheless, while *Politics of Piety* can be credited with invigorating anthropological interest in the study of revivalist movements in Islam, it emphasized a particular mode of Islamic self-cultivation in a way that appeared essentializing and overdeterministic to many other scholars of Islam.[33] Schielke essentially solidified this critique by arguing that the pious self-cultivation described by Mahmood is best understood as a not always achievable ideal rather than as a lived ethnographic fact. Based on his own research with young men who fall in and out of the disciplinary projects of reformist Islam, he argued that ethnographers should pay attention to the ambivalences people feel toward religious discipline and to the fact that more often than not such discipline leads to the fragmentation of people's biographies. Schielke's ethnographically rich argument has been influential within the broader discipline, but it nonetheless contains a problematic slippage: Schielke did not just demonstrate a difference between his field site and that of Mahmood but rather used his own ethnographic data to suggest that the situation described by Mahmood was humanly impossible.

Schielke's critique is only one part of a much broader move within anthropology to document the uncertainties that characterize life for many Muslims in the modern world. An important early example of this trend was Magnus Marsden's lyrical celebration of the vibrancy and autonomy of his Muslim interlocutors' intellectual lives in Pakistan's northwest frontier.[34] In a more recent edited volume, Marsden and cowriter Konstantinos Retsikas have used the idea of "articulation" to see Islam as a "dynamic interface between different dimensions of everyday life, rather than the stable essence against which these are to be compared."[35] Such an approach, they argue, allows us to understand how moral subjects are produced through an engagement with a changing and volatile everyday.[36] Lara Deeb and Mona Harb's *Leisurely Islam* has explored the manner in which Muslims in Beirut do not accept legitimacy unquestioningly but rather negotiate questions of legitimacy and appropriateness through everyday forms of activity, practice, and consumption.[37] They describe a situation in which everybody appreciates that appropriate behavior is crucial to living a good Muslim life, but nobody can agree precisely on what constitutes that behavior. Similarly, Marloes Janson's *Islam, Youth and Modernity in the Gambia* explores how Muslims in West Africa negotiate and debate multiple competing claims to religious authority.[38]

While the above examples are mainly concerned with the question of how people negotiate competing claims to religious authority, a number of ethnographers have also explored how people must balance the demands of religion with effective action in the modern world. A good example is Sarah Tobin's *Everyday Piety*, which examines the anxieties of those who worry about whether they are ever Muslim enough and whose efforts to demonstrate that they practice a real

Islam involve reconciling their piety with matters of money and finance.[39] The result is what Tobin describes as "neoliberal piety," a condition in which people feel "a sense of shortcoming and a desire for more," resulting in a "relentless striving" for both profit and blessings.[40] What is abundantly clear is that for many Muslims in the world today, the complexities of life are in tension with pious ideals that may themselves be indistinct. People must face these challenges, and in doing so, they often come up with creative solutions to the uncertainties of life.[41]

This entire body of literature constitutes a long overdue correction to the anthropological tendency to think of our interlocutors, unlike ourselves, as inhabiting worlds of certainty.[42] It has enabled us to move beyond a crude conceptualization of Islam as an unchanging aspect of people's lives and to resist Orientalizing narratives of fanatical Muslims. Most importantly, it has shown how many Muslims must constantly negotiate questions of legitimacy in religion, both as they navigate the ambiguities of competing claims to authority and as they try to reconcile religious ideals to the complexities of life. The anthropological turn to uncertainty has, in other words, enabled ethnographers to produce ever more detailed, sensitive, and sympathetic descriptions of the lives of the vast majority of Muslims in the world.

The only downside to this trend is that it has resulted in the implicit and widespread acceptance of a set of normative assumptions that make ethnographic descriptions of such communities as the Ahmadiyya Jama'at difficult. This point can be articulated most clearly by reference to a critique by Nadia Fadil and Mayanthi Fernando, who characterize much of the literature just described as constituting a turn to the study of "everyday Islam."[43] They argue that this turn to the everyday emerged partly as a reaction to the reductionist and religion-focused accounts of scholars studying piety movements in Islam.[44] It was, they argue, an attempt to account for the complexities of people's quotidian experiences of being Muslim. The problem that Fadil and Fernando isolate is that these calls to investigate the "ordinary" in Islam have had the effect of equating everyday failure and ambiguity with the reality of human nature and have by extension marked certain forms of pious and disciplined behavior as somehow unreal.[45] In fact, Fadil and Fernando argue that such is the ethical weight placed on the everyday that it has ended up "less as an empirical site of observation than a normative frame that enables the restoration of a conceptualization of agency primarily understood as creative resistance to (religious) norms."[46] The result of this is that accounts of Muslims who do not conform to this humanist vision of ambiguity and failure are routinely discounted. Instead, only those subjects who already resemble the anthropologist are seen as legitimate objects of study, and the disciplined, pious Muslims who seek to subordinate themselves to authority ironically end up banished "from the realm of the human."[47]

For Fadil and Fernando, the normative assumptions of the everyday turn are a result of anthropology's "tacit attachment to a set of secular-liberal sensibilities."[48] I want to suggest, however, that there is an easier explanation for these norms, which does not rely on an assumption of shared ideology across the entire discipline—namely, our poverty of imagination regarding the doubts of others. A substantial impetus behind the turn to the everyday in Islam has been a desire to uncover the uncertainties that Muslims face in daily life. Overwhelmingly, this has resulted in accounts that chart how Muslims challenge, debate, and negotiate religious authority. In other words, it has led to an examination of the ways in which many modern Muslims both question the content of their religion, and question their ability to know that content. After all, with no clear authority to follow, how is a person to know that they believe in the right way? The result is that anthropological accounts of everyday Islam have overwhelmingly embraced the narrow (epistemological) reading of doubt that I outlined in the introduction to this book—that is, a reading in which doubt can only ever be the inverse of belief. This, I think, is a somewhat impoverished way of viewing doubt.

Our poverty of imagination regarding doubt has had two consequences. First, it has led to a situation in which the purpose of anthropological writing becomes a need to identify a doubting subject, through whom we might be made aware of our shared humanity to the Other. This is an old anthropological move, and it echoes how the "suffering subject" became a major object of anthropological study from the late 1990s.[49] As Joel Robbins has so astutely observed, the need for anthropologists to identify suffering in the Other led to a situation in which the goal of anthropological writing was no longer to explore difference but instead to "offer accounts of trauma that make us and our readers feel in our bones the vulnerability we as human beings all share."[50] A similar observation might now be made for the "doubting subject": anthropologists of the everyday have increasingly seen their mission as identifying a particular kind of epistemological doubt everywhere they go. As a result, they have found uncertainty, but the character of that uncertainty has ended up looking very much the same no matter where it is observed. Second, and perhaps more problematically, our poverty of imagination regarding doubt has led to a situation in which we frequently fail to recognize forms of uncertainty that do not fit our paradigm of doubt. As I have shown in the preceding chapters, Qadian's Ahmadis are unusual for the degree to which they feel certain in their access to an authoritative interpretation of Islam that is in harmony with the world. Through the blessings of the caliphate, they feel confident in both their understanding of truth and in the process by which they came to acquire that understanding. By the measure of the everyday Islam literature, the Ahmadis thus appear to live in a world of complete (and hence unreal) certainty. If we think about doubt only as belief's inverse, the Ahmadis will necessarily appear to us as fundamentalist Others. As I have also sought to show, however, Qadian's Ahmadis do have a deeply uncertain relationship to truth. It is just that the uncertainty they feel is about witnessing, proving, and materializing truth, not about believing in it.

Rethinking the Doubting Subject

Much of what I have said so far might be summarized as follows: anthropologists often appear to assume that agentive selfhood depends on a person having a proper relationship to truth; that is, it depends on that person expressing a recognizable form of doubt. Anthropologists are not alone in making such assumptions: the idea that a failure to doubt signals an unfree religious subjectivity has long informed concerns about religious fundamentalism, and it has been particularly important in the criticisms directed at new religious movements (sometimes disparagingly called "cults") by both organized religious groups and secular opponents.[51] Within anthropology, a recognition of the capacity of others for doubt has occasionally been invoked when those others run the risk of being branded fanatical. This is, for example, a tactic employed to great effect by Tanya Luhrmann in *When God Talks Back*, a psychologically informed anthropological study of the relationship that American evangelicals cultivate with God.[52] In writing this book, Luhrmann was acutely aware that many readers—both secular and of a moderate religious persuasion—would find her evangelical interlocutors fanatical, unreasonable, and perhaps even dangerous. The central question of her study was thus to ask how it is that sensible and rational people can come to believe in an invisible God with whom they have a deeply personal relationship and who they believe speaks directly to them.[53] Luhrmann sees doubt as a crucial part of the answer to this question. Her interlocutors, she argues, are fully aware that what they say seems crazy to those on the outside, and they are thus constantly confronted by a paradox that the evidence they have for God is also the clearest evidence of potential folly.[54] Thus, their belief in a "vividly human, deeply supernatural God" emerges "out of an exquisite awareness of doubt."[55] For these evangelicals, a continuous questioning of certainties and sensory experiences is necessary to energize the "work" they do to fully believe in God's presence in their lives. For Luhrmann, doubt thus does for Evangelicals what postmodernism did for intellectuals: "It allows them to waver between the metaphorical and the literal, between what they fear to be true and what they yearn to be true."[56] It is important to note, however, that Luhrmann's interlocutors have an understanding of doubt (*what can I know, and how can I trust my reasons for knowing it?*) that is embedded within the epistemological tradition of doubt that I outlined in the introduction to this book. Luhrmann's ability to humanize these religious Others thus rests on her ability to show that, in contrast to our expectations, they occupy a familiar doubting subjectivity.

What I am arguing for is thus a deeper appreciation for how our estimation of the doubts of others also determines our appreciation for their agency. But why should this be so? The anthropologist Webb Keane has been particularly forceful in arguing that modernity has introduced a moral narrative about self-mastery and agency to many parts of the world. (His own ethnography concerns changes on the Indonesian island of Sumba.)[57] In particular, he argues that the global spread of ideas originating within strands of Protestant thought has led to a moral narrative of modernity in which self-mastery is linked to the discovery of "the true character of human agency."[58] In many places, this has resulted in attacks on indistinct boundaries between humans and their material worlds. The global spread of Protestant ideas has thus provided an ideology by which human agency could be purified of material entanglements, even in places where Christianity did not become dominant. Thus, Keane argues that the Arya Samaj—a Hindu reform group who are historical interlocutors of the Ahmadiyya Jama'at—were involved in Protestant-inspired purification.[59] Indeed, the goal of purification has most commonly been manifested in attacks on fetishisms, idols, and the worship of beings that are seen to intercede in people's lives, in short, objects onto which humans displace their own agency. These fetishisms and idolatries have consequently been identified as threatening human freedom. For Keane, this semiotic ideology has resulted in one of modernity's hallmarks: the idea that a free person is one who understands one's responsibility to one's own agency and who is able to evaluate one's inner thoughts. Within this semiotic ideology, inner meaning is given prominence, and a person's agentive stance toward their own inner beliefs is stressed. Keane argues that while this semiotic ideology was developed most fully within Protestantism, it is now found everywhere, from the U.S. Declaration of Independence to the United Nations Universal Declaration of Human Rights.[60] The reason that Keane's work is important to the present argument is because it helps us to understand how, in much of the modern world, great moral emphasis has been placed on a particular kind of subject who rejects material entanglements and exercises an agentive stance toward belief. This subject is, of course, an individual who also happens to have a relationship to truth that gives rise to very predictable forms of doubt.

But what does religious doubt look like when the kind of interiorized moral selfhood just described is not present? What happens when the doubting subject does not resemble the modern subject that Keane attributes to Protestantism's semiotic ideology? The historian Dipesh Chakrabarty has written about the need to provincialize the European assumption that an "endlessly interiorized subject" represents a culmination of history.[61] Chakrabarty describes how this modern individual is "supposed to have an interiorized 'private' self that pours out incessantly in diaries, letters, autobiographies, novels, and, of course, in what we say to our analyst."[62] There is, of course, a moral celebration attached to this form of subjectivity, for it is seen as modern but also universal. Chakrabarty nonetheless notes the absence of this agonizing sense of private self-reflexivity in Indian autobiographical writing, which seems to constitute a lack or incompleteness in subjectivity, precisely because we have already situated "the modern individual at the very end of history."[63] Rather than keep on searching for this interiorized subject in the Indian archive, Chakrabarty asks whether historians might instead trace historical ambivalences toward it. Only then might they begin to move their writing away from the domination of a "hyperreal Europe."[64] Chakrabarty's model provides us with one possible approach to a new anthropology of doubt. It enables us to question the dominance of an interiorized subject within our own analytical vocabulary, and in doing so, it provides us with a way of writing other histories of uncertainty that do not fall back onto an assumption that those uncertainties are characterized by alterity. Chakrabarty's text, in other words, helps us to ask what it means to be uncertain about religion when one is also highly ambivalent about the agonized interior self as an ideological construct.

Indeed, it is worth asking how widespread the ideal "modern" self just described is, even within Christianity.[65] For example, do forms of Protestantism that emphasize material consumption and accumulation—I think, of course, of the prosperity gospel—produce troubled relationships to truth that are similar to those which I have described in this book?[66] Does the prosperity gospel result in subjects who are concerned only over what they can know, or do the material entanglements that mediate their relationship to truth produce their own forms of uncertainty and their own demands on the subject? Anthropologists are used to analyzing prosperity gospel movements in terms of uncertainty, but in such analyses, the prosperity gospel is almost always presented as a response to other kinds of uncertainty, in particular that emerging out of a neoliberal marketplace.[67] This means that the kinds of uncertainty produced by the prosperity gospel's focus on material consumption as a way of indexing and demonstrating truth have remained remarkably understudied. When the problems of a religion are not understood to be problems of interiorized belief, then the troubles that people experience with truth are going to take on variable forms.

Inevitably, the questions I am raising bring us back to social science's first and most magisterial attempt to think through religious anxiety: Weber's *Protestant Ethic*.[68] In an attempt to understand how Protestantism may have contributed to the rise of modern capitalism, Weber turned to consider the Calvinist doctrine of predestination. This was a doctrine that stressed the unknowable nature of salvation. Whether a person was to enjoy eternal paradise was predetermined, such that good deeds could not purchase salvation but only act as a sign of its possibility. For Weber, the "extreme inhumanity" of this doctrine must necessarily have led its adherents to experience "a feeling of unprecedented inner loneliness of the single individual."[69] Salvation could never be assured, and a person's place within the elect could never be known with certainty. All that could be known were outer signs of worldly success. Excessive accumulation for the sake of accumulation thus became a goal, not because it could in any way prevent damnation but because it was the only way in which people could allay the fear of damnation. For all Weber's potential historical inaccuracies, his astute analysis gives us an archetypal reading of a particular kind of doubt, in which inner life, personal belief, and individual salvation become the sites of deeply troubling anxiety, while the outer material world becomes a place through which people try (in vain) to achieve certainty. For the Calvinists described by Weber, the material world was seen to have no bearing on the ultimate fate of an individual's soul, but it was nonetheless knowable in a way that inner life could never be. In Weber's analysis of Calvinism, material displays are the one thing that can be known with certainty. The question I have attempted to raise in this book is what happens when belief is no longer the problem. What happens if, unlike the situation described by Weber, inner certainty can be achieved, while the entanglements and demands of a material world produce anxieties?

I have made this argument to show how particular idealizations of the doubting subject can obscure our understanding of the ways uncertainty operates in people's lives. Within much Western discourse—both intellectual and popular—a very particular interior-orientated self-doubting subject is often held up as a moral and political exemplar. Once we have provincialized this figure, we might begin to see how quite different archetypes of uncertainty can inform the religious anxiety experienced by our interlocutors. In Qadian, one such figure is the heroic polemicist, who wrestles not with himself but with a world that constantly refuses his attempts to manifest an irrefutable truth. His relationship to truth is one of obligation, and he must fulfill that obligation by demonstrating and witnessing truth in a way that does not simultaneously undermine it. As the anthropologist Mathijs Pelkmans observed, doubt poses methodological challenges for the ethnographer, for it "tends to vanish with articulation."[70] For Qadian's heroic polemicist, it is instead truth that is in danger of disappearing in its moment of articulation.

Qadian's uncertainties are, of course, specific to the particular organizational structure of the Ahmadiyya Jamaʿat and to the unusual position of the town within that system. Other Muslims doubt differently. There are rich histories of skepticism in the Muslim world, which both echo and engage with the Western theological and philosophical approaches to doubt, most significantly because those Islamic discourses have often drawn on the same foundational texts from Greek philosophy. Indeed, as an epistemological tool, doubt has been indispensible for many thinkers within the Muslim world. In a monograph on contemporary Swahili philosophy in Mombasa, for example, Kai Kresse has demonstrated the centrality of doubt as method in what he describes as the "transcultural character of philosophical thought."[71] For Kresse's interlocutors, just like for many Western philosophers, understanding what one does not know is an important starting point for any serious quest for knowledge. What is important is that we realize that this kind of doubt—so reminiscent of our own—is just as much a product of history as that found in Qadian.

Doubting in Qadian

What, then, might a reinvigorated anthropology of doubt look like? This book has shown how, even if Ahmadis occasionally draw on a universal language of belief to explain their doctrine to others, in Qadian, belief does not adequately summarize the relationship that Ahmadis hold to truth. Rather, in Qadian, religious truth is responded to, understood, witnessed, and even practiced to produce a relationship of devotion. For Qadian's Ahmadis, religious authority both staves off a form of doubt that we might find familiar and produces its own forms of uncertainty. Most importantly, these forms of uncertainty are entirely compatible with the deeply felt doctrinal convictions I have also described in these pages. The idea that sincere and sustained conviction should be somehow irreconcilable with the experience of religious uncertainty is, I have argued, a product of our own narrow understanding of what it means to doubt. This book has thus been an attempt to shift anthropological discourse from the question of *why don't these people doubt?* to that of *what kind of relationship do they have with truth?*

What I have shown is that troubled relationships to truth in Qadian emerge out of the fact that a person may know with absolute conviction that they are a Muslim and yet feel great anxiety about their ability to prove this to the world. This has been a book about people faced by an anxiety over how to convert certain knowledge into irrefutable evidence. The long history of anti-Ahmadiyya activity in South Asia means that for Qadian's residents, to talk like Muslims, to act like Muslims, and to engage in ritual practice like Muslims is never enough to convince an outside public that they are, indeed, Muslims. As the example from the Qur'an exhibition in chapter 5 showed, it is the ability of Ahmadis to supposedly appropriate the practice of Muslims that so clearly makes them non-Muslim "provocateurs" in the eyes of many opponents.[72] Ahmadis are thus confronted by a problem: how to evidence truth and prove their own sense of transcendent certainty to a skeptical—and frequently hostile—world. To do this, my Ahmadi interlocutors turn their quotidian existence into a testament to an immaterial relationship of love, devotion, and trust in their caliph. Of the many examples of Ahmadi attempts to materialize this transcendent truth, the mubahala is perhaps the most dramatic. A trial by ordeal initiated by the fourth caliph to make a final argument for the status of his followers as Muslim, the mubahala should supposedly have ended with truth being inscribed in the material world through the death of its participants. In practice, however, the mubahala became a terrain through which members of the Jama'at—including the fourth caliph—argued that it was possible to prove Muslimness, and that the evidence for that Muslimness was to be found in the physical, social, and economic existence of the Ahmadiyya community.

For my Ahmadi interlocutors, this ideal community is produced through their obedience to the caliph, and central to this vision of the social is therefore their willingness to sacrifice (*qurban karna*) their property, their autonomy, their individual aspirations, and ultimately their lives.[73] Following the anthropologist Maya Mayblin, this sacrifice is best understood not as an event or a discourse but as a "lived aesthetic."[74] It is through this aesthetic work that a gift is given to the world: an image of the global, unified Jama'at, the witnessing of which reveals transcendental truth. In return, my interlocutors hope to make their Muslim identity public, verifiable, and authenticated.[75] As is often the case, however, this sacrifice can produce contradictions and paradoxes.[76] The specific paradox of this lived aesthetic is that it produces a truth that is simultaneously potent and unreliable. On the one hand, this sacrificial activity enables the Ahmadis' relationship to the caliph to emerge as a hyperreal fact, which has a potent effect on the world. This relationship of devotion, crystalized in the Jama'at's global system and made visible through proofs and arguments, is felt to impress itself on all who see it and to demand recognition. Once visible, this relationship manifests a transcendent truth that is said to oblige all those who see it to respond. It is a truth that challenges the world and contains a dangerous power, for the consequences of failing to witness it can be fatal. On the other hand, it is in the process of manifesting this truth that my interlocutors' Muslim identity—so firmly held as a private certainty—can be undermined. As we saw in chapter 2's exploration of the "enchanted bureaucracy," my interlocutors' efforts to demonstrate an intimate and direct relationship to the caliph can also expose the necessarily fabricated nature of that relationship. In this sense, from their position in a town that simultaneously lies at the heart and the periphery of the global Jama'at, the act of making truth is also the act of destroying it. As Webb Keane argued is often the case, it is the act of "transducing" the immaterial into the material that generates powerful effects.[77] It is also this process of transduction that threatens the whole ethical project to which my interlocutors are attached.

In many respects, the central problem faced by my interlocutors is one shared by anthropologists. The lived aesthetic of life in Qadian is an attempt to make a relationship knowable: Muslim identity in the town is dependent on this relationship becoming an object that can be witnessed. To prove a relationship in Qadian, however, is also to invent or create it, and this process of invention produces a dangerous possibility that the truth of the relation might be undermined even as it is produced. Qadian's Ahmadis, in other words, are compelled to know and to document relations, but they are also troubled by the ontological status of relations that are both real and invented.[78] In this sense, their religious anxiety is also an anthropological anxiety. It is an anxiety over the ever shifting status of the thing through which each group ensures its continued existence; it is an anxiety about the unstable knowability of the relation.

Counterfeit Proof

Glasgow may be many thousands of miles from Qadian, yet I began this conclusion with the murder of Asad Shah because it epitomizes a concern in Qadian over what I have called counterfeit proof. Shah's death simultaneously proved Ahmadiyyat and undermined it. As a martyrdom, it provided evidence for a truth that could not be ignored, that demanded and received recognition from a wider world. But it also revealed an instability and weakness in the theological claims by which the caliph could demand the obedience and loyalty of his entire global Jama'at. As a martyr, Shah thus both confirmed and rejected the caliphate. His death manifested the caliphate as a relationship while simultaneously unmaking it.

The argument of this book has been that there is something of Shah in the uncertainties felt by every person in Qadian. Through laborious everyday sacrifice, my interlocutors attempt to demonstrate the truth of Ahmadiyyat by making visible a relationship. And yet their efforts to do this always produce a possibility that their connection to the caliph might be too tenuous, implausible, and distant and that their production of this idealized relationship might be an act of imitation and contradiction. This anxiety is not a doubting of truth or a doubting of one's ability to know that truth but a fear that what is known with certainty might ultimately be indemonstrable. As we saw in the previous chapter, even when Ahmadis in Qadian witness images that seem to signify a completely secure Muslim identity, this sense of security is produced out of deeper tensions, ambivalences, and fractures that run through their project of proving a public identity.

Who is a Muslim, and what is Islam? These are questions that this book cannot answer. I have instead focused on one group who strive to prove to a suspicious world that they are Muslim. To cynical readers, the Ahmadis' struggle may appear hopeless, for the more closely they resemble a broader Muslim public, the more their opponents accuse them of being bad copies of original Muslims.[79] While Ahmadis may view these attacks as baseless vitriol, their own religious anxieties nonetheless emerge out of a parallel logic, for their attempts to prove a Muslim identity often seem to lead back to counterfeit proof—that is, proof that undermines itself in its moment of production. Perhaps, however, there is something more Muslim to these counterfeit proofs than even my interlocutors would recognize. In an attempt to give a coherent shape to the extensive and diverse tradition that is Islam, Shahab Ahmed has argued that one central aspect of the tradition is the importance of paradox to its "processes of *meaning–making*."[80] For Ahmed, the long historical tradition of Islam is best characterized by an ability "to live with outright contradiction," in such a way that this contradiction is conceived as "coherent and meaningful" as it arises directly out of Muhammad's revelation.[81] In this sense, it is my interlocutors' ability to live with a meaningful proof that both authenticates and undermines that most clearly places them within the tradition from which so many others have tried to expel them.

Notes

INTRODUCTION

1. "Ahmadiyya Muslim Community," Al Islam: The Official Website of the Ahmadiyya Muslim Community, accessed July 19, 2018, https://www.alislam.org/library/ahmadiyya-muslim-community/. Note that the figure of "tens of millions" of followers is impossible to verify, as no accurate estimate for the global Ahmadiyya population exists.

2. Qasmi, *Politics of Religious Exclusion in Pakistan*.

3. For a comparable use of branded slogans in a South Asian new religious movement, see Lucia, *Reflections of Amma*, 11.

4. Engelke, *God's Agents*.

5. Khan, "Event Nearly a Century in the Making"; Ahmad, "Key to Peace"; Ahmad, "Religion of Peace and Compassion"; Ahmad, "Critical Need of the Time."

6. For an example of the celebration of the Ahmadiyya community in the British Parliament, see HC Deb 11 February 2016, vol 605, cols 679–714WH.

7. "Liberal Party Leader Justin Trudeau at Ahmadiyya Muslim Convention in Canada 2015," posted by Rabwah Times, YouTube, August 29, 2015, https://www.youtube.com/watch?v=apKNeDsLiAs.

8. Mair and Evans, "Ethics across Borders," 215.

9. Lambek, "Living as if It Mattered."

10. Lambek, "Living as if It Mattered."

11. One reason for the anthropological rejection of certainty has been the collapse of our own confidence in the idea of culture as an explanation for what people believe in. Surveying the decline of "shared culture" as an analytical tool available to anthropologists, Joel Robbins has noted how many practitioners of the discipline today "are more interested in documenting the world's chaotic aspects than its structurally predictable or orderly ones." That the world may be more chaotic than we previously thought has, I want to argue, gone together with an assumption that certainty is harder to achieve. Robbins "Where in the World Are Values?" 177.

12. Robinson, "Crisis of Authority."

13. I am here referring to what Nadia Fadil and Mayanthi Fernando have described as the literature on "everyday Islam"; much of which has been inspired by calls made by anthropologists such as Michael Lambek and Veena Das to study "ordinary" ethics. Fadil and Fernando, "Rediscovering the 'Everyday' Muslim"; Lambek, *Ordinary Ethics*; Das, "Ordinary Ethics." In the conclusion to this book, I outline in greater detail my specific criticisms of this body of literature in relation to the anthropological study of doubt. Other parallel criticisms can be found in Robbins, "What Is the Matter with Transcendence?" and Lempert, "No Ordinary Ethics."

14. An example of this, which I explore in greater detail in the conclusion to this book, is Tanya Luhrmann's *When God Talks Back*.

15. The exact figures from the 2011 census are 23,632 residents of whom 3,065 are Muslim. There are very few, if any, non-Ahmadi Muslims in Qadian. During my fieldwork in May 2011, the Ahmadiyya community in Qadian counted its own size at 3,681 due to the large number of temporary residents and students studying in the town.

16. Figures supplied by the Jalsa Salana office in Qadian.

17. The fact that India grants a small number of visas to Pakistanis to visit Qadian is a source of much celebration, for it is the only time when the community in India might be physically united with those from the far larger Ahmadiyya community in Pakistan.

18. See chapter 2 for an explanation of the continued use of fax in Qadian.

19. For an ethnographic account of some of the ways in which people resist these reformist branches of Islam, see Marsden, *Living Islam*.

20. Saeed, "Pakistani Nationalism"; Iqtidar, "State Management of Religion"; Khan, *Muslim Becoming*; Khan, *From Sufism to Ahmadiyya*; Devji, *Muslim Zion*. For an examination of a similar process in which the heterodoxy of the Ahmadiyya community has helped to sediment Sunni orthodoxy in South Africa, see Qadir "How Heresy Makes Orthodoxy."

21. The Arabic phrase *khatam al-nabiyin*, taken from the Qur'an 33:40, literally translates to describe Muhammad as the "seal" of the prophets and is interpreted by most Muslims to mean that Muhammad was the final prophet sent by God to earth. Ahmadis do not dispute that Muhammad was the seal of the prophets but rather argue that this distinction does not preclude other, lesser prophets from following within the teachings revealed to Muhammad.

22. Kamran, "Pre-history of Religious Exclusionism."

23. Munir, *Report of the Court*, 1; Khan, *From Sufism to Ahmadiyya*, 153–54.

24. Munir, *Report of the Court*; Qasmi, *Politics of Religious Exclusion*, 19.

25. Khan, *From Sufism to Ahmadiyya*, 160–61.

26. Qasmi, *Politics of Religious Exclusion*, 7.

27. Qasmi, 219.

28. Khan, *Muslim Becoming*, 114.

29. Irawan, "'They Are Not Muslims,'" 171–72.

30. Qasmi, *Politics of Religious Exclusion*, 223.

31. For a fuller history of the religious exclusion of Ahmadis in Pakistan, readers should turn to Ali Usman Qasmi's superb account in Qasmi, *Politics of Religious Exclusion*.

32. Nelson, "Constitutional Migration."

33. Nelson, "Constitutional Migration."

34. Barker, "Imran Khan Criticised."

35. For an academic examination of this event, see Nijhawan, "'Today, We Are All Ahmadi.'"

36. Many of Qadian's residents had relatives in Pakistan. There were also, however, kinship ties to other countries where Ahmadis have been killed or persecuted, such as Indonesia and Bangladesh. In March 2016, an Ahmadi shopkeeper was murdered in Glasgow for religious reasons: he too had relatives in Qadian. For more details on this last case, see the conclusion to this book.

37. "Religious Fanatics Attack Ahmadis' Houses in Saharanpur, Uttar Pradesh, India; Six Persons Injured," International Press and Media Desk Ahmadiyya Muslim Community, August 27, 2008, http://www.thepersecution.org/world/india/08/08/pr27.html.

38. This is a term used to differentiate the specific variety of Islam practiced by the Ahmadiyya Muslim Community.

39. Gualtieri, *Conscience and Coercion*, 33. Gualtieri refers to this as "a kind of Orwellian attempt at thought control."

40. It is worth noting that my focus on surfaces contrasts with much academic interpretation of the Ahmadiyya Jama'at—for example, Ayesha Jalal's account of Mirza Ghulam Ahmad's reworking of jihad as a peaceful endeavor, which describes Ghulam Ahmad as part of a generation of modernist scholars who rejected an excessive focus on outward ritual practice in favor of a reformation of inner ethics. Other scholars within

this generation included Chiragh Ali and Sayyid Ahmad Khan. Jalal, *Partisans of Allah*, 149–75.

41. The Lahori branch still exists, although it is far smaller than the Jama'at-e-Ahmadiyya. The Lahoris have been written about elsewhere and are not of concern to the present study.

42. Theological arguments for the caliphate can be found in Ahmad, *Anwar-e-Khilafat*; Ahmad, *Mansab-e-Khilafat*.

43. These values are obviously not unique to the Ahmadis: many Muslims subscribe to nonviolence, and Mirza Ghulam Ahmad's call for Muslims to demonstrate loyalty to non-Muslim governments was shared by other Muslim thinkers of his era, most importantly Sir Syed Ahmad Khan. For a critical appraisal of this idea, see Shaz, *Understanding the Muslim Malaise*.

44. *Indian Express*, "Minority in a Minority."

45. Khan, *From Sufism to Ahmadiyya*, 145.

46. "Who Are the Ahmadi?" BBC, May 28, 2010, http://news.bbc.co.uk/1/hi/world/south_asia/8711026.stm.

47. In a newspaper article, an official Jama'at spokesman is quoted as saying that the figure is just over 100,000. Ranal, "Ahmadiyyas Come Out."

48. *Rabwah* means "high or elevated ground" and is taken from the Qur'an 23:50, which Ahmadis translate as: "And We made the son of Mary and his mother a Sign, and gave them shelter on an elevated land of *green* valleys and springs of running water" (emphasis in original). Farīd, *The Holy Qur'ān*, 697.

49. This number is highly significant, being the same as the number of Muslims who under the leadership of Muhammad defeated a much larger force of Meccans at the Battle of Badr in 624.

50. Ahmed, "Paradoxes of Ahmadiyya Identity"; Iqtidar, "State Management of Religion"; Saeed, "Pakistani Nationalism." There have been an increasing number of studies of Ahmadis outside of South Asia: for example, Baer, "Muslim Encounters"; Balzani, "Dreaming, Islam and the Ahmadiyya Muslims"; Nijhawan, "'Today, We Are All Ahmadi'"; Nijhawan, *Precarious Diasporas*; Hanson, *Ahmadiyya in the Gold Coast*.

51. Bajwa, "Historical Visits to Canada and Qadian."

52. Compare Deeb, *An Enchanted Modern*.

53. "Jalsa Salana," Al Islam: The Official Website of the Ahmadiyya Muslim Community, accessed July 12, 2018, http://www.jalsasalana.org/.

54. Prior to my fieldwork, the numbers of converts in India up to the year end of the UK Jalsa Salana were 2,417 for 2008–09 and 2,761 for 2009–10. Figures provided by *da'wat-e-illallah*, Qadian.

55. This refers only to general prayers (du'a) and not the five times daily namaz (*salat*), which must be performed at specific local times.

56. Khan, *From Sufism to Ahmadiyya*, 89.

57. "International Baiat," Al Islam: The Official Website of the Ahmadiyya Muslim Community, accessed August 2, 2018, https://www.alislam.org/library/history/ahmadiyya/103.html.

58. "International Bai'at Jalsa Salana UK 2011: 480,822 Join Islam Ahmadiyyat in One Year," posted by Ahmadiyya Muslim Jama'at, YouTube, July 27, 2011, https://www.youtube.com/watch?v=KGRjQWkj1_w.

59. A copy of the declaration can be found here: "Declaration of Initiation (Bai'at)," Al Islam: The Official Website of the Ahmadiyya Muslim Community, accessed August 2, 2018, https://www.alislam.org/introduction/declaration.pdf.

60. "Jalsa Salana UK 2014: International Ba'ait," posted by mtaOnline1, YouTube, September 18, 2014, https://www.youtube.com/watch?v=Km87rEhuj04; "International

Bai'at (Initiation Ceremony) at Jalsa Salana UK 2013 - Islam Ahmadiyya," posted by Ahmadiyya Muslim Community, YouTube, September 1, 2013, https://www.youtube.com/watch?v=xk7cJZMCvA8.

61. Alexander, "Four Points of the Compass," 93.

62. Alexander, 93.

63. Pelkmans, "Outline for an Ethnography," 4.

64. Pouillon, "Remarks on the Verb 'to Believe,'" 485.

65. Most, *Doubting Thomas*.

66. Most, 226.

67. Hecht, *Doubt*.

68. Hecht, xxi.

69. Roush, "Epistemic Self-Doubt."

70. Owens, "Epistemic Akrasia"; Horowitz, "Epistemic Akrasia."

71. Egan and Elga, "I Can't Believe I'm Stupid."

72. For an anthropological take on this idea, see Pelkmans, "Outline for an Ethnography."

73. Asad, "Reading a Modern Classic"; Lindquist and Coleman, "Introduction: Against Belief?"; Needham, *Belief, Language, and Experience*; Robbins, "Continuity Thinking and the Problem of Christian Culture," Ruel, "Christians as Believers."

74. Wilfred Cantwell Smith, quoted in Ruel, "Christians as Believers," 100.

75. Ruel, 109–10.

76. For more on why Ahmadi religious practice should be seen as an act of "witnessing" truth, see Evans, "Witnessing a Potent Truth."

77. Asad, *Genealogies of Religion*, 43–47.

78. Keane, *Christian Moderns*.

79. In the conclusion to this book, I show precisely how this idea has informed recent anthropological approaches to doubt and uncertainty.

80. Although these terms may be closer than we often image. See Holsinger, *Neomedievalism*.

81. On the "repugnant cultural other," see Harding, "Representing Fundamentalism."

82. Berger and Zijderveld, *In Praise of Doubt*, 101–2, 112–13.

83. For classic examples of social scientists seeking to explain excessive certainty among the adherents of new religious movements, see Bainbridge and Stark, "Scientology"; Festinger, Riecken, and Schachter, "When Prophecy Fails"; Galanter, "Cults"; Iannaccone, "Sacrifice and Stigma"; Zablocki, "Exit Cost Analysis."

84. Snow and Machalek both summarize and critique such assumptions in the article "On the Presumed Fragility."

85. For example, Simmons, "Maintaining Deviant Belief Systems"; Bainbridge and Stark, "Scientology."

86. For a classic approach to these questions, see Kelley, *Why Conservative Churches Are Growing*. For more recent approaches, see Iannaccone, "Why Strict Churches Are Strong"; Stark, "Why Religious Movements Succeed or Fail."

87. The idea of a "plausibility structure" was originally proposed by Peter Berger in the book *The Sacred Canopy*.

88. Spadola, *Calls of Islam*, 4.

89. Andi Muhammad Irawan has shown how these allegations of deceit are not unique to anti-Ahmadiyya discourse in South Asia but can also be found in the discourse of organized opposition to the Jama'at in Indonesia. Irawan, "'They Are Not Muslims.'"

90. Asad, *Genealogies of Religion*. Compare also to the work of Webb Keane on sincerity: for example, Keane, "From Fetishism to Sincerity"; Keane, *Christian Moderns*; Keane, "Sincerity, 'Modernity,' and the Protestants."

91. Asad et al., *Is Critique Secular?* 34–35.

92. Friedmann, *Prophecy Continuous*; Gualtieri, *Ahmadis*; Khan, *From Sufism to Ahmadiyya*; Valentine, *Islam and the Ahmadiyya Jama'at*.

93. Gualtieri, *Ahmadis*, xiii.

94. Abu-Lughod, "Romance of Resistance"; Abu-Lughod, *Veiled Sentiments*; Deeb, *An Enchanted Modern*; Mahmood, "Feminist Theory, Embodiment, and the Docile Agent"; Schulz, "(Re)Turning." For many women who have adopted the veil, this religious identity is explicitly contrasted to an older "cultural" identity.

95. Compare to Marsden, *Living Islam*; Anderson, "'The Piety of the Gift.'"

1. THE HISTORY OF THE AHMADI-CALIPH RELATIONSHIP

1. Ahmed, *What Is Islam?* 81.

2. Mumtaz, "Islamic Fundamentalism." The idea that Aligarh and Deoband represent stark opposites is, of course, a crude simplification. In fact, almost all the significant Islamic movements that arose after the fall of Mughal power engaged with the modern world, and even those that looked most traditional, such as Deoband, represented quite a break from the past. As Barbara Metcalf has argued, the Deobandis emulated many aspects of British bureaucracy and had as their primary goal the combative engagement with European missionary activity. Metcalf, *Islamic Revival in British India*.

3. Ahmad, *Sirat-e-Hadrat Masih Mau'ud*, 1.

4. Ahmad, *Silsila Ahmadiyya*, 1:8.

5. Ahmad, *Tadhkirah*, 8–9.

6. Khan, *From Sufism to Ahmadiyya*, 22.

7. Friedmann, *Prophecy Continuous*, 2–3.

8. For an example of Ahmad's loyalty to the British, see Ahmad, *Tohfa-e-Qaisariyyah*.

9. The full title of this multivolume work is *al-Barahin al-Ahmadiyya 'ala Haqiqatu KitabAllah al-Quran wa an-Nabuwwatu al-Muhammadiyya* (Barahin-e-Ahmadiyya: Arguments in Support of the Holy Quran and the Prophethood of the Holy Prophet Muhammad). The short title is difficult to translate, so much so that the Ahmadis themselves do not do so. Adil Khan translates it as "the proofs of Islam" or "Ahmad's proofs of Islam." Khan, *From Sufism to Ahmadiyya*, 221.

10. Friedmann, *Prophecy Continuous*, 4.

11. Friedmann, 4.

12. Friedmann, 6.

13. Friedmann, 9–10.

14. Powell, "Duties of Ahmadi Women," 129.

15. Ahmad, "Ek Ghalati Ka Izala," 208.

16. This pamphlet is called "Ek Ghalati Ka Izala"; I am here following the interpretation of this pamphlet by my interlocutors in Qadian. As Adil Khan notes, it has been used by others to argue that Ghulam Ahmad was in fact not claiming to be a prophet: "The only reason why this is possible is that Ghulam Ahmad's presentation of his prophetic status remained muddled with contradictions, with clear statements affirming his prophetic status and clear statements denying it." Khan, *From Sufism to Ahmadiyya*, 124.

17. Ahmad, "Ek Ghalati Ka Izala," 207.

18. Ahmad, 212.

19. Friedmann, *Prophecy Continuous*, 186.

20. *The Economist*, "Iran's Multiplicity of Messiahs."

21. Friedmann, "Aḥmadiyya."

22. Ahmad, *Jesus in India*, 73 (emphasis mine).

23. Friedmann, *Prophecy Continuous*; Khan, *From Sufism to Ahmadiyya*.

24. Jones, *Socio-Religious Reform Movements*; Jones, "Swami Dayananda Saraswati's Critique"; Metcalf, "Imagined Community"; Powell, *Muslims and Missionaries*; Van der Linden, *Moral Languages*.

25. Ahmad, *Jesus in India*.

26. Anawati, "'Īsā."

27. Friedmann, *Prophecy Continuous*, 113.

28. Anawati, "'Īsā."

29. Friedmann, *Prophecy Continuous*, 117.

30. Ahmad, *Jesus in India*, 1.

31. For example, Valentine, *Islam and the Ahmadiyya Jama'at*.

32. I expand this idea of an enchanted rationality in the next chapter. Compare to Deeb, *An Enchanted Modern*.

33. Friedmann, *Prophecy Continuous*, 165–76.

34. Friedmann, 172–73.

35. For example, Ahmad, *Murder in the Name of Allah*.

36. On ethical conversation, see Mair and Evans, "Ethics across Borders."

37. Friedmann, "Aḥmadiyya."

38. Ahmad, "Al-Wasiyyat."

39. Khan, *From Sufism to Ahmadiyya*, 74.

40. Ahmad, "Al-Wasiyyat," 305.

41. In the same way that Ghulam Ahmad's birth has become a source of contention, so too has his death. To this day, many opponents continue to make the (hugely insulting) claim that Ghulam Ahmad died of cholera while on the toilet. Ahmadis counter this by arguing that Ghulam Ahmad's body was transported by rail back from Lahore for burial in Qadian. Due to sanitary regulations in British India, transporting a body by rail would have been forbidden by law had he in fact died of cholera. Furthermore, they argue that a doctor provided a certificate that Ghulam Ahmad had not died of a contagious illness, thus proving that he did not die an accursed death. Rehman, *Qadian: A Holy Land*, 44.

42. Khan, *From Sufism to Ahmadiyya*, 64.

43. Tahrik Jadid Anjuman Ahmadiyya Pakistan, *Wasiyyat Rules*, xiii.

44. Nasir, "Nabuwwat-o-Khilafat."

45. For more information on the Lahori sect, see Friedmann, *Prophecy Continuous*; Valentine, *Islam and the Ahmadiyya Jama'at*.

46. Friedmann, "Aḥmadiyya."

47. Khan, *From Sufism to Ahmadiyya*, 66.

48. Nasir, "Nabuwwat-o-Khilafat."

49. Khan, *From Sufism to Ahmadiyya*, 68.

50. Jones, *Socio-Religious Reform Movements*, 200.

51. Ahmad, *Mansab-e-Khilafat*; Ahmad, *Anwar-e-Khilafat*.

52. Zirvi, *Welcome to Ahmadiyyat*, 329.

53. Zirvi, 336.

54. Several academic histories now exist on the spread of Ahmadiyya Islam in West Africa. See Fisher, *Ahmadiyyah*; Hanson, *Ahmadiyya in the Gold Coast*.

55. Jalal, *Self and Sovereignty*, 293.

56. The Jama'at does not tend to use the word *ulema* (a community of scholars in the traditional Islamic sense) to describe its own clerics.

57. Zirvi, *Welcome to Ahmadiyyat*, 362.

58. Tahrik-e-Jadid Anjuman Ahmadiyya Pakistan, *Introduction to Financial Sacrifice*, 37.

59. Tahrik-e-Jadid Anjuman Ahmadiyya Pakistan, 62.

60. This first census put the number of self-declared Ahmadis at just 3,450. Numbers then rose rapidly in each subsequent census, reaching 55,908 by 1931. Powell, "Duties of Ahmadi Women," 129.

61. Khan, *From Sufism to Ahmadiyya*, 78.

62. Khan, 78.

63. Rajeev, "Ahmadiyya Fatwa Muzzles Wedding Bells."

64. Bayoumi, "East of the Sun (West of the Moon)," 255.

65. Bayoumi, 260–61.

66. Ahmad, "Is Music Allowed in Islam?"

67. Another example of a successful African American Ahmadi who is rarely celebrated by the Jama'at is the actor Mahershala Ali, who converted to Ahmadiyyat in 2001. His most prominent role to date has been in *Moonlight*, for which he won an Academy Award. The film explores themes of homosexual love in a way that sits at odds with the social conservatism of the Jama'at. His conversion narrative has been published in Majlis Khuddamul Ahmadiyya USA, *By the Dawn's Early Light*.

68. Ayoob, *Many Faces of Political Islam*, 138.

69. Ayoob, 139.

70. Hashim, *Caliphate at War*, 253.

71. Friedmann, *Prophecy Continuous*, 35.

72. Harris Zafar, "Demystifying 'Caliphate,'" Al Islam: The Official Website of the Ahmadiyya Muslim Community, accessed July 18, 2018, https://www.alislam.org/library /contemporary-issues/demystifying-caliphate/.

73. Qasmi, *Politics of Religious Exclusion*, 203.

74. Ahmad, *Tohfa-e-Qaisariyyah*.

75. One of his most explicit statements was as follows: "According to Islam, therefore, religion has no right to interfere in areas exclusive to the state nor has the state any right to interfere in areas commonly shared by them. Rights and responsibilities are so clearly defined in Islam that any questions of a clash is obviated." Ahmad, *Islam's Response to Contemporary Issues*, 243.

76. Hansen, "Predicaments of Secularism," 257.

77. See, for example, Cantwell Smith, "Aḥmadiyya."

78. On tabarruk, compare to Saniotis, "Enchanted Landscapes."

79. Evans-Pritchard, *Sanusi of Cyrenaica*; Gellner, *Muslim Society*; Hammoudi, *Master and Disciple*.

80. Aquil, *Sufism, Culture, and Politics*; Moin, *Millennial Sovereign*; For an analysis of similar processes in South India, see Bayly, *Saints, Goddesses, and Kings*.

81. Aquil, *Sufism, Culture, and Politics*, 192.

82. Digby, "Sufi Shaykh and the Sultan," 71.

83. Quoted in Digby, 72.

84. Aquil, *Sufism, Culture, and Politics*, 193.

85. Werbner, *Pilgrims of Love*, 5.

86. Werbner, 88.

87. Werbner, 90.

88. For medieval precedents to this, see Alam, *Languages of Political Islam*.

89. For a discussion of Sufis moving into voluntary exile in medieval India, see Aquil, *Sufism, Culture, and Politics*, 196.

90. Ahmad, *Nizam-e-Nau: New World Order of Islam*.

91. During the time of my fieldwork, the caliph made repeated references to the coming of a global crisis in his Friday sermons, and many Ahmadis in Qadian were convinced that World War III was imminent.

92. Metcalf, *Islamic Contestations*, 240.

93. As Francis Robinson has argued, "in its extreme form Islam as an object came to be conceptualised as a system. This was the particular achievement of Maulana Maududi; it grew out of his concern to establish an Islamic vision of life to set against that of the West. He described Islam as a nizām, a system which was comprehensive, complete and covered all aspects of human existence." Robinson, "Islam and the Impact of Print," 91–92.

94. Shepard, "Islam as a 'System.'"

95. The foundations for this way of thinking about the sharia were in many cases laid in the nineteenth century. In the Ottoman Empire, the Tanzimat reforms led to the creation of the *majalla*, a sharia-derived civil code that operated according to a radical principle that anybody would be able to consult it and then conform their behavior to it in the correct way (see Messick, *Calligraphic State*, 54–56). In British India, the development of "Anglo-Muhammadan Law" also helped to create the idea of the sharia as a fixed legal code rather than a discursive process (Zaman, *Ulama in Contemporary Islam*, 32).

96. Ahmad, "Al-Wasiyyat."

97. Ahmad, *Nizam-e-Nau*.

98. Ahmad, *Nizam-e-Nau*, 11.

99. Ahmad, 12.

100. Ahmad, *Nizam-e-Nau*, 14–15.

101. Zaman, *Ulama in Contemporary Islam*, 23.

102. Ahmad, "Khutba Jum'a 25 April 2003," 13.

103. For an extensive anthropological examination of such dream-visions, see Mittermaier, *Dreams That Matter*.

104. Adam, "Hadhrat Khalifatul Masih V."

105. For example, Ahmad, "Letters Sent to World Leaders"; Ahmad, "Letters to World Leaders—Part 2."

106. Compare to Ferguson, "Declarations of Dependence."

107. Since the end of my fieldwork, the administration of India has been divided into two sections for north and south.

108. While Ahmadiyya communities in the West are frequently led by highly educated and affluent Ahmadis, they nonetheless also contain a complex demographic mix in terms of class, education, wealth, and social mobility. For an excellent discussion of these issues, see Balzani, "Two Ahmadiyya Mosques," 52.

109. Because of how this official's presence consumed the complete attention of the entire upper echelons of Qadian's administration, one of my interlocutors cheekily referred to him as a "*chhota* [little] huzur."

2. AN ENCHANTING BUREAUCRACY

1. It seems that the image of Qadian as a self-policing community has been present since before partition. In an unpublished dissertation, Zain Ali Shahryar Shirazi describes a scurrilous work of fiction from the colonial period, titled *Mazhabi Daku* (The dacoit of religion), about murder and deception in Qadian. In the story, a lecherous caliph presides over and controls Qadian, while the British colonial state and police remain completely absent and uninvolved. Shirazi, "'Communal' Public Sphere?" 38–40.

2. Compare to Englund, "Extreme Poverty and Existential Obligations."

3. See Gupta, "Narratives of Corruption."

4. Mazzarella, "Internet X-Ray," 476.

5. Berenschot, "Everyday Mediation"; Berenschot, "Clientelism"; Anjaria, "Ordinary States." On the illegibility of the state, see Das, *Life and Words*.

6. Price, "Kingly Models."

7. My argument thus aligns with anthropological work on Islam that has increasingly sought to complexify associations of subordination with passivity. Mahmood, "Feminist Theory"; Mittermaier, *Dreams That Matter*; Mittermaier, "Dreams from Elsewhere."

8. Hull, *Government of Paper*, 1. See also Tarlo, *Unsettling Memories*.

9. This fact is perhaps less contradictory for a Muslim group than it might appear. Ernest Gellner, for example, has argued that unlike charisma in many European settings, in Muslim societies, charisma does not become tarnished or lose its "glamour" through routinization. In fact, he argues, routinization may paradoxically serve to justify rather than diminish charisma in many Islamic contexts. Gellner, *Muslim Society*, 40.

10. Lara Deeb makes a similar point about the enchanted rationality of her interlocutors through the idea that her Shi'a interlocutors in Lebanon inhabit an "enchanted modern." See Deeb, *An Enchanted Modern*.

11. I take this idea of "selfless munificence" from Piliavsky, "Introduction."

12. Bear and Mathur, "Introduction," 19.

13. The idea that society has been in a state of decline ever since the era of the Prophet Muhammad is in fact a common conception among Muslims. The difference between Ahmadis and other Sunni Muslims is that the Ahmadis see continuous prophecy (in the form of Mirza Ghulam Ahmad and his caliphs) as halting this decline and restoring society to the condition in which it flourished under Muhammad and his caliphs. On the idea of decline in Islam more generally, see Ahmed, *Discovering Islam*.

14. The love that the caliph feels for his followers is said to be profound. He is often imagined, alone in the early hours of the morning, weeping in supplication for his people. This is, moreover, an image that historically has been cultivated by the caliphs, as for example in a poem by the fourth caliph, "Bap ki ek ghum zadah beti." Ahmad, *Kalam-e-Tahir*, 134–35.

15. The report also asks, among many other things, the number of young men who watched the caliph's sermon and the number who showed MTA programs to non-Ahmadis.

16. The extent to which the caliph will respond seems to vary greatly between persons, although it appeared that he was far more likely to respond to letters in Urdu than those in English. Translating letters into Urdu is a major activity for Ahmadi missionaries in India in areas where the language is not well known.

17. I heard a number of stories that stressed the immense personal care the caliph might devote to a single member of the Jama'at; for example, the fourth caliph once heard that a boy in Qadian collected stamps and thus had his staff gather a large number of international stamps from other people's letters, before sending them to the boy in Qadian.

18. This total reorientation of the self through a relationship to the caliph can be compared to the way in which Charles Hirschkind describes his Muslim interlocutors attuning themselves to a knowledge of death and the afterlife such that "fear of death, in this sense, constitutes an adverbial virtue, one that orients the individual to the world by coloring and shaping all his or her actions." The notion of an "adverbial virtue" is drawn from the philosopher Michael Oakeshott to refer to something that instructs us on how we should act rather than what exactly it is we should do. Hirschkind, *Ethical Soundscape*, 181.

19. Bai'at is an oath of allegiance to the caliph, but in the common parlance of the Jama'at it refers to the act of formal conversion. See the introduction for more details.

20. See the previous chapter for the history of this usage of the term waqf within the Jama'at.

21. The Urdu term for these men is *mubaligh*. A more standard translation would be preacher, but the Ahmadis have always used "missionary," a choice that reflects their proselytizing goals.

22. If they wanted to, my interlocutors could trace their own kind of "flat," Actor Network Theory–style description of how events unfold in Qadian. Latour, *Reassembling the Social*.

23. In reading this as an ethnographic account of responsibility rather than rationality (as it is commonly taught in undergraduate courses), I am drawing on a tradition of interpreting Evans-Pritchard that runs through the work of James Laidlaw via Mary Douglas and Max Gluckman. Evans-Pritchard, *Witchcraft, Oracles and Magic*; Laidlaw, "Agency and Responsibility"; Laidlaw, *Subject of Virtue*.

24. This reading of responsibility in the Ahmadiyya Jama'at is inspired by Laidlaw, "Agency and Responsibility." For more on responsibility in Qadian, see Evans "Witnessing a Potent Truth."

25. The primacy of the letter as a form of official communication that required skill and sensitivity again underlines the similarities between the Jama'at system and the bureaucratic apparatus of the Indian state. Describing the everyday work of the state, Nayanika Mathur notes how the primary documentary form of Indian bureaucracy is the letter. These letters fall into multiple genres; they can be introductory, clarificatory, procedural, or photocopied. Often letter writing in government bureaucracies is a form of self-defense, that is, a way of performing duties without performing them. All of these observations also apply to the Jama'at system in Qadian. Mathur, *Paper Tiger*, 97–115.

26. For more on homeopathy in India, see Hausman, "Making Medicine Indigenous"; Frank and Ecks, "Ethnography of Indian Homeopathy."

27. Compare, for example, Brinkley Messick's discussion of the calligraphic state in Yemen. Messick, *Calligraphic State*.

28. Mazzarella, "Internet X-Ray."

29. The notion of *shura*, or consultation, is present in the Qur'an, and the *majlis al-shura* (*majlis-e-shura* in Urdu) has historically been seen as an important consultative device for a caliphate. The term has also come to be used for modern parliaments, e.g., in Pakistan.

30. Gualtieri, *Ahmadis*; Gualtieri, *Conscience and Coercion*.

31. Keane, "Others, Other Minds"; Stasch, "Knowing Minds."

32. Sahlins, *Islands of History*, 35–41.

33. Taneja, "Jinnealogy," 160.

34. Taneja, 162.

35. Thus, for the Ahmadis, an increase in personal agency is, contra much anthropological theory, in no sense a necessarily positive thing. Increased agency does not necessarily bring with it increased freedom or liberation; rather, it can entangle the individual in responsibility for actions that are considered morally dubious. Laidlaw, "Agency and Responsibility."

36. Parry, "'Crises of Corruption.'" Note also Anastasia Piliavsky's distinction between the true patron who is said to act selflessly and the "fixer" who does not. Piliavsky, "Introduction," 23.

37. Malik, "Rules & Regulations."

38. I take my phrasing here from David Graeber. My analysis converges with that of Graeber in seeing an intimate connection between the utopian, "otherwordly perfection of royal courts" and their capacity to inflict arbitrary violence. Graeber, "Divine Kingship of the Shilluk."

39. Herzfeld, *Social Production of Indifference*.

40. Matthew Engelke has described a similar tension for Friday Masowe apostolic Christians in Zimbabwe. Engelke's interlocutors desire a direct and immediate sense of God's presence within their lives, and in order to achieve this, they reject all forms of material mediation, including the Bible. Nonetheless, there are aspects of this "live and

direct" faith, in particular the authority of its prophets, which are in fact possible only because most of the congregants are already aware of the Bible. In other words, the absence of the Bible is really only possible for these Christians because of its unacknowledged presence. This creates a dilemma very similar to that facing my Ahmadi interlocutors, for whom any attempt to create a direct and unmediated relationship with the caliph is always dependent upon the (very material) presence of multiple intermediaries. Engelke, *A Problem of Presence*, 198–99.

41. Mathur, *Paper Tiger*, 25.

42. Mathur, 25.

43. Raman, *Document Raj*, 2–3, 137.

44. Raman, 151.

45. Raman, 140.

46. Veena Das, quoted in Raman, 3.

3. A FAILURE TO DOUBT?

1. The very precise theological distinctions employed by Ghulam Ahmad in his own defense of his prophethood are often overlooked in favor of simplifications in such debates. For Ahmad's precise terminology, see Ahmad, *A Misconception Removed (Eik Ghalatī Kā Izāla)*.

2. Sikand, *Bastions of the Believers*, 104.

3. Sikand, 105.

4. Khan, *Muslim Becoming*, 147–48.

5. For a particularly obvious example of the "exceptionalist" narrative, see Valentine, *Islam and the Ahmadiyya Jama'at*. There is fortunately a large historical narrative that disproves any exceptionalist story. Ayesha Jalal, for example, has analyzed Mirza Ghulam Ahmad and the early Ahmadiyya movement in particular as emplaced and engaged in broader cultural and social changes and events. Jalal, *Self and Sovereignty*; Jalal, *Partisans of Allah*.

6. Parry, "The Brahmanical Tradition," 205.

7. Ahmed, "Specters of Macaulay"; Asad et al., *Is Critique Secular?*

8. For example, Soares and Osella, "Islam, Politics, Anthropology"; Deeb and Harb, *Leisurely Islam*; Janson, *Islam, Youth and Modernity*; Tobin, *Everyday Piety*. See also Katherine Ewing's work for an earlier take on fractured Muslim selfhood. Ewing, *Arguing Sainthood*; Ewing, "Illusion of Wholeness."

9. By ethical, I do not mean that the content of these polemics is about moral action (although it frequently is). Rather, I take inspiration from anthropology's engagement with virtue ethics in order to focus on the practice of polemics as a technique through which Ahmadis cultivate a relationship to their caliph that they see as necessary for human flourishing. In doing this, I draw inspiration from, for example, Hussein Ali Agrama's work to reinterpret fatwa giving not just as a tool for doctrinal adjustment but as an ethical practice of caring for the self. Agrama, "Ethics, Tradition, Authority." For more on virtue ethics and anthropology, see Lambek, "Anthropology of Religion"; Laidlaw, "Anthropology of Ethics and Freedom"; Laidlaw, *Subject of Virtue*; Rogers, *Old Faith*; Mattingly, "Two Virtue Ethics."

10. On questions of ritual, see Bowen, *Muslims through Discourse*. On questions of orthodoxy, see Asad, *Anthropology of Islam*; Hirschkind, "Heresy or Hermeneutics."

11. Mazhari, "Reforming Madrasa Curriculum"; Wasey, "Madrasas in India."

12. Although in the Indian case, such accusations seem to be largely baseless. See Mazhari, "Reforming Madrasa Curriculum."

13. Wasey, "Madrasas in India."

14. Riaz, *Faithful Education*, 50.

15. Robinson, *'Ulama of Farangi Mahall*.

16. Hashmi, *Muslim Response*, 131.

17. Alam, "Enemy Within"; Alam, *Inside a Madrasa*.

18. Zaman, *Ulama in Contemporary Islam*, 126–27.

19. Rahman, "Language, Religion and Identity," 210.

20. Kepel, *Jihad*, 225.

21. On the embodiment of texts, see Eickelman, *Knowledge and Power*; Eickelman, "Mass Higher Education."

22. I use the term "repugnant" in the sense coined by Susan Harding. Harding, "Representing Fundamentalism."

23. Marsden, *Living Islam*.

24. In a later article, Marsden argues that we should deconstruct such categories as Islamist and neofundamentalist, for these labels conceal "the complex and inherently unfinished nature" of responses that people have to processes of Islamization. Marsden demonstrates that even archetypal reformist Muslims switch between various registers of self-presentation in a flexible process that belies the "straightjackets" of "reformism" or "Islamism." Marsden, "Women, Politics and Islamism," 426–27.

25. Zaman, *Ulama in Contemporary Islam*, 50–54.

26. Fischer and Abedi, "Qur'anic Dialogics."

27. Fischer and Abedi, 149.

28. I find problematic Khan's notion that the legal persecution of Ahmadis in Pakistan is due to this form of ethical striving. Nonetheless, I follow Khan in my desire to understand the ethical qualities of forms of Islam that do not conform to a pluralistic liberal outlook. Khan, *Muslim Becoming*.

29. Interestingly, medieval disputations and dialectics, which have always been seen as intellectually productive, have been extensively studied for their ethical and political dimensions. See, for example, Makdisi, *Rise of Colleges*; Stroumsa, "Ibn Al-Rāwandī's Sū' Adab Al-Mujādala."

30. Himal, "Ecumenism and Islam's Enemy Within."

31. The idea that disputation might be a practice for cultivating a relationship to the self opens up the possibility that this "illiberal" activity is in some ways a practice of "freedom." See Laidlaw, "Anthropology of Ethics and Freedom."

32. Muslims for Life (website), Ahmadiyya Muslim Community, accessed March 28, 2014, http://muslimsforlife.org.

33. Iqbal, *Islam and Ahmadism*, 23–24. Naveeda Khan interprets Iqbal's argument as an attempt to justify Muslim exclusion of Ahmadis as a "contemporary need" rather than "a lapse into a medieval inquisitional mode." In this reading, Ahmadiyyat necessarily had to be excluded from definitions of Islam because it substituted the difficult and solitary task of striving to be a better Muslim with mystical guidance. Khan, *Muslim Becoming*, 117–18.

34. Phoenix, *His Holiness*, 153.

35. Jones, *Socio-Religious Reform Movements*; Jones, "Swami Dayananda Saraswati's Critique"; Metcalf, "Imagined Community"; Van der Linden, *Moral Languages*.

36. Metcalf, "Imagined Community," 230. A similar situation has been described in Sri Lanka such that polemical debates between Christian missionaries and Buddhist reformers created an unspoken consensus "that different 'religions' like Buddhism and Christianity were indeed based on different 'doctrines' which were to be found in their 'scriptures', and that each religion's claims to merit were based on the coherence and veracity—or absence of 'error'—of its doctrines." Spencer, "The Politics of Tolerance: Buddhists and Christians, Truth and Error in Sri Lanka," 206.

37. Ahmad, *Revelation, Rationality, Knowledge and Truth*, 633.

38. Ahmad, *Sirat-e-Hadrat Masih Mau'ud*.

39. Alam, *Languages of Political Islam*, 154.

40. Ahmad, *Barāhīn-e-Ahmadiyya*, 74.

41. Ahmad, 79.

42. Rashed, *Ahmadiyyat Ne Dunya Ko Kya Dya?* 37–38.

43. It was in fact necessary for the coherence of Ahmad's own prophethood that Guru Nanak be a Muslim. Ahmad claimed to be a reformer for all the religions he encountered in Punjab. This claim was theologically simple in the case of Hinduism, for Ahmad needed only claim that Krishna was an early prophet of Allah, in much the same way that Muslims see Moses as a prophet before Muhammad. Thus, Hinduism came to be seen as a pre-Islamic religion, to which Ghulam Ahmad was a legitimate reformer in the same way that he presented himself as a reformer to Christianity and Judaism. Sikhism presented a difficult challenge for him because it emerged after Islam, and therefore Ahmad could not claim to be a reformer for the Sikhs while maintaining his claim that his prophethood stemmed from his position within the Prophet Muhammad's sharia. In proving that Baba Nanak was a Muslim saint, he thus established that Baba Nanak brought no new sharia but instead fell within that of the Qur'an. In other words, Guru Nanak being Muslim meant that Ghulam Ahmad could maintain his claim to be the reformer for all religions, including Sikhism.

44. Ahmad, *Silsila Ahmadiyya*, 1:61.

45. As I describe elsewhere with Jonathan Mair, the difference was incommensurated. See Mair and Evans, "Ethics across Borders."

46. Ahmad, *Jesus in India*.

47. Bengalee, *Tomb of Jesus*, 39–40.

48. Ahmad, *Jesus in India*, 14.

49. Adamson, *Mirza Ghulam Ahmad of Qadian*, 71.

50. Evans, "Witnessing a Potent Truth."

51. Ahmad, *Revelation, Rationality, Knowledge and Truth*.

52. In understanding knowledge in this way, the Ahmadis belong to a far longer Islamic tradition, which sees text as fundamentally ambiguous, in such a way that the correct transmission of knowledge and the correct interpretation of scripture can only ever be ensured by relations of discipline. Eickelman, *Knowledge and Power*; Messick, *Calligraphic State*; Robinson, "Technology and Religious Change."

53. Mahmood, "Religious Reason and Secular Affect," 70.

54. Mahmood, 72.

55. It is important to clarify that although Ahmadis understand Ghulam Ahmad to provide a perfect model of how to imitate the Prophet Muhammad, they do not conflate his personhood with that of Muhammad, as has sometimes been assumed in the polemics of opponents and in Pakistani legal discourse. Ahmed, "Paradoxes of Ahmadiyya Identity," 301–3.

56. Ahmed, "Specters of Macaulay," 196.

57. Khan, "Of Children and Jinn," 244.

58. Ataullah and Abdullah, *Qandil sadaqat*.

59. Evans, "Witnessing a Potent Truth."

60. Malabari, *Man That Is Called Jesus*; Jalandhri, *Death on the Cross?*

61. Ahmad, *Revelation, Rationality, Knowledge and Truth*, 682.

62. Compare to Eickelman, *Knowledge and Power*.

63. Evans, "Witnessing a Potent Truth," 362.

64. The importance of witnessing to the anthropological study of Islam has increasingly been recognized. See Mittermaier, *Dreams That Matter*; Mittermaier, "Dreams from Elsewhere."

65. I have previously explored how Ahmadis in Qadian make themselves "susceptible" to potent religious truth in Evans, "Witnessing a Potent Truth" and Evans "Beyond Cultural Intimacy."

66. "Natural Disasters and Divine Punishment: Friday Sermon March 18th, 2011," delivered by Hazrat Mirza Masroor Ahmad. https://www.alislam.org/friday-sermon/2011-03-18.html.

67. "He who follows the right way follows it only for the good of his own soul; and he who goes astray, goes astray only to his own loss. And no bearer of burden shall bear the burden of another, And We never punish until We have sent a Messenger." This translation is taken from an Ahmadi edition of the Qur'an, edited by Malik Ghulam Farid. In the Ahmadi version it is verse 17:16, due to the fact that the Ahmadis follow the convention of counting the bismillah as the first *ayah* of each sura in the Qur'an. Farīd, *Holy Qur'ān*, 552.

68. For the English translation, see Ahmad, *Essence of Islam*, 5:149.

69. Ahmad, *Hazrat Khalifatul Messiah*, 1.

70. Ahmad, *Revelation, Rationality, Knowledge and Truth.*

71. Geertz, *Islam Observed*, 69.

72. Kallon, "Quest for Knowledge."

73. HC Deb 20 October 2010 vol 516 cc 284-304WH.

74. HC Deb 20 October 2010 vol 516 cc 285WH.

75. For more on this, see Evans, "Witnessing a Potent Truth."

76. Lempert, *Discipline and Debate*, 153.

77. Bubandt, *The Empty Seashell.*

78. Bubandt, 15. Bubandt references Latour, *On the Modern Cult.*

79. Bubandt, *The Empty Seashell*, 236.

80. Bubandt, 18.

81. Lambek, "Choking on the Quran."

82. McIntosh, "Reluctant Muslims," 109.

83. For more on the auxiliary organizations, see chapter 1 of this book.

84. I have previously analyzed this event for the purposes of a different argument in Evans, "Witnessing a Potent Truth," 360–61.

85. It is worth comparing the Ahmadi insistence on the moral opacity of others with broader anthropological debates on the opacity of other minds. See Robbins and Rumsey, "Introduction."

4. PRAYER DUELS TO THE DEATH

1. Ahmad, "Khutba Jum'a 3 Jun 1988," 394.

2. Ahmad, "Khutba Jum'a 3 Jun 1988," 394.

3. Ahmad, "Khutba Jum'a 3 Jun 1988," 395.

4. *Haft Rozah Badr Qadian*, July 28, 1988, 3.

5. Schmucker, "Mubāhala."

6. Schmucker, "Mubāhala."

7. This quotation is from a Qur'an published by the Jama'at, translated by Malik Ghulam Farid, which counts the bismillah as the first verse of each chapter. Farid, *Holy Qur'ān*, 142.

8. Schmucker, "Mubāhala."

9. Wahidi, "Mubāhalah di Sosial Media"; Halimi et al., "Assessment of Islamic State's Ideological Threat."

10. See, for example, Hasan, "Salafi Movement in Indonesia."

11. See, for example, Ahmad, "Mubahala Background."

12. Friedmann, *Prophecy Continuous*, 141.

13. Ahmad, *Essence of Islam*, 5:113.

14. *Review of Religion*, "Divine Judgment in Dowie's Death," 119.

15. *Review of Religion*, "Downfall of Dowie."

16. *Haft Rozah Badr Qadian*, December 13, 1984.

17. Cabrita, "An Introduction to the Letters of Isaiah Moteka."

18. Friedmann, *Prophecy Continuous*, 7.

19. Ahmad, *Essence of Islam*, 3:419.

20. For example, Ahmad, 3:382.

21. Ahmad, 3:386.

22. For example, Ahmad, 3:398.

23. Ahmad, 3:392, 415.

24. Ahmad, 3:393, 394, 398, 400, 403.

25. Ahmad, "Khutba Jum'a 3 June 1988," 388.

26. Ahmad, "Mubahala Background."

27. Ahmad, "Mubahala Background," 108.

28. Ahmad, "Khutba Jum'a 3 Jun 1988," 390.

29. Ahmad, "Khutba Jum'a 10 Jun 1988," 403.

30. Ahmad, "Khutba Jum'a 10 Jun 1988," 404.

31. Ahmad, "Khutba Jum'a 10 Jun 1988," 410.

32. Ahmad, "Khutba Jum'a 10 Jun 1988," 414.

33. Ahmad, "Khutba Jum'a 10 Jun 1988," 423.

34. Ahmad, "Khutba Jum'a 10 Jun 1988," 424.

35. For example, *Haft Rozah Badr Qadian*, July 28, 1988, 1.

36. Friedmann, *Prophecy Continuous*, 6–7.

37. Bowen, "Salat in Indonesia"; Simon, "Soul Freed of Cares?"

38. *Haft Rozah Badr Qadian*, September 15, 1988, 4.

39. *Haft Rozah Badr Qadian*, August 25, 1988, 1.

40. Ahmad, "Mubahala Background," 113–14.

41. Ahmad, "Khutba Jum'a 12 Agast 1988," 553.

42. Chaudhry, "Mubahala Challenge."

43. *Haft Rozah Badr Qadian*, August 3, 1989, 1–2.

44. *Haft Rozah Badr Qadian*, August 18, 1988, 2.

45. Chaudhry, "Mubahala Challenge."

46. *Haft Rozah Badr Qadian*, August 18, 1988, 13.

47. *Haft Rozah Badr Qadian*, December 1, 1988, 7.

48. Rahman, *Professor Daktar Tahir ul Qadri ke Khule Khat ke bare men Chand Guzarishat.*

49. "Mubahla between Muhammad Sharif Sahab Ameer of Kababir with an Arab Sheikh {English Subtitles}," posted by True Islam, March 19, 2011, accessed on July 22, 2019, https://www.youtube.com/watch?v=8S9YZQj1pRg.

50. *Haft Rozah Badr Qadian*, September 2, 1999, 3, 16.

51. *Haft Rozah Badr Qadian*, August 12, 1999, 3.

52. *Haft Rozah Badr Qadian*, January 21, 1999, 7.

53. Conversion figures provided by Da'wat-e-Illallah, Qadian.

54. *Haft Rozah Badr Qadian*, May 13–20, 1999, 20.

55. Qureshi, *Hazrat Bani-e-Jama'at-e-Ahmadiyya.*

56. Qureshi, 15.

57. Qureshi, 16.

58. Qureshi, 16.

59. Qureshi, 43–44.

60. *Haft Rozah Badr Qadian*, May 13–20, 1999, 20.

61. *Haft Rozah Badr Qadian*, May 13–20, 1999, 20.

62. *Haft Rozah Badr Qadian*, May 13–20, 1999, 21.

63. *Haft Rozah Badr Qadian*, May 13–20, 1999, 21.

64. *Haft Rozah Badr Qadian*, June 24, 1999, 10.

65. Four days after the performance of the Kodiyathoor mubahala, a notice was published on the front page of *Badr* recording the time, date, and place of the mubahala and requesting prayers from all Ahmadis. The mubahala was understood to extend far beyond just those who had been in Kodiyathoor on that day, for its success rested on the backing of the unified Jama'at. *Haft Rozah Badr Qadian*, June 1, 1989, 1.

66. *Haft Rozah Badr Qadian*, June 15, 1989, 1, 2, 14.

67. Yusef, *Yugarashmi: Kannada Quarterly*.

68. *Haft Rozah Badr Qadian*, June 15, 1989, 1, 2.

69. e.g. *Haft Rozah Badr Qadian*, June 22, 1989, 9.

70. Chaudhry, "Mubahala Challenge."

71. *Haft Rozah Badr Qadian*, June 15, 1989, 1.

72. *Haft Rozah Badr Qadian*, June 22, 1989, 9–10.

73. Chaudhry, "Mubahala Challenge."

74. Asad, *Genealogies of Religion*, 90.

75. Interestingly, this involves performatively defining infelicities that are both misfires and abuses in Austin's terminology. Austin, *How to Do Things*, 16.

76. Evans-Pritchard, *Witchcraft, Oracles and Magic*, 155.

77. Ahmed, "Paradoxes of Ahmadiyya Identity," 281–82.

78. Ahmed, 282–83.

79. Ahmed, 306.

80. Cavell, "Epistemology and Tragedy," 43.

81. Tahir Ahmad's use of the mubahala thus echoes arguments made within the anthropology of religion that we have to stop seeing the materialities of religion only as evidence for immaterial belief. Keane, "Evidence of the Senses."

82. Devji, *Muslim Zion*.

83. Devji, 47.

84. Devji, 48.

85. Devji, 158.

86. For a critique of this idea that Pakistan was "insufficiently imagined" prior to partition, see Dhulipala, *Creating a New Medina*.

5. TELEVISING ISLAM

1. Cook, *Forbidding Wrong in Islam*, 57–63.

2. Ahmed, *What Is Islam?* 281.

3. Ahmed, 385.

4. Ahmad, *Islami Usul Ki Falasafi*.

5. The Jama'at is vocal in its condemnation of the caste system. In-group marriage nonetheless remains a norm for many Ahmadis in India, frequently justified by notions of suitability rather than by direct reference to caste.

6. This, of course, is a wonderfully ambiguous statement. It could mean that the converts do not know who Mirza Ghulam Ahmad is. But it could also mean that they have not yet realized that the Ahmadis' prophet is the same as the prophet of all Muslims: Muhammad.

7. An apocryphal story that was told to me by an Ahmadi missionary was that Jinnah started wearing his distinctive qaraqul cap after having been given it by an Ahmadi. My

interlocutor thus claimed that this distinctively Pakistani marker of identity was initiated by the Ahmadis.

8. Baer, "Muslim Encounters," 145.

9. Osella and Osella, "Introduction."

10. Introductory footage to the caliph's *khitab*, Qadian Jalsa Salana 2011, first broadcast December 28, 2011.

11. In this sense, MTA's ability to transmit the caliph's voice to the whole world is understood as the culmination of a prophecy given to Mirza Ghulam Ahmad in 1886: "I will deliver your message to the ends of the earth [teri da'wat ko dunya ke kanaron tuk pahuncha dega]." Ahmad, *Tadhkirah*, 179.

12. For example, in his book *The Criterion of Religion* (*Mi'yarul Madhahib*), Ahmad wrote, "Also, Jesus could not describe himself as good, for people knew that he was a known drunkard and this misconduct seems to have been there since the beginning and not something that developed after his claim to divinity. Hence his claim to divinity can only be an evil consequence of alcoholism." I spoke to a number of Ahmad missionaries about this statement, and they were clear that Ahmad was talking about the Jesus of the Bible, not the Jesus of the Qur'an who they believe to be a real historical prophet and therefore most definitely not a drunkard. Ahmad, *Criterion for Religion*, 29.

13. Gualtieri, *Conscience and Coercion*.

14. Although Ahmadis believe that Ahmad was a prophet after Muhammad, this young missionary's statement that there is no prophet after Muhammad was not a mistake. It was, rather, an attempt to second-guess the opponents' use and understanding of the term *nabi* (prophet). For Ahmadis, Ahmad is a prophet only by virtue of his annihilation of the (self) *fana'* in the Prophet Muhammad (see Ahmad, "Ek Ghalati Ka Izala," 207–12). Ahmad is understood to be a prophet of a lower status to Muhammad, in that he brought no new law but fell within the sharia of Muhammad. The young missionary's statement that there is no prophet after Muhammad was an attempt, in the middle of a very heated and potentially violent situation, to explain without subtlety the fact that, for Ahmadis, there can never be another prophet of the same status as Muhammad.

15. Chowdhury, "Ahmadiyyas Face Protest"; Tankha, "Exhibition on Teachings."

16. Mahmood, *Politics of Piety*, 119.

17. For another ethnographic description of these Peace Symposia, see Mair and Evans, "Ethics across Borders."

18. The Jama'at in the United Kingdom is far more successful than that in India at attracting high-profile guests, such as MPs. This is, of course, another example of the relative marginality of the Indian Jama'at compared to its international cousins, particularly the Jama'ats in the United Kingdom, Germany, and Canada.

19. Compare Shryock, "Double Remoteness of Arab Detroit."

20. Khan, "Event Nearly a Century in the Making."

21. Khan, 11.

22. This is a turn of phrase I have taken from Simon Coleman's description of the aesthetics of charismatic Christians who strive for an "unproblematic reception of the Word." Coleman, *Globalisation of Charismatic Christianity*, 152.

23. The photo can be seen at the following website, http://www.reviewofreligions.org /7846/notes-and-comments-28/ (accessed July 23, 2019).

24. Khan, "Event Nearly a Century in the Making," 13.

25. Khan, "Eyewitness Account," 22.

26. Khan, 25.

27. Rashed, "Reflections," 67.

28. Qamar, "Reflections," 72.

29. Spadola, *Calls of Islam*, 3.

30. "Etiquette of Attending Jalsa Salana," Al Islam: The Official Website of the Ahmadiyya Muslim Community, accessed July 23, 2019, http://www.jalsasalana.org/etiquette .html.

31. Compare to Deger, *Shimmering Screens*, 173.

32. Coleman, *Globalisation of Charismatic Christianity*.

33. Coleman, 172.

34. Coleman, 172.

35. Mauss, *The Gift*.

36. For a similar discussion of the gifting of words in an Islamic setting, see Anderson, "'The Piety of the Gift.'"

37. Coleman, *Globalisation of Charismatic Christianity*, 202.

38. Rashid, *Darul Aman*, 68.

39. Ahmad, *British Government and Jihad*, 18.

40. Wedeen, *Ambiguities of Domination*.

41. Wedeen, 12.

42. For example, Friedmann, *Prophecy Continuous*.

43. Shryock, "Other Conscious/Self Aware:," 3.

44. Shryock, "Double Remoteness of Arab Detroit," 286. For the similar problem in writing anthropologically about groups that make particular political claims to victimhood, see Jeffery and Candea, "Politics of Victimhood."

45. Herzfeld, *Cultural Intimacy*.

46. Mittermaier, "Dreams from Elsewhere"; see also Mittermaier, *Dreams That Matter*; Mittermaier, "Invisible Armies"; Mittermaier, "How to Do Things."

47. Mittermaier, "Dreams from Elsewhere," 259

48. Mittermaier, 258 (italics in original).

49. Vlad Naumescu draws explicitly on Mittermaier's ideas to describe a similar moral project among Russian Old Believers in Romania. He argues that "the space of human agency is defined in relation to divine justice: the world acts upon Old Believers to challenge and prove their faith in anticipation of the end times." The importance of being acted upon, in other words, may a more common feature of religious ethics than anthropologists have previously acknowledged. For Naumescu, such moral projects are best described as "an ethics of passion, a relational mode of constituting ethical personhood which displaces intentionality from self to other." Naumescu, "The End Times and the Near Future," 326.

CONCLUSION

1. Brooks, "Shunned for Saying They're Muslims."

2. BBC, "Asad Shah Killing"; Curtis, "Uber Driver Pleads Guilty."

3. Brooks, "Shunned for Saying They're Muslims."

4. Mughal, "Anti-Ahmadi Hate Crime."

5. Curtis, "Uber Driver Pleads Guilty"; Mughal, "Anti-Ahmadi Hate Crime."

6. My thanks to Patrick O'Hare and Dominic Martin for suggesting this point.

7. Ahmad, "Khutba Jum'a 1 April 2016."

8. Kermani, "Why Was Shopkeeper Asad Shah Murdered?"

9. *Asad Shah* [channel], YouTube, joined November 4, 2013, accessed August 7, 2018, https://www.youtube.com/channel/UC6visj4FWeSs9GZnMmUA2dw.

10. Kermani, "Why Was Shopkeeper Asad Shah Murdered?"

11. Faith Matters, "How Tanveer Ahmed (and Others)"; Jalal, *Self and Sovereignty*, 295–96.

12. Kermani, "Why Was Shopkeeper Asad Shah Murdered?"

13. Bennett Jones, "How Punjab Governor's Killer Became a Hero."

14. Kermani, "Why Was Shopkeeper Asad Shah Murdered?"

15. A form of action that has historically caused much confusion for commentators in the West. See, Asad et al., *Is Critique Secular?*

16. Friedmann, *Prophecy Continuous.*

17. Jamal, *Divine Manifestation in Mauritius.*

18. For example, Sherwood, "'It's a Beautiful Thing.'"

19. Brooks, "Scottish Muslim Groups Fail to Attend."

20. Carrell, "Man Who Murdered Glasgow Shopkeeper."

21. I take this phrasing from Clifford Geertz, who in a discussion of religious belief, described how people are increasingly "holding religious views rather than being held by them." Geertz, *Islam Observed*, 17.

22. Berthomé, Bonhomme, and Delaplace, "Preface," 130. For an earlier attempt to understand the production of certainty, see James, "Introduction."

23. Carey, "'The Rules' in Morocco?"

24. Samimian-Darash, "Governing Future Potential Biothreats"; Samimian-Darash and Rabinow, *Modes of Uncertainty*; Keck, "Sentinel Devices."

25. The most famous argument in the Western canon for skepticism being a necessary tool for the acquisition of knowledge is, of course, Descartes's *Meditations on First Philosophy.*

26. Pelkmans, *Fragile Conviction*, 170.

27. Aishima and Salvatore, "Doubt, Faith, and Knowledge"; Engelke, "Early Days of Johane Masowe"; Strhan, *Aliens and Strangers?*; see also Schielke, "Being a Nonbeliever."

28. Willerslev and Suhr, "Is There a Place?" 74.

29. Pelkmans, "Ethnography of Doubt."

30. Kloos and Beekers, "Introduction"; Soares and Osella, "Islam, Politics, Anthropology"; Deeb and Harb, *Leisurely Islam*. For other examples, see Simpson, "Changing Perspectives"; Al-Mohammad and Peluso, "Ethics and the 'Rough Ground'"; Schielke, "Being Good in Ramadan"; Schielke, "Being a Nonbeliever"; Schielke and Debevec, *Ordinary Lives and Grand Schemes.*

31. Mahmood, *Politics of Piety*; Schielke, "Being Good in Ramadan."

32. For example, Laidlaw, *Subject of Virtue.*

33. Soares and Osella, "Islam, Politics, Anthropology," S11.

34. Marsden, *Living Islam.*

35. Marsden and Retsikas, "Introduction," 4.

36. Marsden and Retsikas, 8.

37. Deeb and Harb, *Leisurely Islam.*

38. Janson, *Islam, Youth and Modernity.*

39. Tobin, *Everyday Piety*, 3. Observations across the Muslim world have shown how religious identities are increasingly being structured through acts of consumption; see, for example, Maqsood, "Buying Modern."

40. Tobin, *Everyday Piety*, 6.

41. See, for example, Debevec, "Postponing Piety," 45, who analyzes the postponing of prayers in Burkina Faso as an example of a successful "solution" to this conflict.

42. Lambek, "Choking on the Quran," 259.

43. Fadil and Fernando, "Rediscovering the 'Everyday' Muslim."

44. The most significant of which are Mahmood, *Politics of Piety*; Hirschkind, *Ethical Soundscape.*

45. Fadil and Fernando, "Rediscovering the 'Everyday' Muslim," 61.

46. Fadil and Fernando, 65.

47. Fadil and Fernando, 74.

48. Fadil and Fernando, 61.

49. Robbins, "Beyond the Suffering Subject."

50. Robbins, 455.

51. Emerson and Hartman, "Rise of Religious Fundamentalism"; Robbins and Anthony, "Cults, Porn, and Hate"; Zablocki and Looney, "Research on New Religious Movements"; Zablocki, "Blacklisting of a Concept."

52. Luhrmann, *When God Talks Back*.

53. Luhrmann, xi.

54. Luhrmann, 316.

55. Luhrmann, 301.

56. Luhrmann, 322.

57. Keane, "Self-Interpretation, Agency"; Keane, *Christian Moderns*.

58. Keane, *Christian Moderns*, 6.

59. Keane, 78.

60. Keane, 76.

61. Chakrabarty, "Postcoloniality."

62. Chakrabarty, 9.

63. Chakrabarty, 10.

64. Chakrabarty, 17.

65. For an interesting discussion on this topic, see Hann, "Heart of the Matter."

66. See, for example, Coleman, "Borderlands."

67. Comaroff and Comaroff, "Occult Economies"; Comaroff and Comaroff, "Millennial Capitalism."

68. Weber, *Protestant Ethic*.

69. Weber, 60.

70. Pelkmans, "Ethnography of Doubt," 5.

71. Kresse, *Philosophising in Mombasa*, 2.

72. See also Nelson, "Constitutional Migration."

73. I do not mean this in the sense of dying for the Jama'at, although martyrdom is obviously an ever-present possibility, particularly for Ahmadis in Pakistan. Rather I refer to the idea of giving one's life (zindagi) as an endowment (waqf) in an almost unbreakable bond of devotion and service.

74. Mayblin, "Untold Sacrifice," 356.

75. For a discussion of "authentication," see Deeb, *An Enchanted Modern*.

76. Derrida, *The Gift of Death*. On the related question of the gift, see Parry, "Gift, the Indian Gift"; Laidlaw, "Free Gift Makes No Friends."

77. Keane, "On Spirit Writing."

78. Compare to Wagner, *Invention of Culture*. See also the 2010 GDAT (Group for Debates in Anthropological Theory) debate for an anthropological deconstruction of the distinctions between "invention" and "discovery" in the study of relations. Venkatesan et al., "The Task of Anthropology Is to Invent Relations."

79. There is a postcolonial fear of mimicry behind many of these accusations. Taussig, *Mimesis and Alterity*; Gable, "Bad Copies."

80. Ahmed, *What Is Islam?* 401 (italics in original).

81. Ahmed, 404.

Bibliography

Abu-Lughod, Lila. "The Romance of Resistance: Tracing Transformations of Power through Bedouin Women." *American Ethnologist* 17, no. 1 (1990): 41–55. https://doi.org/10.1525/ae.1990.17.1.02a00030.

———. *Veiled Sentiments: Honor and Poetry in a Bedouin Society*. Updated edition with a new preface. Berkeley: University of California Press, 1999.

Adam, Abdul Wahab. "Hadhrat Khalifatul Masih V: Service in Ghana." *Review of Religions* 103, no. 5 (2008): 7–14.

Adamson, Iain. *Mirza Ghulam Ahmad of Qadian*. Old Woking, UK: Elite International Publications, 1989.

Agrama, Hussein Ali. "Ethics, Tradition, Authority: Toward an Anthropology of the Fatwa." *American Ethnologist* 37, no. 1 (2010): 2–18. https://doi.org/10.1111/j.1548-1425.2010.01238.x.

Ahmad, Basheer ud-Din Mahmood. *Anwar-e-Khilafat*. Qadian, India: Nazarat Nashr-o-Isha'at, 2007.

———. *Mansab-e-Khilafat*. Qadian, India: Nazarat Nashr-o-Isha'at, 2007.

———. *Nizam-e-Nau*. Qadian, India: Nazarat Nashr-o-Isha'at, 2005.

———. *Nizam-e-Nau: New World Order of Islam*. Translated by Chaudhry Muhammad Zafrullah Khan. Tilford, UK: Islam International Publications, 2005.

———. *Sirat-e-Hadrat Masih Mau'ud*. Qadian, India: Nazarat Nashr-o-Isha'at, 2001.

Ahmad, Mirza Bashir. *Silsila Ahmadiyya*. Vol. 1. Qadian, India: Nazarat Nashr-o-Isha'at, 2008.

Ahmad, Mirza Ghulam. *A Misconception Removed [Eik Ghalatī Kā Izāla]*. Translated by Munawar Ahmed Saeed. Tilford, UK: Islam International Publications, 2007.

———. "Al-Wasiyyat." In *Ruhani Khazain*, 20:299–332. Rabwah, Pakistan: Nazarat Ishaat, 2008. First published 1905.

———. *Barāhīn-e-Ahmadiyya: Arguments in Support of the Holy Quran and the Prophethood of the Holy Prophet Muhammad*. Parts I & II. Translated by Mirza Anas Ahmad and Sayyed Atiq Ahmad. Surrey, UK: Islam International Publications, 2012.

———. "Ek Ghalati ka Izala." In *Ruhani Khazain*, 18:313–452. Rabwah, Pakistan: Nazarat Ishaat, 2008. First published 1901.

———. "Islami Usul ki Falasafi." In *Ruhani Khazain*, 10:206–16. Rabwah, Pakistan: Nazarat Ishaat, 2008. First published 1905.

———. *Jesus in India: Jesus' Deliverance from the Cross and Journey to India*. Edited by Chaudhry Muhammad Ali. Translated by Qazi Abdul Hamid. Tilford, UK: Islam International Publications, 2003.

———. *Tadhkirah: English Rendering of the Divine Revelations, Dreams and Visions Vouchsafed to Ḥaḍrat Mirza Ghulam Ahmad of Qadian, the Promised Messiah and Mahdi, on Whom Be Peace*. Edited by Munawar Ahmed Saeed. Translated by Muhammad Zafrulla Khan. Tilford: Islam International Publications, 2009.

———. *The British Government and Jihad*. Translated by Tayyba Seema Ahmed and Lutfur Rahman. Tilford, UK: Islam International Publications, 2006.

——. *The Criterion for Religion: A Comparative Study of Religions on the Basis of Natural Criteria*. Translated by M. J. As'ad. Tilford, UK: Islam International Publications Ltd, 2007.

——. *The Essence of Islam*. Vol. 3. Translated by Chaudhry Muhammad Zafrullah Khan. Tilford, UK: Islam International Publications, 2005.

——. *The Essence of Islam*. Vol. 5. Edited by Sayyed Mir Dawud Ahmad. Translated by Saleem Rahman. Tilford, UK: Islam International Publications, 2007.

——. "Tohfa-e-Qaisariyyah." In *Ruhani Khazain*, 12:251–316. Rabwah, Pakistan: Nazarat Ishaat, 2008. First published 1897.

Ahmad, Mirza Masroor. "Islam—a Religion of Peace and Compassion." *Review of Religions* 108, no. 9 (2013): 46–61.

——. "Khutba Jum'a 1 April 2016." Accessed July 24, 2019. https://www.alislam.org/urdu/khutba/2016-04-01/.

——. "Khutba Jum'a 25 April 2003." In *Khutbat-e-Masroor*, 7:3–13. Rabwah, Pakistan: Islam International Publications. 2003.

——. "Letters Sent to World Leaders." *Review of Religions* 107, no. 4 (2012): 8–18.

——. "Letters to World Leaders—Part 2." *Review of Religions* 107, no. 8 (2012): 30–57.

——. "The Key to Peace—Global Unity." *Review of Religions* 108, no. 2 (2013): 42–63.

——. "World Peace—the Critical Need of the Time." *Review of Religions* 109, no. 3 (2014): 48–58.

Ahmad, Mirza Tahir. "Is Music Allowed in Islam?" *Review of Religions* 105, no. 1 (2010): 51–52.

——. *Islam's Response to Contemporary Issues*. Tilford, UK: Islam International Publications, 2007.

——. *Kalam-e-Tahir*. 4th ed. Qadian, India: Nazarat Nashr-o-Isha'at, 2004.

——. "Khutba Jum'a 3 Jun 1988." In *Khutbat-e-Tahir*, 7:387–407, Tahir Foundation. n.d.

——. "Khutba Jum'a 10 Jun 1988." In *Khutbat-e-Tahir*, 7:409–28, Tahir Foundation. n.d.

——. "Khutba Jum'a 12 Agast 1988." In *Khutbat-e-Tahir*, 7:547–58, Tahir Foundation. n.d.

——. "Mubahala Background: Darsul Quran by Hadrat Khalifatul Masih IV on 14th and 15th May 1988." Translated by Amatul Majeed Chaudhary. *Review of Religions*, March 23, 1989, (special centenary number), 107–17.

——. *Murder in the Name of Allah*. Translated by Syed Barakat Ahmad. Rev. ed. Amritsar, India: Nazarat Nashr-o-Isha'at, 1990.

——. *Revelation, Rationality, Knowledge and Truth*. Tilford, UK: Islam International Publications, 1998.

Ahmad, Shiraz. *Hazrat Khalifatul Messiah V's(Atba) Important Instruction to Ahmadi Students*. Qadian, India: Nazarat Taleem, n.d.

Ahmed, Akbar S. *Discovering Islam: Making Sense of Muslim History and Society*. Rev. ed. London: Routledge, 2002.

Ahmed, Asad Ali. "Specters of Macaulay: Blasphemy, the Indian Penal Code, and Pakistan's Postcolonial Predicament." In *Censorship in South Asia: Cultural Regulation from Sedition to Seduction*, edited by Raminder Kaur and William Mazzarella, 172–205. Bloomington: Indiana University Press, 2009.

——. "The Paradoxes of Ahmadiyya Identity: Legal Appropriation of Muslim-ness and the Construction of Ahmadiyya Difference." In *Beyond Crisis: Re-Evaluating Pakistan*, edited by Naveeda Ahmed Khan, 273–314. London: Routledge, 2010.

Ahmed, Shahab. *What Is Islam? The Importance of Being Islamic*. Princeton, NJ: Princeton University Press, 2015.

Aishima, Hatsuki, and Armando Salvatore. "Doubt, Faith, and Knowledge: The Reconfiguration of the Intellectual Field in Post-Nasserist Cairo." *Journal of the Royal Anthropological Institute* 15 (2009): S41–56. https://doi.org/10.1111/j.1467-9655.2009.01541.x.

Alam, Arshad. *Inside a Madrasa: Knowledge, Power and Islamic Identity in India*. London: Routledge, 2011.

———. "The Enemy Within: Madrasa and Muslim Identity in North India." *Modern Asian Studies* 42, no. 2–3 (2008). https://doi.org/10.1017/S0026749X07003113.

Alam, Muzaffar. *The Languages of Political Islam: India 1200–1800*. London: Hurst, 2004.

Alexander, James. "The Four Points of the Compass." *Philosophy* 87, no. 1 (2012): 79–107. https://doi.org/10.1017/S0031819111000568.

Al-Mohammad, Hayder, and Daniela Peluso. "Ethics and the 'Rough Ground' of the Everyday: The Overlappings of Life in Postinvasion Iraq." *HAU: Journal of Ethnographic Theory* 2, no. 2 (2012): 42–58. https://doi.org/10.14318/hau2.2.004.

Anawati, G. C. "'Īsā." In *Encyclopaedia of Islam*, 2nd ed., edited by P. Bearman, T. Bianquis, C. E. Bosworth, E. van Donzel, and W. P. Heinrichs. Brill Online, 2014.

Anderson, Paul. "'The Piety of the Gift': Selfhood and Sociality in the Egyptian Mosque Movement." *Anthropological Theory* 11, no. 1 (2011): 3–21. https://doi.org/10.1177/1463499610395441.

Anjaria, Jonathan Shapiro. "Ordinary States: Everyday Corruption and the Politics of Space in Mumbai." *American Ethnologist* 38, no. 1 (2011): 58–72. https://doi.org/10.1111/j.1548-1425.2010.01292.x.

Aquil, Raziuddin. *Sufism, Culture, and Politics: Afghans and Islam in Medieval North India*. New Delhi: Oxford University Press, 2007.

Asad, Talal. *Genealogies of Religion: Discipline and Reasons of Power in Christianity and Islam*. Baltimore: Johns Hopkins University Press, 1993.

———. "Reading a Modern Classic: W. C. Smith's 'The Meaning and End of Religion.'" *History of Religions* 40, no. 3 (2001): 205–222.

———. *The Idea of an Anthropology of Islam*. Occasional Papers Series. Washington, DC: Centre for Contemporary Arab Studies, Georgetown University, 1986.

Asad, Talal, Wendy Brown, Judith Butler, and Saba Mahmood. *Is Critique Secular? Blasphemy, Injury, and Free Speech*. 2nd rev. ed. New York: Fordham University Press, 2013.

Ataullah, Kaleem, and Abdullah Wagishauser. *Qandil Sadaqat*. 2nd ed. Qadian: Nazarat Nashr-o-Isha'at, 2008.

Austin, J. L. *How to Do Things with Words*. Oxford: Clarendon Press, 1965.

Ayoob, Mohammed. *The Many Faces of Political Islam: Religion and Politics in the Muslim World*. Ann Arbor: University of Michigan Press, 2008.

Baer, Marc David. "Muslim Encounters with Nazism and the Holocaust: The Ahmadi of Berlin and Jewish Convert to Islam Hugo Marcus." *American Historical Review* 120, no. 1 (2015): 140–71. https://doi.org/10.1093/ahr/120.1.140.

Bainbridge, William Sims, and Rodney Stark. "Scientology: To Be Perfectly Clear." *Sociological Analysis* 41, no. 2 (1980): 128–36. https://doi.org/10.2307/3709904.

Bajwa, Fauzia. "Historical Visits to Canada and Qadian." *Review of Religions*, Khilafat: Special Edition 8 (2008): 32–35.

Balzani, Marzia. "A Tale of Two Ahmadiyya Mosques: Religion, Ethnic Politics, and Urban Planning in London." *Laboratorium: Russian Review of Social Research* 7, no. 3 (2015): 49–71.

———. "Dreaming, Islam and the Ahmadiyya Muslims in the UK." *History and Anthropology* 21, no. 3 (2010): 293–305. https://doi.org/10.1080/02757206.2010.496783.

Barker, Memphis. "Imran Khan Criticised for Defence of Pakistan Blasphemy Laws." *The Guardian*, July 9, 2018, sec. World News. http://www.theguardian.com/world/2018/jul/09/imran-kahn-accused-over-defence-of-pakistan-blasphemy-laws.

Bayly, Susan. *Saints, Goddesses, and Kings: Muslims and Christians in South Indian Society, 1700–1900*. Cambridge: Cambridge University Press, 1989.

Bayoumi, Moustafa. "East of the Sun (West of the Moon): Islam, the Ahmadis, and African America." *Journal of Asian American Studies* 4, no. 3 (2001): 251–63. https://doi.org/10.1353/jaas.2001.0024.

BBC. "Asad Shah Killing: 'Disrespecting Islam' Murderer Jailed." BBC News. Accessed August 9, 2016. http://www.bbc.co.uk/news/uk-scotland-glasgow-west-37021385.

Bear, Laura, and Nayanika Mathur. "Introduction." *Cambridge Journal of Anthropology* 33, no. 1 (2015): 18–34. https://doi.org/10.3167/ca.2015.330103.

Bengalee, Sufi Mutiur Rahman. *The Tomb of Jesus*. 3rd ed. Ahmadiyya Muslim Association UK, 2001.

Bennett Jones, Owen. "How Punjab Governor's Killer Became a Hero." BBC News, January 9, 2012, sec. Magazine. http://www.bbc.co.uk/news/magazine-16443556.

Berenschot, Ward. "Clientelism, Trust Networks, and India's Identity Politics: Conveying Closeness in Gujarat." *Critical Asian Studies* 47, no. 1 (2015): 24–43. https://doi.org/10.1080/14672715.2015.997075.

——. "Everyday Mediation: The Politics of Public Service Delivery in Gujarat, India." *Development and Change* 41, no. 5 (2010): 883–905. https://doi.org/10.1111/j.1467-7660.2010.01660.x.

Berger, Peter L. *The Sacred Canopy: Elements of a Sociological Theory of Religion*. New York: Anchor Books, 1990.

Berger, Peter, and Anton Zijderveld. *In Praise of Doubt: How to Have Convictions without Becoming a Fanatic*. New York: HarperOne, 2010.

Berthomé, François, Julien Bonhomme, and Grégory Delaplace. "Preface: Cultivating Uncertainty." *HAU: Journal of Ethnographic Theory* 2, no. 2 (2012): 129–37. https://doi.org/10.14318/hau2.2.008.

Bowen, John R. *Muslims through Discourse: Religion and Ritual in Gayo Society*. Princeton, NJ: Princeton University Press, 1993.

——. "Salat in Indonesia: The Social Meanings of an Islamic Ritual." *Man* 24, no. 4 (1989): 600–619. https://doi.org/10.2307/2804290.

Brooks, Libby. "Scottish Muslim Groups Fail to Attend Ahmadi Anti-Extremism Event." *The Guardian*, April 18, 2016, sec. UK News. https://www.theguardian.com/uk-news/2016/apr/18/scottish-muslim-groups-ahmadi-anti-extremism-campaign-launch-glasgow.

——. "Shunned for Saying They're Muslims: Life for Ahmadis after Asad Shah's Murder." *The Guardian*, April 9, 2016, sec. World News. https://www.theguardian.com/world/2016/apr/09/shunned-for-saying-theyre-muslims-life-for-ahmadis-after-asad-shahs.

Bubandt, Nils. *The Empty Seashell: Witchcraft and Doubt on an Indonesian Island*. Ithaca, NY: Cornell University Press, 2014.

Cabrita, Joel. "An Introduction to the Letters of Isaiah Moteka: The Correspondence of a Twentieth-Century South African Zionist Minister." *Africa: The Journal of the International African Institute* 84, no. 2 (2014): 163–98. https://doi.org/10.1017/S0001972014000011.

Cantwell Smith, Wilfred. "Aḥmadiyya." In *Encyclopaedia of Islam*, 2nd ed., edited by P. Bearman, T. Bianquis, C. E. Bosworth, E. van Donzel, and W. P. Heinrichs. Brill Online, 2014.

Carey, Matthew. "'The Rules' in Morocco? Pragmatic Approaches to Flirtation and Lying." *HAU: Journal of Ethnographic Theory* 2, no. 2 (2012): 188–204. https://doi.org/10.14318/hau2.2.011.

Carrell, Severin. "Man Who Murdered Glasgow Shopkeeper Asad Shah in Sectarian Attack Jailed." *The Guardian*, August 9, 2016. https://www.theguardian.com/uk-news/2016/aug/09/tanveer-ahmed-jailed-for-murder-glasgow-shopkeeper-in-sectarian-attack.

Cavell, Stanley. "Epistemology and Tragedy: A Reading of Othello." *Daedalus* 108, no. 3 (1979): 27–43.

Chakrabarty, Dipesh. "Postcoloniality and the Artifice of History: Who Speaks for 'Indian' Pasts?" *Representations* 37 (1992): 1–26. https://doi.org/10.2307/2928652.

Chaudhry, Rashid Ahmad. "The Mubahala Challenge and the Response of Mullahs." Al Islam: The Official Website of the Ahmadiyya Muslim Community. Accessed July 25, 2019. http://www.alislam.org/library/links/00000170.html.

Chowdhury, Shreya Roy. "Ahmadiyyas Face Protest at Peace Mission." *Times of India*, September 24, 2011. https://timesofindia.indiatimes.com/city/delhi/Ahmadiyyas-face -protest-at-peace-mission/articleshow/10099709.cms.

Coleman, Simon. "Borderlands: Ethics, Ethnography and 'Repugnant' Christianity." *HAU: Journal of Ethnographic Theory* 5, no. 2 (2015): 275–300. https://doi.org/10.14318 /hau5.2.016.

——. *The Globalisation of Charismatic Christianity*. Cambridge: Cambridge University Press, 2007.

Comaroff, Jean, and John L. Comaroff. "Millennial Capitalism: First Thoughts on a Second Coming." *Public Culture* 12, no. 2 (2000): 291–343. https://doi.org/10.1215 /08992363-12-2-291.

——. "Occult Economies and the Violence of Abstraction: Notes from the South African Postcolony." *American Ethnologist* 26, no. 2 (1999): 279–303. https://doi.org/10.1525 /ae.1999.26.2.279.

Cook, Michael. *Forbidding Wrong in Islam*. Cambridge: Cambridge University Press, 2003.

Curtis, Joseph. "Uber Driver Pleads Guilty to 'Despicable' Murder of Glasgow Shopkeeper Asad Shah Because He Belonged to Minority Muslim Sect." *Daily Mail*, July 7, 2016. http://www.dailymail.co.uk/news/article-3678547/Taxi-driver-pleads-guilty-killing -Glasgow-shopkeeper-Asad-Shah-wished-Christian-customers-happy-Easter.html.

Das, Veena. *Life and Words: Violence and the Descent into the Ordinary*. Berkeley: University of California Press, 2007.

——. "Ordinary Ethics." In *A Companion to Moral Anthropology*, edited by Didier Fassin, 1st ed., 133–149. Chichester: Wiley-Blackwell, 2012.

Debevec, Liza. "Postponing Piety in Urban Burkina Faso: Discussing Ideas on When to Start Acting as a Pious Muslim." In *Ordinary Lives and Grand Schemes: An Anthropology of Everyday Religion*, edited by Joska Samuli Schielke and Liza Debevec, 33–47. New York: Berghahn Books, 2012.

Deeb, Lara. *An Enchanted Modern: Gender and Public Piety in Shi'i Lebanon*. Princeton, NJ: Princeton University Press, 2006.

Deeb, Lara, and Mona Harb. *Leisurely Islam: Negotiating Geography and Morality in Shi'ite South Beirut*. Princeton, NJ: Princeton University Press, 2013.

Deger, Jennifer. *Shimmering Screens: Making Media in an Aboriginal Community*. Minneapolis: University of Minnesota Press, 2006.

Derrida, Jacques. *The Gift of Death*. Chicago: University of Chicago Press, 1996.

Descartes, René. *Meditations on First Philosophy: With Selections from the Objections and Replies*. Edited by John Cottingham. Cambridge: Cambridge University Press, 2013.

Devji, Faisal. *Muslim Zion: Pakistan as a Political Idea*. London: Hurst, 2013.

Dhulipala, Venkat. *Creating a New Medina: State Power, Islam, and the Quest for Pakistan in Late Colonial North India*. Delhi: Cambridge University Press, 2015.

Digby, Simon. "The Sufi Shaykh and the Sultan: A Conflict of Claims to Authority in Medieval India." *Iran* 28 (1990): 71–81. https://doi.org/10.2307/4299836.

The Economist. "Iran's Multiplicity of Messiahs: You're a Fake." *The Economist*, April 27, 2013. http://www.economist.com/news/middle-east-and-africa/21576700-authorities -think-too-many-people-are-claiming-be-mahdi-youre.

Egan, Andy, and Adam Elga. "I Can't Believe I'm Stupid." *Philosophical Perspectives* 19, no. 1 (2005): 77–93. https://doi.org/10.1111/j.1520-8583.2005.00054.x.

Eickelman, Dale F. *Knowledge and Power in Morocco: The Education of a Twentieth-Century Notable*. Princeton, NJ: Princeton University Press, 1985.

——. "Mass Higher Education and the Religious Imagination in Contemporary Arab Societies." *American Ethnologist* 19, no. 4 (1992): 643–55. https://doi.org/10.1525/ae.1992.19.4.02a00010.

Emerson, Michael O., and David Hartman. "The Rise of Religious Fundamentalism." *Annual Review of Sociology* 32 (2006): 127–44. https://doi.org/10.1146/annurev.soc.32.061604.123141.

Engelke, Matthew. *A Problem of Presence: Beyond Scripture in an African Church*. Berkeley: University of California Press, 2007.

——. *God's Agents: Biblical Publicity in Contemporary England*. Berkeley: University of California Press, 2013.

——. "The Early Days of Johane Masowe: Self-Doubt, Uncertainty, and Religious Transformation." *Comparative Studies in Society and History* 47, no. 4 (2005): 781–808. https://doi.org/10.1017/S0010417505000356.

Englund, Harri. "Extreme Poverty and Existential Obligations: Beyond Morality in the Anthropology of Africa?" *Social Analysis* 52, no. 3 (2008): 33–50. https://doi.org/10.3167/sa.2008.520302.

Evans, Nicholas H.A. "Beyond Cultural Intimacy: The Tensions that Make Truth for India's Ahmadi Muslims." *American Ethnologist* 44, no. 3 (2017): 490–502. https://doi.org/10.1111/amet.12524.

——. "Witnessing a Potent Truth: Rethinking Responsibility in the Anthropology of Theisms." *Journal of the Royal Anthropological Institute* 22, no. 2 (2016): 356–72. https://doi.org/10.1111/1467-9655.12380.

Evans-Pritchard, E. E. *The Sanusi of Cyrenaica*. Oxford: Clarendon Press, 1949.

——. *Witchcraft, Oracles and Magic among the Azande*. Oxford: Clarendon Press, 1976.

Ewing, Katherine P. "The Illusion of Wholeness: Culture, Self, and the Experience of Inconsistency." *Ethos* 18, no. 3 (1990): 251–78. https://doi.org/10.1525/eth.1990.18.3.02a00020.

Ewing, Katherine Pratt. *Arguing Sainthood: Modernity, Psychoanalysis, and Islam*. Durham, NC: Duke University Press, 1997.

Fadil, Nadia, and Mayanthi Fernando. "Rediscovering the 'Everyday' Muslim: Notes on an Anthropological Divide." *HAU: Journal of Ethnographic Theory* 5, no. 2 (2015): 59–88. https://doi.org/10.14318/hau5.2.005.

Faith Matters. "How Tanveer Ahmed (and Others) Exploit Religious Sentiment to Justify Murder." *Faith Matters* (blog), October 3, 2016. http://faith-matters.org/2016/10/03/tanveer-ahmed-others-exploit-religious-sentiment-justify-murder/.

Farīd, Malik Ghulām, ed. *The Holy Qur'ān: Arabic Text with English Translation and Short Commentary*. Tilford, UK: Islam International Publications, 2002.

Ferguson, James. "Declarations of Dependence: Labour, Personhood, and Welfare in Southern Africa." *Journal of the Royal Anthropological Institute* 19, no. 2 (2013): 223–42. https://doi.org/10.1111/1467-9655.12023.

Festinger, Leon, Henry Riecken, and Stanley Schachter. *When Prophecy Fails*. Minneapolis: University of Minnesota Press, 1956.

Fischer, Michael M. J., and Mehdi Abedi. "Qur'anic Dialogics: Islamic Poetics and Politics for Muslims and for Us." In *The Interpretation of Dialogue*, edited by Tullio Maranhão, 120–53. Chicago: University of Chicago Press, 1990.

Fisher, H. J. *Ahmadiyyah: A Study in Contemporary Islam on the West African Coast*. London: Oxford University Press, 1963.

Frank, Robert, and Stefan Ecks. "Towards an Ethnography of Indian Homeopathy." *Anthropology and Medicine* 11, no. 3 (2004): 307–26. https://doi.org/10.1080/1364847042000296581.

Friedmann, Yohanan. "Aḥmadiyya." In *Encyclopaedia of Islam, THREE*, edited by Gudrun Krämer, Denis Matringe, John Nawas, and Everett Rowson. Brill Online, 2014.

——. *Prophecy Continuous: Aspects of Ahmadi Religious Thought and Its Medieval Background*. 2nd ed. New Delhi: Oxford University Press, 2003.

Gable, Eric. "Bad Copies: The Colonial Aesthetic and the Manjaco-Portuguese Encounter." In *Images and Empires: Visuality in Colonial and Postcolonial Africa*, edited by Deborah D. Kaspin and Paul Stuart Landau, 294–319. Berkeley: University of California Press, 2002.

Galanter, Marc. *Cults: Faith, Healing, and Coercion*. New York: Oxford University Press, 1989.

Geertz, Clifford. *Islam Observed: Religious Development in Morocco and Indonesia*. New Haven, CT: Yale University Press, 1968.

Gellner, Ernest. *Muslim Society*. Cambridge: Cambridge University Press, 1981.

Graeber, David. "The Divine Kingship of the Shilluk: On Violence, Utopia, and the Human Condition; or, Elements for an Archaeology of Sovereignty." *HAU: Journal of Ethnographic Theory* 1, no. 1 (2011): 1–62. https://doi.org/10.14318/hau1.1.002.

Gualtieri, Antonio R. *Conscience and Coercion: Ahmadi Muslims and Orthodoxy in Pakistan*. Montreal: Guernica, 1989.

——. *The Ahmadis: Community, Gender, and Politics in a Muslim Society*. London: McGill-Queen's University Press, 2004.

Gupta, Akhil. "Narratives of Corruption: Anthropological and Fictional Accounts of the Indian State." *Ethnography* 6, no. 1 (2005): 5–34.

Halimi, M., M. Sudiman, and A. Hassan. "Assessment of Islamic State's Ideological Threat." *Counter Terrorist Trends and Analyses* 11, no.1 (2019): 86–90.

Hammoudi, Abdellah. *Master and Disciple: The Cultural Foundations of Moroccan Authoritarianism*. Chicago: University of Chicago Press, 1997.

Hann, Chris. "The Heart of the Matter: Christianity, Materiality, and Modernity." *Current Anthropology* 55, no. S10 (2014): S182–92. https://doi.org/10.1086/678184.

Hansen, Thomas Blom. "Predicaments of Secularism: Muslim Identities and Politics in Mumbai." *Journal of the Royal Anthropological Institute* 6, no. 2 (2000): 255–72. https://doi.org/10.1111/1467-9655.00015.

Hanson, John H. *The Ahmadiyya in the Gold Coast: Muslim Cosmopolitans in the British Empire*. Bloomington: Indiana University Press, 2017.

Harding, Susan F. "Representing Fundamentalism: The Problem of the Repugnant Cultural Other." *Social Research* 58, no. 2 (1991): 373–93.

Hasan, Noorhaidi. "The Salafi Movement in Indonesia: Transnational Dynamics and Local Development." *Comparative Studies of South Asia, Africa and the Middle East* 27, no. 1 (2007): 83–94. https://doi.org/10.1215/1089201x-2006-045.

Hashim, Ahmed. *The Caliphate at War: The Ideological, Organisational and Military Innovations of Islamic State*. London: Hurst, 2018.

Hashmi, Syed Masroor Ali Akhtar. *Muslim Response to Western Education: A Study of Four Pioneer Institutions*. New Delhi: Commonwealth, 1989.

Hausman, Gary J. "Making Medicine Indigenous: Homeopathy in South India." *Social History of Medicine* 15, no. 2 (2002): 303–22. https://doi.org/10.1093/shm/15.2.303.

Hecht, Jennifer Michael. *Doubt: A History*. New York: HarperOne, 2004.

Herzfeld, Michael. *Cultural Intimacy: Social Poetics in the Nation-State*. London: Routledge, 1997.

——. *The Social Production of Indifference: Exploring the Symbolic Roots of Western Bureaucracy*. Chicago: University of Chicago Press, 1993.

Himal. "Ecumenism and Islam's Enemy Within." *Himal Southasian*, March 2004. http://old.himalmag.com/component/content/article/1738-.html.

Hirschkind, Charles. "Heresy or Hermeneutics: The Case of Nasr Hamid Abu Zayd." *Stanford Humanities Review* 5, no. 1 (1995): 35–49.

——. *The Ethical Soundscape: Cassette Sermons and Islamic Counterpublics*. New York: Columbia University Press, 2006.

Holsinger, Bruce. *Neomedievalism, Neoconservatism, and the War on Terror*. Paradigm 29. Chicago: Prickly Paradigm, 2007.

Horowitz, Sophie. "Epistemic Akrasia." *Noûs* 48, no. 4 (2014): 718–44. https://doi.org/10.1111/nous.12026.

Hull, Matthew S. *Government of Paper: The Materiality of Bureaucracy in Urban Pakistan*. Berkeley: University of California Press, 2012.

Iannaccone, Laurence R. "Sacrifice and Stigma: Reducing Free-riding in Cults, Communes, and Other Collectives." *Journal of Political Economy* 100, no. 2 (1992): 271–291. https://doi.org/10.1086/261818.

——. "Why Strict Churches Are Strong." *American Journal of Sociology* 99, no. 5 (1994): 1180–1211. https://doi.org/10.1086/230409.

Indian Express. "Minority in a Minority." *Indian Express*, August 5, 2016. http://indianexpress.com/article/opinion/editorials/ahmadiyya-community-census-india-muslims-2954285/.

Iqbal, Muhammad. *Islam and Ahmadism: A Reply to Questions Raised by Pandit Jawahar Lal Nehru*. Edited by Zafarul Islam Khan. New Delhi: Pharos Media, 2010.

Iqtidar, Humeira. "State Management of Religion in Pakistan and Dilemmas of Citizenship." *Citizenship Studies* 16, no. 8 (2012): 1013–28. https://doi.org/10.1080/13621025.2012.735026.

Irawan, Andi Muhammad. "'They Are Not Muslims': A Critical Discourse Analysis of the Ahmadiyya Sect Issue in Indonesia." *Discourse and Society* 28, no. 2 (2017): 162–81. https://doi.org/10.1177/0957926516685462.

Jalal, Ayesha. *Partisans of Allah: Jihad in South Asia*. Cambridge, MA: Harvard University Press, 2008.

——. *Self and Sovereignty: Individual and Community in South Asian Islam since 1850*. London: Routledge, 2000.

Jalandhri, Abul Ata. *Death on the Cross? Ten Arguments from the Holy Bible*. 8th ed. Amritsar, India: Printwell, 2012.

Jamal, Fazil. *The Divine Manifestation in Mauritius: A Response to Certain Questions Raised by Ahmadi Brothers and Sisters*. Vol. 1. India: Jamaat Ul Sahih Al Islam International, 2012.

James, Wendy. "Introduction: Whatever Happened to the Enlightenment?" In *The Pursuit of Certainty: Religious and Cultural Formulations*, edited by Wendy James, 1–14. London: Routledge, 1995.

Janson, Marloes. *Islam, Youth and Modernity in the Gambia: The Tablighi Jama'at*. New York: Cambridge University Press, 2014.

Jeffery, Laura, and Matei Candea. "The Politics of Victimhood." *History and Anthropology* 17, no. 4 (2006): 287–96. https://doi.org/10.1080/02757200600914037.

Jones, Kenneth. *Socio-Religious Reform Movements in British India*. Cambridge: Cambridge University Press, 1989.

——. "Swami Dayananda Saraswati's Critique of Christianity." In *Religious Controversy in British India: Dialogues in South Asian Languages*, edited by Kenneth Jones, 52–74. Albany: State University of New York Press, 1992.

Kallon, Tommy. "Islam and the Quest for Knowledge." *Review of Religions* 106, no. 2 (2011): 54–63.

Kamran, Tahir. "The Pre-history of Religious Exclusionism in Contemporary Pakistan: Khatam-e-Nubuwwat 1889–1953." *Modern Asian Studies* (2015): 1–35. https://doi.org/10.1017/S0026749X14000043.

Keane, Webb. *Christian Moderns: Freedom and Fetish in the Mission Encounter.* Berkeley: University of California Press, 2007.

——. "From Fetishism to Sincerity: On Agency, the Speaking Subject, and Their Historicity in the Context of Religious Conversion." *Comparative Studies in Society and History* 39, no. 4 (1997): 674–93. https://doi.org/10.1017/S0010417500020855.

——. "On Spirit Writing: Materialities of Language and the Religious Work of Transduction." *Journal of the Royal Anthropological Institute* 19, no. 1 (2013): 1–17. https://doi.org/10.1111/1467-9655.12000.

——. "Others, Other Minds, and Others' Theories of Other Minds: An Afterword on the Psychology and Politics of Opacity Claims." *Anthropological Quarterly* 81, no. 2 (2008): 473–82.

——. "Self-Interpretation, Agency, and the Objects of Anthropology: Reflections on a Genealogy." *Comparative Studies in Society and History* 45, no. 2 (April 2003): 222–48. https://doi.org/10.1017/S0010417503000124.

——. "Sincerity, 'Modernity,' and the Protestants." *Cultural Anthropology* 17, no. 1 (2013): 65–92. https://doi.org/10.1525/can.2002.17.1.65.

——. "The Evidence of the Senses and the Materiality of Religion." *Journal of the Royal Anthropological Institute* 14 (2008): S110–27. https://doi.org/10.1111/j.1467-9655.2008.00496.x.

Keck, Frédéric. "Sentinel Devices: Managing Uncertainty in Species Barrier Zones." In *Modes of Uncertainty: Anthropological Cases,* edited by Limor Samimian-Darash and Paul Rabinow, 165–81. Chicago: University of Chicago Press, 2015.

Kelley, Dean M. *Why Conservative Churches Are Growing: A Study in Sociology of Religion.* New York: Harper & Row, 1972.

Kepel, Gilles. *Jihad: The Trail of Political Islam.* Cambridge, MA: Harvard University Press, 2002.

Kermani, Secunder. "Why Was Shopkeeper Asad Shah Murdered?" BBC News. Accessed July 7, 2016. http://www.bbc.co.uk/news/uk-scotland-36732596.

Khan, Adil Hussain. *From Sufism to Ahmadiyya: A Muslim Minority Movement in South Asia.* Bloomington: Indiana University Press, 2015.

Khan, Amjad Mahmood. "An Event Nearly a Century in the Making: Khalifatul Masih V's Visit to U.S. Capitol Hill." *Review of Religions* 107, no. 9 (2012): 8–13.

Khan, Anwer Mahmood. "An Eyewitness Account of the Address at Capitol Hill: A Grand Manifestation of the Prophecy: 'You Have Been Helped with Prestige.'" Translated by Nakasha Ahmad. *Review of Religions* 107, no. 9 (2012): 20–25.

Khan, Naveeda. *Muslim Becoming: Aspiration and Skepticism in Pakistan.* Durham, NC: Duke University Press, 2012.

——. "Of Children and Jinn: An Inquiry into an Unexpected Friendship during Uncertain Times." *Cultural Anthropology* 21, no. 2 (2006): 234–264. https://doi.org/10.1525/can.2006.21.2.234.

Kloos, David, and Daan Beekers. "Introduction: The Productive Potential of Moral Failure in Lived Islam and Christianity." In *Straying from the Straight Path: How Senses of Failure Invigorate Lived Religion,* edited by Daan Beekers and David Kloos, 90–106. New York, Bergahn Books, 2017.

Kresse, Kai. *Philosophising in Mombasa: Knowledge, Islam and Intellectual Practice on the Swahili Coast.* Edinburgh: Edinburgh University Press, 2007.

Laidlaw, James. "A Free Gift Makes No Friends." *Journal of the Royal Anthropological Institute* 6, no. 4 (2000): 617–34. https://doi.org/10.1111/1467-9655.00036.

——. "Agency and Responsibility: Perhaps You Can Have Too Much of a Good Thing." In *Ordinary Ethics: Anthropology, Language, and Action*, edited by Michael Lambek, 143–64. New York: Fordham University Press, 2010.

——. "For an Anthropology of Ethics and Freedom." *Journal of the Royal Anthropological Institute* 8, no. 2 (2002): 311–32. https://doi.org/10.1111/1467-9655.00110.

——. *The Subject of Virtue: An Anthropology of Ethics and Freedom.* Cambridge: Cambridge University Press, 2014.

Lambek, Michael. "Choking on the Quran and Other Consuming Parables from the Western Indian Ocean Front." In *The Pursuit of Certainty: Religious and Cultural Formulations*, edited by Wendy James, 258–81. London: Routledge, 1995.

——. "The Anthropology of Religion and the Quarrel between Poetry and Philosophy." *Current Anthropology* 41, no. 3 (2000): 309–20. https://doi.org/10.1086/300143.

——. *Ordinary Ethics: Anthropology, Language and Action.* Edited by Michael Lambek. New York: Fordham University Press, 2010.

——. "Living as if It Mattered." In Michael Lambek, Veena Das, Didier Fassin, and Webb Keane, *Four Lectures on Ethics: Anthropological Perspectives*, Masterclass Series (Vol. 3). Chicago: HAU Books, 2015. https://haubooks.org/viewbook/four-lectures-on-ethics/04_ch01.

Latour, Bruno. *On the Modern Cult of the Factish Gods.* Durham, NC: Duke University Press Books, 2010.

——. *Reassembling the Social: An Introduction to Actor-Network-Theory.* Oxford: Oxford University Press, 2005.

Lempert, Michael. *Discipline and Debate: The Language of Violence in a Tibetan Buddhist Monastery.* Berkeley: University of California Press, 2012.

——. "No Ordinary Ethics." *Anthropological Theory* 13, no. 4 (2013): 370–93. https://doi.org/10.1177/1463499613505571.

Lindquist, Galina, and Simon Coleman. "Introduction: Against Belief?" *Social Analysis* 52, no. 1 (2008): 1–18. https://doi.org/10.3167/sa.2008.520101.

Lucia, Amanda J. *Reflections of Amma: Devotees in a Global Embrace.* Berkeley: University of California Press, 2014.

Luhrmann, Tanya M. *When God Talks Back: Understanding the American Evangelical Relationship with God.* New York: Knopf, 2012.

Mahmood, Saba. "Feminist Theory, Embodiment, and the Docile Agent: Some Reflections on the Egyptian Islamic Revival." *Cultural Anthropology* 16, no. 2 (2001): 202–36. https://doi.org/10.1525/can.2001.16.2.202.

——. *Politics of Piety: The Islamic Revival and the Feminist Subject.* Princeton, NJ: Princeton University Press, 2005.

——. "Religious Reason and Secular Affect: An Incommensurable Divide?" In Talal Asad, Wendy Brown, Judith Butler, and Saba Mahmood, *Is Critique Secular? Blasphemy, Injury, and Free Speech*, 2nd rev. ed., 58–94. New York: Fordham University Press, 2013.

Mair, Jonathan, and Nicholas H.A. Evans. "Ethics across Borders: Incommensurability and Affinity." *HAU: Journal of Ethnographic Theory* 5, no. 2 (2015): 201–25. https://doi.org/10.14318/%x.

Majlis Khuddamul Ahmadiyya USA, ed. *By the Dawn's Early Light: Short Stories by American Converts to Islam.* Chauncey, OH: Fazl-e-Umar Press, 2009.

Makdisi, George. *The Rise of Colleges: Institutions of Learning in Islam and the West.* Edinburgh: Edinburgh University Press, 1981.

Malabari, A. R. *A Man That Is Called Jesus.* Cannanore, India: Wisdom Printers, 1981.

Malik, Mubarik Ahmad. "Rules and Regulations Qadha'a Board USA, Dispute Resolution and Jama'at Involvement." Ahmadiyya Muslim Community: United States of America (website). Accessed August 1, 2018. https://www.ahmadiyya.us/documents/depart ments/qadha-a/1192-rules-and-regulations-qadha-a-board-usa-2017/file.

Maqsood, Ammara. "Buying Modern: Muslim Subjectivity, the West and Patterns of Religious Consumption in Lahore, Pakistan." *South Asianist* 1, no. 2 (2012).

Marsden, Magnus. *Living Islam: Muslim Religious Experience in Pakistan's North-West Frontier.* New Delhi: Cambridge University Press, 2005.

——. "Women, Politics and Islamism in Northern Pakistan." *Modern Asian Studies* 42, Special Double Issue 2–3 (2008): 405–29. https://doi.org/10.1017/S0026749X07003174.

Marsden, Magnus, and Konstantinos Retsikas. "Introduction." In *Articulating Islam: Anthropological Approaches to Muslim Worlds*, edited by Magnus Marsden and Konstantinos Retsikas, 1–31. Dordrecht, Netherlands: Springer, 2013.

Mathur, Nayanika. *Paper Tiger: Law, Bureaucracy and the Developmental State in Himalayan India.* Cambridge Studies in Law and Society. Delhi: Cambridge University Press, 2016.

Mattingly, Cheryl. "Two Virtue Ethics and the Anthropology of Morality." *Anthropological Theory* 12, no. 2 (2012): 161–84. https://doi.org/10.1177/1463499612455284.

Mauss, Marcel. *The Gift: Forms and Functions of Exchange in Archaic Societies.* Translated by W. D. Halls. London: Routledge, 2001.

Mayblin, Maya. "The Untold Sacrifice: The Monotony and Incompleteness of Self-Sacrifice in Northeast Brazil." *Ethnos* 79, no. 3 (2014): 342–64. https://doi.org/10.1080 /00141844.2013.821513.

Mazhari, Waris. "Reforming Madrasa Curriculum." In *Madrasas in India: Trying to Be Relevant*, edited by Akhtarul Wasey, 37–49. New Delhi: Global Media Publications, 2005.

Mazzarella, William. "Internet X-Ray: E-governance, Transparency, and the Politics of Immediation in India." *Public Culture* 18, no. 3 (2006): 473–505. https://doi.org/10 .1215/08992363-2006-016.

McIntosh, Janet. "Reluctant Muslims: Embodied Hegemony and Moral Resistance in a Giriama Spirit Possession Complex." *Journal of the Royal Anthropological Institute* 10, no. 1 (2004): 91–112. https://doi.org/10.1111/j.1467-9655.2004.00181.x.

Messick, Brinkley Morris. *The Calligraphic State: Textual Domination and History in a Muslim Society.* Berkeley: University of California Press, 1993.

Metcalf, Barbara Daly. "Imagining Community: Polemical Debates in Colonial India." In *Religious Controversy in British India: Dialogues in South Asian Languages*, edited by Kenneth Jones, 229–240. Albany: State University of New York Press, 1992.

——. *Islamic Contestations: Essays on Muslims in India and Pakistan.* New Delhi: Oxford University Press, 2010.

——. *Islamic Revival in British India: Deoband, 1860–1900.* Princeton, NJ: Princeton University Press, 1982.

Mittermaier, Amira. "Dreams from Elsewhere: Muslim Subjectivities beyond the Trope of Self-Cultivation." *Journal of the Royal Anthropological Institute* 18, no. 2 (2012): 247–65. https://doi.org/10.1111/j.1467-9655.2012.01742.x.

——. *Dreams That Matter: Egyptian Landscapes of the Imagination.* Berkeley: University of California Press, 2011.

——. "How to Do Things with Examples: Sufis, Dreams, and Anthropology." *Journal of the Royal Anthropological Institute* 21, no. S1 (2015): 129–43. https://doi.org/10.1111 /1467-9655.12170.

——. "Invisible Armies: Reflections on Egyptian Dreams of War." *Comparative Studies in Society and History* 54, no. 2 (2012): 392–417. https://doi.org/10.1017 /S0010417512000084.

Moin, A. Azfar. *The Millennial Sovereign: Sacred Kingship and Sainthood in Islam.* New York: Columbia University Press, 2012.

Most, Glenn W. *Doubting Thomas.* Cambridge, MA: Harvard University Press, 2007.

Mughal, Fiyaz. "Anti-Ahmadi Hate Crime Has Gone Unchecked for Too Long—and the Consequences Are Terrifying." *The Independent*, October 11, 2016. http://www .independent.co.uk/voices/ahmadi-muslim-hate-crime-murder-asad-shah -murder-tanvaar-qadri-islam-gone-unchecked-uk-too-long-a7355401.html.

Mumtaz, Ahmad. "Islamic Fundamentalism in South Asia: The Jamaat-i-Islami and the Tablighi Jamaat of South Asia." In *Fundamentalisms Observed*, edited by Martin E. Marty and R. Scott Appleby, 487–500. Chicago: University of Chicago Press, 1991.

Munir, Muhammad. *Report of the Court of Inquiry Constituted under Punjab Act II of 1954 to Enquire into the Punjab Disturbances of 1953.* Lahore, Pakistan: Government Printing, Punjab, 1954.

Nasir, Mir Mahmood Ahmad. "Nabuwwat-o-Khilafat Ke Mut'alliq Ahl-e Paigham Ka Mauqif (13 March 1914 Ke b'ad)." In *Nabuwwat-o-Khilafat*, 32–39. Qadian, India: Nazarat Nashr-o-Isha'at, 2000.

Naumescu, Vlad. "The End Times and the Near Future: The Ethical Engagements of Russian Old Believers in Romania." *Journal of the Royal Anthropological Institute* 22, no. 2 (2016): 314–331. https://doi.org/10.1111/1467-9655.12379.

Needham, Rodney. *Belief, Language, and Experience.* Oxford: Blackwell, 1972.

Nelson, Matthew J. "Constitutional Migration and the Meaning of Religious Freedom: From Ireland and India to the Islamic Republic of Pakistan." *Journal of Asian Studies*, forthcoming.

Nijhawan, Michael. *The Precarious Diasporas of Sikh and Ahmadiyya Generations: Violence, Memory, and Agency.* New York: Palgrave Macmillan, 2016.

——. "'Today, We Are All Ahmadi': Configurations of Heretic Otherness between Lahore and Berlin." *British Journal of Middle Eastern Studies* 37, no. 3 (2010): 429–47. https://doi.org/10.1080/13530194.2010.524443.

Osella, Filippo, and Caroline Osella. "Introduction: Islamic Reformism in South Asia." *Modern Asian Studies* 42, nos. 2–3 (2008): 247–57. https://doi.org/10.1017 /S0026749X07003186.

Owens, David. "Epistemic Akrasia." *The Monist* 85, no. 3 (2002): 381–97. https://doi.org /10.5840/monist200285316.

Parry, Jonathan. "The Brahmanical Tradition and the Technology of the Intellect." In *Reason and Morality*, edited by Joanna Overing, 198–222. London and New York: Tavistock Publications, 1985.

——. "The 'Crises of Corruption' and 'The Idea of India': A Worm's-Eye View." In *Morals of Legitimacy: Between Agency and System*, edited by Italo Pardo, 27–55. New York: Berghahn Books, 2000.

——. "The Gift, the Indian Gift and the 'Indian Gift.'" *Man* 21, no. 3 (1986): 453–73. https://doi.org/10.2307/2803096.

Pelkmans, Mathijs. *Fragile Conviction: Changing Ideological Landscapes in Urban Kyrgyzstan.* Ithaca, NY: Cornell University Press, 2017.

——. "Outline for an Ethnography of Doubt." In *Ethnographies of Doubt: Faith and Uncertainty in Contemporary Societies*, edited by Mathijs Pelkmans, 1–42. London: I. B. Tauris, 2013.

Phoenix. *His Holiness: A Fearless and Frank Exposition of the Hollowness of Mirza Ghulam Ahmad's Claim to Prophethood.* Lahore, Pakistan: The Islamic Literature Publishing House, 1970.

Piliavsky, Anastasia. "Introduction." In *Patronage as Politics in South Asia*, edited by Anastasia Piliavsky, 1–35. New Delhi: Cambridge University Press, 2014.

Pouillon, Jean. "Remarks on the Verb 'to Believe.'" *HAU: Journal of Ethnographic Theory* 6, no. 3 (2016): 485–92. https://doi.org/10.14318/hau6.3.034.

Powell, Avril. "'Duties of Ahmadi Women': Educative Processes in the Early Stages of the Ahmadiyya Movement." In *Gurus and Their Followers: New Religious Reform Movements in Colonial India*, edited by Antony Copley, 128–56. Delhi: Oxford University Press, 2000.

———. *Muslims and Missionaries in Pre-mutiny India*. Surrey, UK: Curzon, 1993.

Price, Pamela G. "Kingly Models in Indian Political Behavior: Culture as a Medium of History." *Asian Survey* 29, no. 6 (1989): 559–72. https://doi.org/10.2307/2644752.

Qadir, Ali. "How Heresy Makes Orthodoxy: The Sedimentation of Sunnism in the Ahmadi Cases of South Africa." *Sociology of Islam* 4, no.4 (2016): 345–367. https://doi.org/10.1163/22131418-00404001.

Qamar, Naseer Ahmad. "Reflections on the Historic European Parliament Event." Translated by Tariq H. Malik. *Review of Religions* 108, no. 2 (2013): 72–75.

Qasmi, Ali Usman. *The Ahmadis and the Politics of Religious Exclusion in Pakistan*. London: Anthem, 2015.

Qureshi, Muhammad Azmatullah. *Hazrat Bani-e-Jama'at-e-Ahmadiyya per Maulvi Muhamad Sho'aibullah Miftahi Deobandi Ke Jhute Ilzamat Ka Tehqiqi Jawab*. Qadian, India: Nazarat Nashr-o-Isha'at, 1998.

Rahman, Mujeebur. *Professor Daktar Tahir ul Qadri Ke Khule Khat Ke Bare Men Chand Guzarishat*. Hvidovre, Denmark: Ahmadiyya Muslim Mission, Copenhagen, 1988.

Rahman, T. "Language, Religion and Identity in Pakistan: Language-Teaching in Pakistan Madrassas." *Ethnic Studies Report* 16, no. 2 (1998): 197–214.

Rajeev, K. R. "Ahmadiyya Fatwa Muzzles Wedding Bells." *Times of India*, May 12, 2012.

Raman, Bhavani. *Document Raj: Writing and Scribes in Early Colonial South India*. South Asia across the Disciplines. Chicago: University of Chicago Press, 2012.

Ranal, Yudhvir. "Ahmadiyyas Come Out against Abolition of Triple Talaq." *Times of India*, April 27, 2017. http://timesofindia.indiatimes.com/city/amritsar/ahmadiyyas-come-out-against-abolition-of-triple-talaq/articleshow/58388606.cms.

Rashed, Ataul Mujeeb. *Ahmadiyyat Ne Dunya Ko Kya Dya?* Qadian, India: Nazarat Nashr-o-Isha'at, 2003.

———. "Reflections on the Historic European Parliament Event." *Review of Religions* 108, no. 2 (February 2013): 67–69.

Rashid, Abdul. *Darul Aman*. Self-published pamphlet, n.d.

Rehman, M. Abdu. *Qadian: A Holy Land*. Kannur, India: Samayam, 2007.

Review of Religions. "Divine Judgment in Dowie's Death." *Review of Religions* 6, no. 4 (1907): 117–29.

———. "Downfall of Dowie." *Review of Religions* 5, no. 7 (1906): 281–86.

Riaz, Ali. *Faithful Education: Madrassahs in South Asia*. New Brunswick, NJ: Rutgers University Press, 2008.

Robbins, Joel. "Beyond the Suffering Subject: Toward an Anthropology of the Good." *Journal of the Royal Anthropological Institute* 19, no. 3 (2013): 447–462. https://doi.org/10.1111/1467-9655.12044.

———. "Continuity Thinking and the Problem of Christian Culture: Belief, Time, and the Anthropology of Christianity." *Current Anthropology* 48, no. 1 (2007): 5–38. https://doi.org/10.1086/508690.

———. "What Is the Matter with Transcendence? On the Place of Religion in the New Anthropology of Ethics." *Journal of the Royal Anthropological Institute* 22, no. 4 (2016): 767–81. https://doi.org/10.1111/1467-9655.12494_7.

———. "Where in the World Are Values? Exemplarity, Morality, and Social Process." In *Recovering the Human Subject: Freedom, Creativity and Decision,* edited by James

Laidlaw, Barbara Bodenhorn, and Martin Holbraad, 174–192. Cambridge: Cambridge University Press, 2018.

Robbins, Joel, and Alan Rumsey. "Introduction: Cultural and Linguistic Anthropology and the Opacity of Other Minds." *Anthropological Quarterly* 81, no. 2 (2008): 407–20.

Robbins, Thomas, and Dick Anthony. "Cults, Porn, and Hate: Convergent Discourses on First Amendment Restriction." In *New Religious Movements in the Twenty-First Century: Legal, Political, and Social Challenges in Global Perspective*, edited by Phillip Charles Lucas and Thomas Robbins, 329–39. London: Routledge, 2004.

Robinson, Francis. "Crisis of Authority: Crisis of Islam?" *Journal of the Royal Asiatic Society* 19, no. 3 (2009): 339–54. https://doi.org/10.1017/S1356186309009705.

——. "Islam and the Impact of Print in South Asia." In *Islam and Muslim History in South Asia*, 66–104. Delhi: Oxford University Press, 2003.

——. "Technology and Religious Change: Islam and the Impact of Print." *Modern Asian Studies* 27, no. 1 (1993): 229–51. https://doi.org/10.1017/S0026749X00016127.

——. *The 'Ulama of Farangi Mahall and Islamic Culture in South Asia*. Delhi: Permanent Black, 2001.

Rogers, Douglas. *The Old Faith and the Russian Land: A Historical Ethnography of Ethics in the Urals*. Ithaca, NY: Cornell University Press, 2009.

Roush, Sherrilyn. "Epistemic Self-Doubt." In *The Stanford Encyclopedia of Philosophy*, edited by Edward N. Zalta, Winter 2017. Metaphysics Research Lab, Stanford University, 2017. https://plato.stanford.edu/archives/win2017/entries/epistemic-self-doubt/.

Ruel, Malcolm. "Christians as Believers." In *A Reader in the Anthropology of Religion*, edited by Michael Lambek, 99–113. Oxford: Wiley, 2002.

Saeed, Sadia. "Pakistani Nationalism and the State Marginalisation of the Ahmadiyya Community in Pakistan." *Studies in Ethnicity and Nationalism* 7, no. 3 (2007): 132–52. https://doi.org/10.1111/j.1754-9469.2007.tb00166.x.

Sahlins, Marshall David. *Islands of History*. Chicago: University of Chicago Press, 1985.

Samimian-Darash, Limor. "Governing Future Potential Biothreats: Toward an Anthropology of Uncertainty." *Current Anthropology* 54, no. 1 (2013): 1–22. https://doi.org/10.1086/669114.

Samimian-Darash, Limor, and Paul Rabinow, eds. *Modes of Uncertainty: Anthropological Cases*. Chicago: University of Chicago Press, 2015.

Saniotis, Arthur. "Enchanted Landscapes: Sensuous Awareness as Mystical Practice among Sufis in North India." *Australian Journal of Anthropology* 19, no. 1 (2010): 17–26. https://doi.org/10.1111/j.1835-9310.2008.tb00103.x.

Schielke, Samuli. "Being a Nonbeliever in a Time of Islamic Revival: Trajectories of Doubt and Certainty in Contemporary Egypt." *International Journal of Middle East Studies* 44, no. 2 (2012): 301–20. https://doi.org/10.1017/S0020743812000062.

——. "Being Good in Ramadan: Ambivalence, Fragmentation, and the Moral Self in the Lives of Young Egyptians." *Journal of the Royal Anthropological Institute* 15 (2009): S24–S40.

Schielke, Samuli, and Liza Debevec. *Ordinary Lives and Grand Schemes: An Anthropology of Everyday Religion*. New York: Berghahn Books, 2012.

Schmucker, W. "Mubāhala." In *Encyclopaedia of Islam*, 2nd ed., edited by P. Bearman, T. Bianquis, C. E. Bosworth, E. van Donzel, and W. P. Heinrichs. Brill Online, 2013.

Schulz, D. E. "(Re)Turning to Proper Muslim Practice: Islamic Moral Renewal and Women's Conflicting Assertions of Sunni Identity in Urban Mali." *Africa Today* 54, no. 4 (2008): 21–43.

Shaz, Rashid. *Understanding the Muslim Malaise: A Conceptual Approach in the Indian Context*. New Delhi: Milli, 2001.

Shepard, William E. "Islam as a 'System' in the Later Writings of Sayyid Qutb." *Middle Eastern Studies* 25, no. 1 (1989): 31–50. https://doi.org/10.1080/00263208908700766.

Sherwood, Harriet. "'It's a Beautiful Thing': Ahmadi Muslims Find Strength at UK Gathering." *The Guardian*, August 12, 2016, sec. World News. https://www.theguardian.com/world/2016/aug/12/ahmadi-ahmadiyya-muslims-islam-jalsa-salana-hampshire.

Shirazi, Zain Ali Shahryar. "A 'Communal' Public Sphere? Print, Debate and Hindu-Muslim Discourses in Colonial North India, c. 1880–1930." MPhil diss., University of Cambridge, unpublished.

Shryock, Andrew. "In the Double Remoteness of Arab Detroit: Reflections on Ethnography, Culture Work, and the Intimate Disciplines of Americanization." In *Off Stage / On Display: Intimacy and Ethnography in the Age of Public Culture*, edited by Andrew Shryock, 279–314. Stanford, CA: Stanford University Press, 2004.

——. "Other Conscious/Self Aware: First Thoughts on Cultural Intimacy and Mass Mediation." In *Off Stage / On Display: Intimacy and Ethnography in the Age of Public Culture*, edited by Andrew Shryock, 3–28. Stanford, CA: Stanford University Press, 2004.

Sikand, Yoginder. *Bastions of the Believers: Madrasas and Islamic Education in India*. New Delhi: Penguin Books India, 2005.

Simmons, J. L. "On Maintaining Deviant Belief Systems: A Case Study." *Social Problems* 11, no. 3 (1964): 250–56. https://doi.org/10.2307/798723.

Simon, Gregory. "The Soul Freed of Cares? Islamic Prayer, Subjectivity, and the Contradictions of Moral Selfhood in Minangkabau, Indonesia." *American Ethnologist* 36, no. 2 (2009): 258–75. https://doi.org/10.1111/j.1548-1425.2009.01134.x.

Simpson, Edward. "The Changing Perspectives of Three Muslim Men on the Question of Saint Worship over a 10-Year Period in Gujarat, Western India." *Modern Asian Studies* 42, nos. 2–3 (2008): 377–403. https://doi.org/10.1017/S0026749X07003216.

Snow, David A., and Richard Machalek. "On the Presumed Fragility of Unconventional Beliefs." *Journal for the Scientific Study of Religion* 21, no. 1 (1982): 15–26. https://doi.org/10.2307/1385566.

Soares, Benjamin, and Filippo Osella. "Islam, Politics, Anthropology." *Journal of the Royal Anthropological Institute* 15 (2009): S1–23. https://doi.org/10.1111/j.1467-9655.2009.01539.x.

Spadola, Emilio. *The Calls of Islam: Sufis, Islamists, and Mass Mediation in Urban Morocco*. Bloomington: Indiana University Press, 2013.

Spencer, Jonathan. "The Politics of Tolerance: Buddhists and Christians, Truth and Error in Sri Lanka." In *The Pursuit of Certainty: Religious and Cultural Formulations*, edited by Wendy James, 195–214. London: Routledge, 1995.

Stark, Rodney. "Why Religious Movements Succeed or Fail: A Revised General Model." *Journal of Contemporary Religion* 11, no. 2 (1996): 133–46. https://doi.org/10.1080/13537909608580764.

Stasch, Rupert. "Knowing Minds Is a Matter of Authority: Political Dimensions of Opacity Statements in Korowai Moral Psychology." *Anthropological Quarterly* 81, no. 2 (2008): 443–53.

Strhan, Anna. *Aliens and Strangers? The Struggle for Coherence in the Everyday Lives of Evangelicals*. Oxford: Oxford University Press, 2015.

Stroumsa, S. "Ibn Al-Rāwandī's Sū' Adab Al-Mujādala: The Role of Bad Manners in Medieval Disputations." In *The Majlis: Interreligious Encounters in Medieval Islam*, edited by Hava Lazarus-Yafeh, Mark R. Cohen, Sasson Somekh, and Sidney H. Griffith, 66–83. Wiesbaden, Germany: Harrassowitz Verlag, 1999.

Tahrik Jadid Anjuman Ahmadiyya Pakistan. *Wasiyyat Rules*. Tilford, UK: Raqeem, 2010.

Tahrik-e-Jadid Anjuman Ahmadiyya Pakistan. *An Introduction to Financial Sacrifice*. Tilford, UK: Islam International, 2005.

Taneja, Anand Vivek. "Jinnealogy: Everyday Life and Islamic Theology in Post-Partition Delhi." *HAU: Journal of Ethnographic Theory* 3, no. 3 (2013): 139–65. https://doi.org/10.14318/hau3.3.007.

Tankha, Madhur. "Exhibition on Teachings of Quran Denounced." *The Hindu*, September 24, 2011.

Tarlo, Emma. *Unsettling Memories: Narratives of the Emergency in Delhi*. Berkeley: University of California Press, 2001.

Taussig, Michael. *Mimesis and Alterity: A Particular History of the Senses*. New York: Routledge, 1993.

Tobin, Sarah A. *Everyday Piety: Islam and Economy in Jordan*. Reprint ed. Ithaca, NY: Cornell University Press, 2016.

Valentine, Simon Ross. *Islam and the Ahmadiyya Jama'at: History, Belief, Practice*. London: Hurst, 2008.

Van der Linden, Bob. *Moral Languages from Colonial Punjab: The Singh Sabha, Arya Samaj and Ahmadiyahs*. New Delhi: Manohar, 2008.

Venkatesan, Soumhya, Matei Candea, Casper Bruun Jensen, Morten Axel Pedersen, James Leach, and Gillian Evans. "The Task of Anthropology Is to Invent Relations: 2010 Meeting of the Group for Debates in Anthropological Theory." *Critique of Anthropology* 32, no. 1 (2012): 43–47. https://doi.org/10.1177/0308275X11430873.

Wagner, Roy. *The Invention of Culture*. Englewood Cliffs, NJ: Prentice-Hall, 1975.

Wahidi, R. "Mubāhalah di Sosial Media: Kasus-kasus di Indonesia dalam Dimensi Qur'ani." *ITQAN: Jurnal Ilmu-Ilmu Kependidikan* 9, no.1 (2018): 95–105.

Wasey, Akhtarul. *Madrasas in India: Trying to Be Relevant*. New Delhi: Global Media, 2005.

Weber, Max. *The Protestant Ethic and the Spirit of Capitalism*. London: Routledge, 2001.

Wedeen, Lisa. *Ambiguities of Domination: Politics, Rhetoric, and Symbols in Contemporary Syria*. Chicago: University of Chicago Press, 1999.

Werbner, Pnina. *Pilgrims of Love: The Anthropology of a Global Sufi Cult*. London: Hurst, 2003.

Willerslev, Rane, and Christian Suhr. "Is There a Place for Faith in Anthropology? Religion, Reason, and the Ethnographer's Divine Revelation." *HAU: Journal of Ethnographic Theory* 8, no. 1–2 (2018): 65–78. https://doi.org/10.1086/698407.

Yusef, Muhammad. *Yugarashmi: Kannada Quarterly*. Mangalore, India: Jubilee, 1990.

Zablocki, Benjamin. "Exit Cost Analysis: A New Approach to the Scientific Study of Brainwashing." *Nova Religio: The Journal of Alternative and Emergent Religions* 1, no. 2 (1998): 216–249. https://doi.org/10.1525/nr.1998.1.2.216.

——. "The Blacklisting of a Concept: The Strange History of the Brainwashing Conjecture in the Sociology of Religion." *Nova Religio: The Journal of Alternative and Emergent Religions* 1, no. 1 (1997): 96–121. https://doi.org/10.1525/nr.1997.1.1.96.

Zablocki, Benjamin, and J. Anna Looney. "Research on New Religious Movements in the Post-9/11 World." In *New Religious Movements in the Twenty-First Century: Legal, Political, and Social Challenges in Global Perspective*, edited by Phillip Charles Lucas and Thomas Robbins, 313–28. London: Routledge, 2004.

Zaman, Muhammad Qasim. *The Ulama in Contemporary Islam: Custodians of Change*. Princeton, NJ: Princeton University Press, 2007.

Zirvi, Karimullah. *Welcome to Ahmadiyyat, the True Islam*. Silver Spring, MD: Ahmadiyya Movement in Islam, USA, 2002.

Index

accountability. *See* responsibility

aesthetics of Muslimness, 18–20, 143–47, 162–64, 166–67, 183–84

Ahmad, Mirza Basheer ud–Din Mahmood, 12–14, 39–50, 52–56, 58, 61, 99, 172

Ahmad, Mirza Ghulam, 49; and British Empire, 1, 27, 33–34, 49; claims to special spiritual standing, 8, 34–38, 99, 171, 199n43; death, 192n41; family (*khandan*), 58–59; fulfillment of prophecy, 164–66; life of, 32–39; and the mubahala, 116–18, 120; as polemicist, 96–102; revelations of, 17, 98, 120, 130, 135, 141–42

Ahmad, Mirza Masroor, 10, 13, 57, 59, 156–58

Ahmad, Mirza Tahir, 10, 43, 49, 52, 72, 79, 102, 105, 111; and the mubahala, 115–16, 119–29, 131–33

Ahmadiyya Muslim Community: boundaries of, 45–47; establishment of, 39–45; size, 187n1, 14. *See also* Jamaʻat system

Ahmed, Shahab, 32, 141, 185

annual gathering. See *jalsa salana*

anti-Semitism, 28, 121–22, 146

argumentation. *See* disputation

Asad, Talal, 24, 28, 137

Atham, Abdullah, 118

baiʻat. See initiation

Bangalore, 129–33

Barelvi, 136

belief, vii–viii, 4, 22–28, 87, 91, 109–14, 178, 182; knowability of, 138–39; and modernity, 179

blasphemy, 10, 171

Bubandt, Nils, 109–10

bureaucracy. *See* Jamaʻat system

caliph, the, 5–7, 48–62, 56–62; broadcast image, 146, 161–62; election of, 58–59; exile of, 10, 15, 59; history of, 12–13, 39–45; infallibility of, 81–86; legitimacy of, 172; love for followers, 20, 67–69; office and individual, 56–59, 72; as patron, 63–65; private secretary, 69, 72, 77–79; and Muslimness, 12–14, 50; sermons of, 39, 57, 68–70, 104,

119–24, 129, 142, 170, 193n91, 195n15; sovereignty of, 51–52, 64, 78–79; superhuman attributes of, 70–71, 77–80; unity under, 101–102, 129, 132–33, 136; visits to Qadian, 15–16

caste, 202n5

Cavell, Stanley, 138–39

certainty. *See* conviction

Chakrabarty, Dipesh, 179–80

chanda. See finance of Ahmadiyya Jamaʻat

Chinioti, Manzoor, 121–24, 132

Christians and Christianity, 22–24, 36–38, 53, 98–99, 101, 128–29, 147; in Qadian, 107–108; in the Qurʼan, 116–21

class, 62, 74, 93, 144, 194n108; struggle, 55

Coleman, Simon, 163–164, 203n22

colonialism, 55–56, 86

communalism. *See* sectarianism

conversion, 18, 42, 47, 71, 101, 129; recent converts, 144, 159

conviction, vii, 3, 25–27, 60, 87, 129, 173–78; doctrinal, 3–4; as reconcilable with uncertainty, 182–84

corruption, 63–64, 83–84

courts: Indian, 107–108; sharia, 84

cultural intimacy, 167

curses, 117–23, 126, 128, 133–36

debate. *See* disputation

Deoband, 32, 90, 92–93, 130

derwesh, 15, 62, 142

Devji, Faisal, 139

disputation, 3, 147; in colonial Punjab, 34–36, 96; as exemplary action, 36, 94–102; public debate, 131–32; refusal to debate, 102–103, 149–52; silencing of opponents, 88–91, 101, 105–106, 111–12, 128; types of, 125

dissimulation, 9–11, 27–28, 138, 149, 166, 185

divine retribution, 66, 103–104, 145; and the mubahala, 120–21, 124, 129–30, 134

doubt, 3–4, 22–27, 91, 109–14, 143, 164; in anthropological theory, 87, 173–78, 187n13; failure to, 93–94; rethinking, 178–84. *See also* uncertainty

Lightning Source UK Ltd.
Milton Keynes UK
UKHW010753200520
363319UK00012B/176